RAYMOND MASON

1. Raymond Mason, Arts Club, New York, 1993. Photo: Rob Kenmonth

Michael Edwards

RAYMOND MASON

THAMES AND HUDSON

This book has been published thanks to the support of
Gilbert Lloyd, Barbara Lloyd and Pierre Levai,
Marlborough Gallery, London, New York, Tokyo, Madrid

Publishing co-ordinator: Paola Gribaudo

Special thanks are due to the photographer François Delagenière

British Library Cataloguing-in-Publication Data

A catalogue record for this book is available from the British Library

ISBN 0-500-09245-1

Library of Congress Catalog Card Number: 94-68190

Printed and bound in Italy
Stamperia Artistica Nazionale - Turin

TABLE OF CONTENTS

I

BIRMINGHAM, OXFORD, LONDON, PARIS

The first encounter with Raymond Mason — with the works or with the man — can leave one durably surprised. Here are sculptures, paintings, drawings, which are not only figurative but, in his own word, realist. Many of the sculptures are polychrome as well, and some represent crowds of people, processing through a market carrying lifelike fruit and vegetables, or standing stunned and waiting for news after a mining disaster. Humans and objects in this art are abruptly, oddly, there, and so are their meanings. A man in the monument for Birmingham who symbolises the city, the 'heart of England', has his hand on his heart, and behind him are a car, a jeweller, a factory. One senses a disturbing open-handedness towards the viewer, and a desire also to involve him in the work, to draw him into a narrative, into an identifiable scene of human activity and human emotion. So straightforward is the recognition of a real world, in fact, that one discovers a powerful realist representation at a time when both realism and the shared world on which it depends could well seem to be no longer available. And once the introductions are over, one learns progressively the inexhaustible nature of a unique life-work, violently alive and hugely ambitious, not for an abundance of items but for the abundant, commanding statements of a number of master-pieces on a large scale, produced by a larger-than-life figure whose enthusiasm goes spontaneously to artists of scope and above all of energy: to Michelangelo, Hugo, Beethoven. That first encounter is with precisely the kind of art for which one was not prepared, and which can slowly persuade one to question and to enlarge one's convictions, as one ponders works which are apparently regressive and yet profoundly, radically, new.

If the works are colourful, so is the man. Mason has vivid views on a great many subjects and a gift for stating them brusquely and memorably. He describes always with telling phrases — the smooth, aristocratic, 'porcelain face' of Churchill, for example, encountered briefly while in the Navy; or with speaking gestures —

twinkling finger movements up and down a small piece of imagined clay to convey Giacometti at work. A direct and essential eloquence turns all the incidents of his life, and especially his meetings with the famous, into moments of charged significance or uproarious and inventive scenes of the human comedy. He has written of Giacometti in a recent unpublished study that he was not tragic but 'tonic', and he is himself tonic and life-enhancing. (Our own first meeting was in October 1989 in the crypt of the Madeleine church in Paris, after a poetry reading by Yves Bonnefoy. It was Bonnefoy who introduced us, in fact, and appropriately so, since for many years, despite the great difference between Mason's art and his own poetry and poetics, Bonnefoy had been advancing Mason's claims in a series of the most probing writings on his work. There is a photograph of Mason and myself a few moments after shaking hands where we are laughing like old friends, at something, certainly, which he must have said.) It is not a question of exploring the man so as to understand the works — though even that discredited idea may seem to revive in his case — but of seeing, if one happens to know him, that the work is alive in the same way, being everywhere forceful, decisive, big, immediately present and absolutely itself.

The works can also shock by seeming gross, loud and outmoded, and many reviewers of his exhibitions have said as much, indulging their initial reaction as if it were sufficient. It is no doubt the fact of producing such work at such a time, against the current of so much of the sculpture that one comes across in the contemporary rooms of museums and galleries, along with his being unclassifiable through belonging to no group or tendency, which have made Mason at once world-famous and virtually unknown. He has held major exhibitions in many countries, including retrospectives in London, Paris and Birmingham, and his dealer is the prestigious Marlborough Gallery. There are works of his in cities around the world: monuments, for instance, in Birmingham, Montreal and Washington, and other large sculptures in public sites in Paris and New York. Above all he is highly regarded by numerous fellow artists, including many of the finest and the most renowned, and is popular with the public, who come to his retrospectives in large crowds. It is the journalists and other makers of reputation who, with some notable exceptions, have ignored or disparaged him, with the result that one of the greatest living British artists and arguably the finest English sculptor of the century with Henry Moore is not considered with due seriousness and has yet to enter the public discussions of modern art.

Mason's work is diverse — it includes monuments and other sculptures, free-standing and in relief and in various media, oil paintings and water-colours, hundreds of drawings and a number of book illustrations, three major series of lithographs and a single, spectacular theatrical design — but one comes gradually to realise that it develops massively as a coherent whole, just as it is sustained by a complex and coherent body of ideas. Mason's writings are actually quite numerous: not only do they offer an aesthetic to explore but they re-draw certain areas of the art-historical map and they make one look again in particular at the history of English painting. What is at stake in his art and in the reflection accompanying it can only appear through the analysis of the works, which are strenuous acts of renewal and recovery, of re-opening sculpture to its own most generous possibility and to the whole human condition which gives it meaning. He reconstructs the notion that a sculpture is not an object, and cannot survive if it takes autonomy to the point of autism, but rather treats it as a vehicle of human thought and emotion. The inner thought, if sufficiently rich, continues to reveal itself, while the emotion, or the sentiment properly so-called, appeals to the human need, not for the sensational but for those true relationships which make for 'a warmer life'. That many inferior artists will agree with the latter idea, and many critics find it hackneyed, increases the challenge for Mason to create an 'art of sentiment' which is at the same time utterly serious. It can also make it expedient for anyone to reflect on the possible danger of a sophistication of taste which closes one in art to the emotions one maybe relies on in life.[1] He also revives the great tradition of sculpture, in its figurative intention and its polychromy, while equally finding for colour entirely new ways of combining with sculpture, and while refreshing figuration continually, on occasion by pushing it to unforeseen limits. For there is a large adventurousness in his work, and an exacting aesthetic resolve which makes his realism anything but easy-going. And he reclaims the idea of the masterpiece. Far from producing series of works which are variations on the same theme, he singularises each work into its own specialness and often

makes of it one of the extremes within his work as a whole; he also aims not for a minimal but for a 'maximal' art, containing not as little as possible but 'everything', and achieving a complexity which he calls, in a word that his friend Fernando Botero has also used, 'symphonic'.[2]

He likewise restores contact with a non-human as well as a human reality beyond the work, through seeking 'to express and, if possible, to exalt' the world immediately surrounding him,[3] whether the crowd-filled architecture of Paris or the countryside in the south of France. The turning outward of the artist and of his art comes from an unashamedly elevated and in its way religious conviction that 'painting' (but for the context he might have said 'sculpture') is 'an act of worship'.[4] And he rediscovers the viewer as someone whose claims are intrinsic to the work. In the presentation of an unrealised project, a monument to a heroic episode in the history of Guadeloupe, he states (in French): 'As for its being understood, at least in part, by everybody, I consider this to be the major difficulty in art and I have always sought to overcome it.' Rather than expressing the artist or expressing itself, rather than drawing the world towards itself for the production of a succession of 'Masons', of works signifying essentially their author, here is an art which endeavours to leave the self and go out towards others, to make itself understood — to quote one of Mason's many vulnerable expressions for which one may come eventually to re-learn respect — by his 'fellow men'. And this despite the large exuberance of the man. To adapt a well-known declaration of T. S. Eliot's in the essay on 'Tradition and the Individual Talent': while the laying aside of self for the other is always a good, in the realm of art the foregoing only of strong selves and plentiful personalities is instructive to the observer.

Much is at stake here, in an art which flies in the face of a great deal of the art currently being produced by many big names in the present star system, of whom Mason has often chosen to make public his forthright and reasoned disapproval. This is his affair, and I shall not join in. I know from another art how foolish a critic shows himself to be when he claims to tell poets their business, and I have no intention of passing judgment on any artist pursuing an art contradictory to Mason's — leaving aside the fact that his perspective is not always mine. The problems of sculpture, of painting, of drawing can only be resolved by sculptors, painters and draughtsmen, and while anyone thinking well may contribute something useful, their quarrels will not be settled by poets and professors. I would simply note that much of the art which Mason's own art actively repudiates seems to rely for its value on the texts which surround it, and that to the old and vexing question: how can you demonstrate the superiority of good art over bad? — of *Coriolanus*, for example, over *Coronation Street* — at least there is a serviceable answer. What an intelligent person can say about the TV serial may well be more interesting than the serial, whereas one cannot imagine anything being said about Shakespeare's play that could be as interesting as the play itself.

Only when Mason's art has worked as art does it invite one, not to spin thoughts around it but to explore the large thinking which it performs itself. And this is hardly surprising when one begins to take its measure and to appreciate something of its stature. For I see Mason as one of the last great representatives of the Ecole de Paris. Like Giacometti and like Balthus to a degree, both of whom he admires foremost among his contemporaries along with another friend, Francis Bacon, he belongs there as a member of that fraternity which he once called, in a simple and memorable phrase, 'the foreigners of Paris'.[5] His art is different, moreover, in any company. When finally rejected for an exhibition in Paris with the title *La création artistique en France 1960-1972*, a period which includes two of his most important works, he made this proud and accurate rejoinder: 'Je vous mets au défi de me signaler ailleurs une oeuvre qui ressemble à la mienne'[6] — I challenge you to show me anywhere work like mine.

His work is full of such certainties, and also of proper hesitations. Both are visible from the beginning. Born in 1922 to a Scottish father, who had been a pioneer motor-mechanic and taxi-driver, and to an English mother, the daughter of a local publican, he spent hours of his childhood at the downstairs window of the house in Wheeleys Lane where, fighting asthma, he would sit gazing at the passers-by and at the redbrick factory opposite — so authoritative a scene of creative origin that we shall need to explore it to the full later. We should also note what he says of the drawings he did while at elementary school:

> From my earliest childhood I had drawn . . . But, unlike other children, what I produced were not the flamboyant creations seemingly at the threshold of modern art but painstaking copies of this and that. My only originality afterwards was that I would glue the watercolours on to wood and then cut them out with a fret-saw to make an object in relief. A miniature form of what, sixty years later, I am still occupied in doing.[7]

The move from a flat to a relieved surface is basic to his art, and he has called his sculpture, including the high reliefs which he does indeed elaborate by advancing figures progressively further away from a background, 'a translation of a painter's vision into three dimensions'.[8] Even the last of his large compositions, a monument appropriately to Birmingham, incorporates perspective despite the fact that it stands free. A spatial world flattened pictorially and then coming alive through re-entering the real world of the whole body moving through time: here is the core of his imagining of space and of his feeling for the viewer. And there is something else to learn about Mason's art, and perhaps also about genuine election in the arts, from his taking pains, not to pursue his vision or to advance the frontiers of drawing but, as an initial step, to flatter the reality of a world beyond the self — of the 'this' and 'that' which chance to fall under the gaze — by attempting to imitate it.

A scholarship to study painting took him in 1937 to the Birmingham School of Arts and Crafts, to which he returned after a period in the Navy (he was invalided out in 1942 through being short-sighted) so as to win a Royal Scholarship for Painting at the Royal College of Art. After an 'unsuccessful term' at the College, then evacuated to Ambleside in the Lake District, he again went back to Birmingham. Of the six months during which he shared a flat in Pershore Road with the Swedish painter Sven (or Harry) Blomberg, and of the small exhibition they mounted there, we might remark, first, Mason's uncertainty. It was Blomberg who was producing 'beautiful cityscapes', whereas Mason did 'nothing but portraits, still lifes and an occasional view from the window' — only his 'occasional' work homing to what would later belong to his true concern: the city scene. Blomberg, moreover, whose 'interest was the dirty, dipping streets of lower Birmingham', was painting 'their gleaming damp bricks in deep reds with dark skies and the black accents of doors and windows'. Mason is remembering those works many years after having painted his own gleaming wet cobblestones in *A Tragedy in the North*, and especially the dipping streets and the redbrick houses with black doors and windows of *Birmingham. In Memoriam*. If his memory is as accurate as it is generous, one can assume the presence of Blomberg in his work, and trace it right through to *Forward*, the Birmingham monument completed in 1991.

In 1943 Mason left the RCA for Oxford, where he became a student of the evacuated Slade School and the Ruskin School combined. It was here that he produced what he considers his first works of interest, including a 1943 *Oxford Landscape* described in a letter as 'deep greens with shots of buildings in luminous pinks and ochres'. Signed 'RM', it was hanging in his mother's house after the War but had disappeared at the time of her death in 1958. More to our purpose is a painting of the Cadena Café in the High Street, which was

2. *Mother and Child,* 1944

actually executed back in Pershore Road and was also probably lost from his mother's house. It was an adaptation to his own circumstances of Manet's *Un Bar aux Folies-Bergère*, whose impress on Mason's representation of space was decisive. It apparently shows Mason himself in the foreground, seated at a table and being served by a young woman with a chignon and wearing a velvet dress with a lace collar. They are reflected in the mirror behind them, along with the interior of the café and the other customers illuminated by chandeliers. Mason describes the work in one of his key essays, 'Manet et Cézanne' (1981), as the 'prototype' of all that has followed, because of its organisation of foreground figures, a mid-ground, and a background bristling with a multiplicity of further figures, shrunk 'in the painting by the withdrawal of the reflection in the mirror' just as in his large sculptures such figures are shrunk 'by a perspective accelerated so as to cover 200 metres in a metre and a half'.[9] To that copiousness in recession as a sign of his later work one might add what he

also stresses in the Manet painting: its 'frontality', the impression it gives of drawing the viewer in but also, and most strikingly, of looming towards him. It is also remarkable that, in re-working what was for him the most important painting of one of the most important painters, Mason included a self-portrait. This is not, as far as anyone can know, the vanity of the twenty-one-year-old. A sign of Mason's several liminal works is that he places himself in them, directly or indirectly, not at all so as to contemplate himself in a pleasing phantasm but, on the contrary, to interrogate himself and to ask his way. Mason writes of the painting that it was the last he produced when he still thought of himself as a painter; it stands as a threshold to his sculpture.

Before we consider the turn to sculpture there are two further and later paintings to mention: *Mother and Child*, a portrait of Paulette Scott, the wife of a friend, nursing her baby, which was painted in London in 1944 and came into Mason's possession again in 1989 as the earliest example of his work known to have survived;

10

and a portrait of the French violonist Ginette Neveu, whom Mason had met after a concert she had given in Birmingham where she had played the Beethoven violin concerto. The latter portrait, painted in 1945 when Mason was mainly sculpting but also producing paintings under the impact of the Picasso-Matisse exhibition that year at the Victoria and Albert Museum, hangs in the Swindon Museum and Art Gallery, as one of the deplorably few Mason works in public collections in this country.

The most forceful and forward-looking 'work' of the period, however, is an article, 'British Art Schools — Augustus John', which Mason published in the Autumn 1945 issue of *New Phineas*, the magazine of University College, London, to which the Slade School is affiliated. It seems to derive from the unruliness of Mason's young manhood, and its immediate effect, since it was an attack on John and on the Slade in John's time, was to make him no longer welcome in the School. Yet it is also an extraordinarily clear-sighted rejection of a lower rule for a higher. Mason refuses the idea that 'technique' is something to be learnt during one's student days — and perhaps even acquired as 'technique' itself, as something already existing and available to be appropriated — and that 'talent' can be defined as the ability to perfect a technique while young and then apply it for the rest of one's career, arguing instead that an artist has to 'construct for himself a language of paint' in the light of his own 'personal feelings' and of 'how the physical world itself is expressed in terms of colour, rhythm, balanced mass, line and texture'. To achieve such a language, he writes, 'demands from the artist unremitting work over the span of his life', and he gives the prerequisites for making worthwhile art as 'a belief and ever-growing interest in art as a whole, and one's own expressive medium in particuliar', along with 'an unfailing determination to produce'. Despite the fact that he is writing as a painter, this essay by a twenty-three-year-old reveals an exemplary clarity of purpose and power of conviction: an awareness both of himself and of a whole world to be known, a willingness to turn his eyes to all the art there is, and an authentic vocation, not to 'be an artist' but to make, unfailingly and without cease for the whole of his life, works of art. One thinks of the boy from Birmingham, the city of work, and also of the fulfilment, in the works before us, of that prophetic determination.

He also argues that 'the comprehension of the literary and philosophical content of the picture is simple', and that the 'content' itself is relatively unimportant: 'for the task of describing and sublimating it into the terms of the personal painting technique is infinitely longer in time and more difficult in execution.' It is just as true, however, that such content is 'all-important', since 'without its initial entry, painting is abstraction'. Mason will continue to reflect over the years on the paradox, which many practitioners in all the arts will recognise, of the concurrent supremacy of both the subject, the reference outwards from the work, and the work itself, the sculpture as sculpture, the poem as poem. We shall consider his reflections, and more particularly the works themselves, where the paradox is elucidated. He also takes it for granted that 'the basic emotions of life' are 'common to all men', and will continue to say so, as part of a humanism which we shall also have occasion to examine, which has proved difficult to sustain in our time, but on which one might think that the communicability of art nevertheless depends.

The turn to sculpture, a move of the first importance, is something about which Mason has often questioned himself and which retains its mystery. It occurred at the Slade where, in his own words, the Principal, Randolph Schwabe (who, with Albert Rutherston, Director of the Ruskin School, was paying his fees), 'convinced me . . . I have no real idea why . . . that I'd be a better sculptor than a painter'.[10] Mason acknowledges that at the time he lacked a painter's 'fluidity' and 'touch', but feels that this is no longer the case, and seems to sense that the explanation fails to find the cause. He also recalls that he was earning money as a fire-watcher in the Ashmolean Museum, where the Ruskin School was located, and that at six o'clock each evening he was locked up for the night 'with all this Mediterranean sculpture', the paintings having been removed because of the war; but he will only say of those exalting summer evenings, which certainly nourished his taste, that they 'coincided' with the change to sculpture. That there was a change is of interest because, in a way, it has never ceased to occur. It is not simply that Mason, having begun as a painter, was led to colour his sculptures — though that in itself is no small affair in the history of modern art. Many of his sculptures are pictorial reliefs, and very few are fully free-standing. Even the large compositions, whose size might have been expected to encourage Mason to work on them from all sides, habitually have a background and a perspective which rises towards it. Even the three torsos of *The Falling Man*, which search the tradition of Western sculpture, are incomplete behind and require to be viewed from the front. His work occupies a new ground, in fact, a space explored for the first time, with unflagging persistence and with a prodigiously varied inventiveness, between the pictorial and the sculptural.

The first two sculptures were realist works in clay, and were produced at Oxford under the tutelage of Ralph Nuttall-Smith, the Slade secretary who had

11

studied under Despiau. They recalled the forms of Despiau and Maillol, one being a nude, the other a slightly larger than life-size half-figure of a fellow-student, Barbara Rennie, which convinced everyone, Mason writes in a letter, including Mason himself, that 'he had something to say in this discipline'. Although there are photographs, the works themselves are now lost, as indeed are all those made subsequently in London. The considerable significance of the latter, however, can be gauged from another photograph and from Mason's description of them. He left for London in advance of the return there of the Slade School and worked alone for a year, making sculptures in plaster and also drawing in the streets and painting. On the Slade's return he began carving in the School and in what had been the shop premises of 'Sun House', a large house he had acquired in Fane Street, West Kensington. (It was from this address that he applied in November 1945 for membership of the Artists International Association, describing his 'Type of Work', in an order which remains undecided, as 'Painting, sculpture & drawing'.)[11] The London works, including the portrait of Ginette Neveu, became Mason's contribution to an exhibition which he held with Sven Blomberg and the latter's French wife, Mimi, at Brown's Hotel in London in 1946. Although he was unaware of the fact, the exhibition occurred shortly before his departure for Paris, and contained certain essentials of his sculpture which were only to come fully into view many years later.

Belsen Head of 1945, in Hopton stone, suggests most evidently a kind of art which he did not pursue. He was not to be a carver, and the highly stylized, hardly European treatment of the head will not return in subsequent work. Yet the head itself will be one of his main concerns as a sculptor, and will furnish part of the means for his entry, in 1952, on his major work. The deeply gouged eyes also suggest those infinitely seeing gazes which will take so many later figures into their own minds and into the viewer's mind, and out from the sculpture into the space before them. Even its expressionistic quality — it was made under the impact of the first images of the concentration camps arriving in London — will return in a number of works which constitute a second and indeed alternative art to Mason's other products of the 1950s.

The plaster sculptures in the exhibition included a *Miner*, which showed the influence of Van Gogh, and a full-sized *Mandrill*, based on an animal seen at London Zoo and painted red, black and purple. For the startling fact about these works is that, as well as being figurative, they were polychrome. If only for a short period Mason addressed himself, quite early in his career, to what was eventually to become the most evident task, at once revolutionary and restorative, of his whole oeuvre. Immediately prior to uprooting himself he confronted what really mattered, without as yet realising its significance.

Belsen Head is unlikely to have been destroyed and might still reappear. The coloured works, on the other hand, which were sent to Sweden to be sold, have probably failed to survive because of the materials with which they were made.

The move to France was occasioned by the fact that Sven and Mimi Blomberg were going to Paris and invited Mason to accompany them. It was motivated, as Mason remembers it, by a desire to leave England and to see 'the wide world after the War'. The choice of Paris in particular was that of his friends, and he had no intention of staying there; he did so eventually because the city was good for his asthma.[12] Yet there is also a deeper answering to desire: 'When my feelings were beginning to crystallise artistically my earliest admiration was obviously for Van Gogh who had lived and portrayed the industrial scene with what seemed contemporary rigour ... Of course, Van Gogh was also France and its painting so, progressively, I lifted my eyes from my home town to look abroad'.[13] This is a later reflection; here is Mason in 1945, the year before his crossing to France, describing in the article on Augustus John, where the hero in France is Picasso, the same gesture of the eyes and head: 'We leave the shabbiness of British contemporary painting and trace the comparison which is to give this article true dimensions. With the raising of our eyes to the continental scene, we are dazzled by the colour and vigour of that brilliant world.' We might remember also that Mason's father had travelled, being a native of Scotland and not of Birmingham, and reflect, if we care to speculate about such things, that travelling for Mason, the leaving of one place for another, may well have had a more hidden, existential purpose, and have been the search, at this deeper level, for a site of greater reality. So much of the work, after all, of this artist whose subject is Man, is also a probing of Place.

In Paris, where he arrived in late July, 1946, Mason lived in a series of tiny lodgings in the Latin Quarter and on the Ile St Louis — at one point handing his room over when leaving to Eduardo Paolozzi, a friend from Slade School days — and began to meet numerous artists and writers, beginning with Alexander Calder. He was awarded a scholarship to the Ecole des Beaux-Arts on the personal intervention of De Gaulle, who happened to be a friend of Randolph Schwabe; he left after twenty-four hours, because of 'incompatibility', he has said, with the Beaux-Arts mentality. Since his living conditions made sculpture impossible, for a year he drew and painted, often working, as in Birmingham and London, in the streets. On moving, however, with his painter friends Jacques Lanzmann and Serge Rezvani to the derelict mansion of the Yourievitch family on the quai du 4 septembre at Boulogne-sur-Seine, he at last found space to work and produced, of all things, abstract sculpture. Mason's passage through abstraction had actually begun in London, where, after seeing another 1945 exhibition, the Klee retrospective in December at the National Gallery, he had spent some six months doing 'colourful, geometric semi-abstract' paintings.[14] His abstract period was in no way an aberration and became in his later thinking a necessary and fortunate engagement with the abstract or formal element of all art, including the figurative. He was now trying to combine Klee with Brancusi, making sculptures which were 'simple forms, coloured brightly . . . They were clearly defined, but they weren't sharp-edged',[15] and they consisted of two sculptures in wood and of a large pipe-shaped work in plaster painted blue, which included a smoothed and hollowed groove designed to enhance its colour with the entry of the light. All have disappeared, though there are photographs of one of the wooden pieces and of the 'pipe', and also a photograph of Mason working on the latter, in the company of Jacques Lanzmann, which appeared in *France-Illustration*. It was no doubt the painter in Mason which led him to colour these works, so that, although he was only to turn or return to polychrome sculpture in the late 1960s, he had in fact already explored this fundamental of his art by 1947, and had done so, moreover, in both figurative sculpture and abstract.

In that year, from 17 October to 15 November, he showed the works in a joint exhibition with Lanzmann and Rezvani, organised by the as yet relatively unknown dealer Aimé Maeght under the title *Les Mains éblouies*, 'the dazzled hands'. He also showed an embroidered tapestry sewn on to a red flag, which he named, with good cause, *An Improvement of the Red Flag*. He delivered a speech, moreover, in a debate on the exhibition at the Boeuf sur le Toit restaurant. The speech was published in part in the Maeght Gallery review,[16] and this second of Mason's texts is as interesting in its way and as far-reaching into his later work as the essay on Augustus John. For while it offers itself as a defence of abstraction, the abstraction which it defends reeks of the human and of the phenomenal world. Abstract art may well imply for others, he writes, 'a work devised by the brain [and] detached from humanity, [which] emerges from nothing, serves no end and will inevitably fall into the void', just as 'pure painting' may well be taken to mean 'painting stripped of human

3. *Belsen Head,* 1945

elements'. His own commitment is, on the contrary, to an abstraction, a purity, which convey in strict artistic terms the response of the whole person to a reality outside. 'We are in love with this world', he writes, and even adds: 'We are capable of loving everything there is on earth and are ready to defend the integrity of each individual and each object — for if our first emotion is love, our second is respect.' The 'integrity' of 'each' and 'each': here is already that close adhesion to the immediacy of the multiple facets of the real which will never cease to give ethical and ontological authority to Mason's art. It explains his attack on figuration, which fails a chair, for example, by allowing 'only one side of it in a painting with the other three merely suggested', and it will soon lead him, not to a revised form of Cubism as one sees that it might have done, but to his own quite different though equally demanding realism, based on the laws of optics and the moving eye. Even in a text discussing a kind of art that he will shortly

4. *Tree Form,* 1947

reject, he defends what truly counts for him and seems, even here, to know the way forward, while he concludes with a sentence which might serve as an epigraph to his whole work: 'Without delirium, without myth, we shall practise a human art.'

Mason continued as an abstract sculptor until 1949, though here again the work he remembers in particular (which was eventually cast into bronze, passed through the Galerie Claude Bernard in Paris and is presumably still in existence) was an 'abstract construction' of 1947 or 1948 'based on a tree form and the open-

ing chestnut buds' seen before his window, on the edge of the Seine opposite St Cloud. The photograph shows an abstraction engaging with forms, and indeed with life, beyond the work, while the description (from a letter) places the abstraction in a very real geography.

Abstraction, however incomplete, may have been a means for Mason to focus, over a short period, cleanly on the fact that for art to celebrate life it must also celebrate itself. The return to figuration was greatly influenced by his companion, Mimi Fogt, and by the example of Giacometti, of whom Paolozzi had said that he was 'the essential man' and whom Mason had met in 1948. This was the first of a small number of decisive meetings, in fact, and Giacometti would remain a major point of reference. The first work actually inspired by Giacometti, *House of the Soul*, a wooden sculpture of 1949-1950 which recalls his 1932 *The Palace at 4 a.m.*, could have inaugurated, like the very different *Belsen Head*, a kind of art which Mason did not in the end pursue. Yet even in this isolated work, of which only the photograph survives, the pegged-up spiral representing passers-by establishes a form which will go to the centre of Mason's science of composition, while the staircase recalls the one leading to his studio Place de la Sorbonne. The whole work, indeed, is a synthesis of everything that greets the eye in the Latin Quarter. It discovers, quite suddenly, Mason's subject — a human, inhabited place, a house for the soul — and will reappear in spirit in a host of subsequent works, including *Latin Quarter* itself forty years later. It was not, however, what he was by now searching for. Giacometti himself climbed up to see the work, and it may have been his nettling Mason by asking what it was and speculating that it might be a theatre set, which convinced Mason, who was by now 'bored stiff with abstraction, the self-invented forms',[17] that what he desired was not even semi-abstract forms referring to the visible world from a considerable representational distance, but an art of figuration where reference begins, at least, in the seeing of the customary eye.

At the same time, since, as far as Mason was concerned, Giacometti was above all drawing and working with white plaster, he was also the occasion for Mason's loss of involvement, for many years, with colour.

In a few short years in Paris, Mason had made his way in the artistic and intellectual web of that dense, small, infinite city (having also met Jean Cocteau, Gilles Deleuze, Jean Cau and Claude Lanzmann, the brother of Jacques, among others), and had slowly begun to show his work. After the Galerie Maeght in 1947, he appeared at the Salon de mai in 1948 and the Salon des Réalités Nouvelles in 1949, with abstract monotypes. In 1950, Mason shared a joint exhibition with Mimi Fogt, at the Hôtel Crystal, rue St Benoît, showing the embroidery, monotypes and linocuts, as well as *The House of the Soul*. He also began to travel, to Barcelona in 1950 and to Greece and Italy in 1951. In 1952, at the age of thirty, he was to find himself making what was for him a new kind of work, a low-relief sculpture of a man in a street, which goes back via Oxford and Manet to an origin in the pictorial fretworks of his childhood, and which he is surely right to see as the beginning.

Notes on Chapter I

[1] See Mason's 'A Tragedy in the North. Winter, Rain and Tears', in Birmingham 1989, p. 98.

[2] See Raymond Mason, ' . . . et pour quand?', in *Revue des deux mondes*, November 1992, p. 90.

[3] 'Responses', in Arts Council 1982, p. 12.

[4] From Mason's text on Miklos Bokor written for the latter's exhibition in 1964 at the Galerie Janine Hao.

[5] While speaking at the Tate Gallery on 18 June 1993, in the course of a conference on 'Paris Post War: Matter and Memory'.

[6] From a letter to François Mathey of 15 February 1972, quoted in Centre Georges Pompidou 1985, p. 150.

[7] 'My Early Artistic Life in Birmingham', in Birmingham 1989, p. 12. I continue to quote from this text unless otherwise stated.

[8] 'Responses', in Arts Council 1982, p. 13.

[9] 'Manet et Cézanne', in Centre Georges Pompidou 1985, p. 79.

[10] From an interview given to Michael Brenson in 1976, shortened and translated in Claude Bernard 1977.

[11] The application form is in the AIA collection at the Tate Gallery Archive (TGA 7043.1.580).

[12] 'The Torrent of Life', in Birmingham 1989, p. 34.

[13] 'My Early Artistic Life in Birmingham', in Birmingham 1989, p. 15.

[14] Sarah Wilson, 'Raymond Mason – An Exalting Life', in Birmingham 1989, p. 16.

[15] From an interview given to Cynthia Nadelman in 1984, published in Marlborough 1985.

[16] 'Les Mains éblouies', in *Derrière le miroir*, no. 9, Galerie Maeght, Paris, 1948. Reprinted in Centre Georges Pompidou 1985, pp. 75–6.

[17] In Marlborough 1985.

5. *House of the Soul*, 1949

6. *Man in a Street,* 1952

II

THE ART OF PLACE

ason found what he was looking for, in combination with what he was daily looking at, in a series of street reliefs, in fact, executed in plaster between 1952 and 1959 and only later, because of the expense, cast into bronze. He discovered his first subject: human presence outside in the light and in the city, while perhaps remembering himself as a child living and playing in the streets of Birmingham. He then explored, from a quite different vantage with each new work, the meanings of human place and the art of representing it. And according to chance, which sometimes goes by nobler names and seems to enter like an impersonal blessing into all of our acts which finally count, he only came upon what he wanted by trying to do something else. He was thinking of Giacometti, whose influence had been decisive in proving by example that the exacting aesthetic demands which had led Mason for a while in the direction of abstraction could still be met in a figurative art attentive to a world existing prior to the work and independently of it. Mason writes in an unpublished appreciation of Giacometti of 1987 that in 'post-war Paris he was a figure to whom a young artist in love with the outer world yet desirous of real art could turn'. In his responses to questions by Michael Peppiatt in 1982 Mason even calls Giacometti 'the saviour, the only rallying-point possible in the luxurious art-world of Paris. He was the example for a young man who felt that the image of the world had to be worshipped. He showed that it was possible'.[1] So Mason sculpted a head, yet soon realised not only that it would probably not do in the company of Giacometti's heads and the intense study over years which had gone to their making, but that, by itself, it failed to satisfy. As he told Michael Brenson, although out of admiration for Giacometti he was attempting to 'concentrate', this was not his way, because he needed, and needs, 'multiplicity', or rather 'elements acting on one another', since 'to get a spark, one thing has to strike another'. So: 'I sculpted the head and straightaway I put the façade of a house behind it . . . And that's how it started'.[2]

One thing acting on another: this is essential to Mason's art and to the contrast and the energy which animate it. And by striking the rounded forms of the head against the flats and angles not only of a façade but of the corner of a building, he began, in a work which he would call *Man in a Street* and in the most concise way imaginable, to plot his understanding of the geometries of Paris and his particular definition of sculpture as changing forms in space, as well as probing his central theme. Of the relatively homogeneous and planned city of Paris, he has often remarked that the full presence of doors and windows on the façades along which one travels gives way excitingly down sudden side-streets to the same rectangles clustering together into slits or (interesting word) 'stigmata'.[3] Here, the box of the relief contains another, architectural 'box', where a single door and window establish the forms of the visual world crossing one's gaze while the forms of the same world, foreshortened as it withdraws rapidly down a perspective, are slits literally. The two sides of the building also suggest, in a sculpture which requires to be viewed from the front, the total change through ninety degrees — as a kind of paradigm or extreme of sculptural metamorphosis when the viewer moves — of a postcard, now a rectangle, now a line,[4] and indeed of a Giacometti bust, where the narrow, deep head and wide, shallow shoulders invert and exchange their forms as they turn.

While adding the building Mason also humanises it, by giving it, like the man, two gouged 'eyes', though the visual pun serves also to remind one that a building is already a sign and indeed a receiver of human presence. If Mason's unceasing concern for architecture is certainly artistic and is focused through sculpture, it is also inseparable from his humanism. His theme, as he first seizes it in the very title of the first low relief, is not the street — and nor is it unlocated Man — but man in a street. And that move from modelling in the round to low relief also enables him to begin to map the dynamics of his sculptural space. The façade receding, as it were, in profile, deepens the perceptual world and draws the viewer into it, while the man, whose head is framed in part against that recession, pulls the scene by contrast towards the viewer, as he approaches with that advancing presence which Mason had recognised in Manet and which, in work after work and in a great variety of ways, will be his own means of reaching out to the viewer across the intervening space.

What appeals in the work, however, is surely a strangeness, a sense of presence but also of absence. This was not, I believe, intended. In the catalogue of his Arts Council retrospective of 1982, Mason comments: 'As the title goes, the simplest possible description of the artist himself'.[5] By adding the façade Mason takes his concern for sculpture out of the artist's studio, according to the ethical principle of his work: the awaking to a world and the *outering* of vital interest, and becomes man in a street, a seeing eye and a living 'I' outside. He then expresses the man's belonging in a city thoroughfare by the care of the composition, which causes so many lines of force to pass through both the building and the head, and which repeats the rectangular shape of the whole in the cross on the man's forehead and in the combination of his horizontal eyes with the vertical 'eyes' of the façade. Yet the work could all be in the man's thought. What we see as we look beyond him, situated as he is in the lower third of the work and to the right of centre, is at once the place where he is and his image of the place. The building emerges, moreover, from only one side of his head, what emerges from the other being the silence of the street, which one might understand as the silence of the sculpture. Much of the work is empty, and there is only one figure, so that we are at the same time in an outer and an inner world, an urban scene and a psychology. The work is Mason's, and could not be taken for a Giacometti or a de Chirico, yet it has the isolation of the one and something of the disquiet of the other.

The street has no right-hand side, moreover, and no further distance, since where it meets the back of the sculpture all one sees is a surface interestingly treated but figuring nothing. Strictly speaking there is no street, as the cavernous doorway has no door. And what of the eyes? The man certainly advances most vividly through them, and although by their size and their depth they again recall Giacometti, they also belong fully to Mason's art. They are the sculptural equivalent of the black pools of ink by which he suggests intense and living gazes in his drawings, and are a means of calling shadow into the orbits and thereby 'colouring' them (as he has described it in conversation) and sending infinite looks towards the viewer. Their physical hollowness serves to fill them with mental presence. Just as the man

thinks the sculpture, however, the three dimensions of the work — in the horizontal line occurring where the road meets the rear of the box, and the vertical and receding diagonal lines delimiting the side of the building — all pass through his eyes, so that the work in its entirety stares at the viewer.

The gaping doorway, the blank window, the infinite eyes in this first sculpture where they appear, open, it seems, to the otherness of an unconscious. At this critical moment when Mason finds himself crossing the threshold into his own art, the anxiety of liminal experiences becomes visible in a certain haunting vacancy of the work. The building lacks continuity, moreover, with the rest of a city; the street is peopled by a solitary individual. If the work looks at the viewer, it also looks at the sculptor, now thirty years old, and asks him what he intends to do, and who, as an artist, he is. The street too, one realises, is as yet unnamed.

Mason begins his major work with a head, a sculptural form which, from *Belsen Head* (1946) and from before the brief engagement with Giacometti, has always been one of his prime concerns. He states many years later, in his unpublished Hayward Gallery lecture of 1986, 'Rodin. An occasion to discuss sculpture', that the 'most interesting, the most difficult thing in art is the human head', adding, in a phrase which one can apply to him at this decisive moment in his career, that it is also 'the extremity to which the great artist always moves when fleeing abstract forms of art'. The head was not only and not chiefly what he needed, however, in this first series of reliefs, and although what first strikes the viewer in the next one, *Place Saint-Germain-des-Prés* (1953), is again the bust of a man looking this way from a similar position in the work, one is also aware — in a sculpture which has significantly replaced a 'portrait' format by a 'landscape' — of an enlargement and multiplication of the scene. The new work is more clearly a pictorial relief, and suggests that his early practice as a painter is enabling Mason to construct a complex, perspective view independent of the consciousness of the human figures within it. The scene is a genuine outside with a life of its own, as in the architectural detail of the façade on the right (which succeeds the flat inner side of the frame in *Man in a Street*), the spreading out of the distant façades, or the alluring disappearance of the far streets, the result of which is that buildings are placed within the scape of a square and by implication of a whole city. Behind the advancing head is a copious background where, rather than merely remembering Manet, one discovers for the first time, in the repeated windows especially, Mason's particular insistence on 'numbering the streaks of the tulip',[6] as he looks and looks again at a world available to sight. The scene is named, furthermore, as an actual Parisian square.

The relief is not simply, however, a realistic piece of reporting. The scene is instilled with thought, in the figure, for example, of the cyclist. Having begun with a single character Mason adds a second, and how odd is their relation. As soon as he places two figures in a sculpture they pull away from each other and create the first of those tension points which will bring energy and movement to so many later works. Turning his back on the viewer and moving away from him, the cyclist likewise announces numerous later figures, including figures in the next two reliefs, who similarly draw the viewer into the fictive scene. And if the gaze of the central character is along an axis advancing towards the viewer, the cyclist's gaze can be imagined prolonging it backwards into the depth of the work. This is why it matters that certain of the perspective lines of the work attract one's eyes to his small head, which one sees on its blind side and which is situated almost exactly at the work's centre. The scene converges on his head, not necessarily as something in his mind but as that wide portion of the visual world which is at the disposition of his looks.

His being perched on the man's shoulder, moreover, suggests that they are more inwardly related. The relation is clearly of importance, since it produces the only moment in the work where distance is indicated not by perspective but by a juxtaposition of incompatible scales which calls attention to the work's surface. The relation may also recall the more enigmatic dimension of *Un Bar aux Folies-Bergère*, the link, that is, between the young woman looking candidly at the viewer and her reflection seen from the back, in a mirror unrealistically curved round. There, she returns the intimate, intent gaze of a man standing close, whose quite illogical presence could be explained if he and the reflection were the woman's reverie, the life of another self hidden from view, though not from vision, behind her social appearance. The relation in the relief is equally mysterious — why a cyclist? Why so near? — and seems to concern not the psyche of one of the characters but the creative process itself. To the extent that *Place Saint-Germain-des-Prés* could be considered nevertheless as existing in the head of the man facing us and in the head of the cyclist, it does so as memory. The man remembers the scene, at which he is not looking, rather as the artist produces it. The scene is already there, a square in Paris viewed from the north, yet the artist re-models it in plaster according to his idea of seeing it, rather as memory, which is a re-creative rather than a passive faculty, re-models it in the mind. Through the eyes of

7. *Queue at the Opéra,* 1953

the man we see, as it were, the mental fashioning of the scene, as he looks at the viewer rather than the square, while the cyclist is his memory as such, riding back into the scene and gazing at it for him.

The thought of the work is also in the dog. Its look is the first of many which traverse a sculpture so as to underline the spreading of the scene across the visual plane, and it serves here to emphasize the different construction of space from that of *Man in a Street*. Of the watercolour *Wheeleys Lane, Birmingham*, however, of 1958, Mason will say that the boy in the picture is himself and the dog is 'his' dog; of *Place Saint-Germain-des-Prés* he almost says, on the actual work, that the dog is himself, for it is just underneath the dog that he writes his own name. This is the only boxed relief where he places his signature inside the work rather than on the lower frame, and even if this were fortuitous, the mere presence of a dog and its forming a small triangle with the two men suggest its participation in a force field where Mason is situating some urgent concern. Perhaps, in this first sculpture (after *House of the Soul*) where he celebrates the Latin Quarter, meets its spirit in the young man facing him and voyages out into it through

8. *Place Saint-Germain-des-Prés,* 1953

the cyclist (the single two-way movement explaining again the proximity of the two figures), he is led to the consciously remembered or obscurely operative emotions of childhood, in the streets of Birmingham, and so to the neighbours' dog. Here, indeed, is another of the 'characters', a car, which is linked to the other figures by the surprising angle of turn of its front wheels and which could well stand for Mason's father. Perhaps it is also significant that, while the bust of Mabillon and the wall in which it is set evoke the church of Saint-Germain, the church itself does not figure in the work, so that while GOD is absent on the left, a DOG is present on the right, as the oblique and quizzical sign of a different creed.

The work opens widely to a world outside, yet does not entirely dispel disquiet. Mason imagines himself seated at the Café Bonaparte underneath the window

of Sartre's flat and across from the concentrated intelligence of his interlocutor, while the view of his adopted city, prodigious and available, spreads out in front of him; yet the scene is abnormally still. The immobility of the parked cars is increased by their number, as that of the busts of a crowd seated at the terrace of a far café is emphasized by the actual bust opposite, alone in its niche. Only the cyclist moves, and with a motion which seems precarious in such pervading stillness. The scene is also, for the most part, empty, and even the young man's head can be disturbing, with its lunar shape and lunar shadows. One thinks of de Chirico, especially as Mason acknowledges a 'likely . . . echo' of him both in the next street relief, *Barcelona Tram,* and in the earlier *House of the Soul.*[7] Even more in *Place Saint-Germain-des-Prés* one recalls the paintings of his first manner, with their city squares, blatant perspectives, box-like architecture, and the distribution over their vacancy of a small number of heterogeneous figures and objects. Maybe the tall rounded arch in the façade to the right, modified from the arch on the actual square, remembers, with whatever degree of consciousness, the inordinately high arches of *The Mystery and Melancholy of a Street* and of other paintings of the years 1911 to 1917.

Nevertheless, the differences are notable and instructive. Whereas de Chirico displays and systematically undermines the perspective of the fifteenth century, through unaccountable eye levels, for example, wilfully long-cast shadows, and a deliberate failure to model in the round (having studied, it would seem, the overstressing and ominous falsification of perspective in Uccello), Mason espouses perspective, carefully contrived, and so reverses de Chirico's programmatic, modernist refusal of illusion. The viewer no longer contemplates abandonment in a brightly lit but enigmatic and menacing endlessness of space and time but is restored to what 'looks like' the real world. Everything in the work is visually possible, according to that particular realism which most surprises in Mason's art, in a century which

has accustomed us to more distant relations between a visual art and a visible world. For Mason it is important not only to believe that a world exists outside the world or worlds that we carry around in our heads or in our language, but to devise an art which gives access to that world in a way that, on one level at least, anyone can understand. The work is still exploring, in part, a state of mind, an inward atmosphere, and continues to look questioningly at the artist himself, through the intent eyes of the young man and their repetition (again) in the windows of the front two cars. The young man turns his head, however, rather than confronting the artist or the viewer full-square, and in the expansive world beyond him are hints of the final overcoming of self-interrogation and disquiet in a confident outgoing to the abundance and depth of the real. The huddle of tiny customers away in the *Deux-Magots* are the sign, in hindsight, of Mason's approaching great theme: the crowd. The curving disappearance of the far streets, which joins the reality of the here and now to a larger reality into which it continues, also intimates an elsewhere within the world itself, while the movement of the work as a whole is towards the 'fortunate' right.

9. *Barcelona,* 1952

By folding out the volumes of the city blocks across the work, *Place Saint-Germain-des-Prés* organizes space into alternating and contrasting passages of horizontal planes and rapidly withdrawing depths. The area between the picture frame and this activity, which occurs at the rear, is measured by the contracting or expanding façade on the right, while the whole sculpture is drawn forward towards the viewer by the head and the look of the young man. It is not perspective as such that is in question, but a way of articulating space: crosswise, backward and forward, so that the viewer should scan the work, gaze into it and be greeted by it.

The next work, *Barcelona Tram*, of which the Tate Gallery has a fine cast, dates also from 1953, is much larger, and is the first high relief. The change of form was a response to the given of a perceptual world — Mason made a second trip to Barcelona in 1952 and 'when I began to draw the Catalan scene,' he writes, 'the strong sun and the opulent, sculptural forms of the people, particularly the women . . . impelled the idiom of high-relief upon me'[8] — and the work's sudden multiplicity of figures, along with its real as well as imagined depth of field, are the sign, after two questioning low reliefs, of a new assurance in the meeting and the representing of a world outside. The move to high relief was not definitive, and a similar unconstrained celebration of a visible world brimming with thought returns in subsequent low reliefs. It already announces, nevertheless, in this earliest of Mason's major works, the devising of the great, large compositions.

This is also the first sculpture in which something like a crowd appears, and where this central subject is suddenly discovered and established. Most of the figures, though not yet gathered into a single event or story, are nonetheless assembled for a purpose, that of travelling. Here again, Mason moves forward — in a seminal piece belonging to a series where otherwise individuals and crowds are simply *there*, on a city square or street — to the narrative organization of much later pieces. And as in many of these, the idea of theatre is also present. Mason saw the passengers in real-life Barcelona trams, seated behind the unusual glass-less windows, as 'spectators in theatre boxes'. In his sculpture, for several figures in the queue glancing in at them, they become themselves a spectacle. Those figures queueing are equally on display, to the viewer, and they even repeat the situation of the viewer as someone looking in at people looking out. The work in its box is already, in fact, a kind of peep-show, as an anticipation of *St Mark's Place, East Village, New York City* of 1972, and is much concerned with looking and being looked at, in a world of unending visibility. The plotting of numerous acts of looking, as they cross at all angles with

10. *Barcelona Tram,* 1953

considerable, satisfying complexity, is a further index of the artist's quite unperturbed pleasure in looking and looking again.

So, it seems, is the spreading-out of the work across one's view, which marks, for Mason, the beginning of his complete 'detachment from the art of Giacometti'. Its horizontality is enforced by repetition — the façade of the station and the side of the tram, the rows of passengers and of people queueing, the tram-lines and the passenger island which reaches almost to the limits — and is augmented by the stretching of the work between the woman looking out on the left and the tram

moving off to the right. No one — surprisingly, after the two previous reliefs — advances towards the viewer. This is not the case with one of the accompanying drawings of 1953, where a woman carrying a baby detaches herself from a similarly shaped scene and walks forward; nor with one of the 1952 drawings, a view from the Barcelona Post Office done on site in a jostling crowd, which perhaps acknowledges and if so transforms the influence of de Chirico in the fact that a vast shadow falls across the somnolent square but is perfectly explicable and produces no sense of the strange, and where a very separate figure stepping out of the shadow in our

direction was an afterthought. The advancing figure is a deep requirement of Mason's imagination, and its absence from the sculpture means not that he is unconcerned to reach out towards the viewer but that he is fully engaged in scrutinising a world 'out there'. The work does not turn its back on the viewer, but by turning most of the figures' backs towards him it establishes a world beyond the self which the viewer is invited to recognise and to enter.

Not that the people in the scene are as yet individuals. Even before he turns to the expressive humanism of *The Departure of Fruit and Vegetables* and its

11. *Paris,* 1953

successors, Mason will acknowledge that in these reliefs of the street he is essentially an artistic observer of the life around him. In the case of *Barcelona Tram* in particular there is a revealing sentence in his letter to the Tate Gallery: 'My personages stood as little statues until the tramcar came — and then away.' Is he alluding to the actual scene or to his representation of it? The people of Barcelona, viewed from a distance, are already seen as statues, and when he transfers them to his sculpture he sets them on a plinth.

At the same time, in only the previous sentence he describes the arrival of the trams before the station as 'irresistible'. This is the first of many instances where the origin of a work lies in something, which exists beyond Mason and in advance of art, imposing itself on his attention. So he was conscious in the work of dealing with 'reality at its strongest', and it seems to have been, indeed, the 'strength' of the sun, along with the 'opulence' of human forms, that, more successfully than the place Saint-Germain-des-Prés, called him fully outwards into the scene, and enabled him to overcome the intensity of *Man in a Street* — whose delimiting lines converge on a single pair of eyes — for a kind of extensity, a plenitude of place. And it is right that, as he responds to the otherness of a world, whatever enters

the sculpture through a process of representation ('I just made a box', he writes, 'and put into it all that had caught my eye') should encounter the demands of art and hence of mind. Or, as Mason himself will express it (in French, and when presenting the work of the American painter Anne Harvey in his own gallery in 1961), an 'authentic work is, and has always been, both figuration and abstraction, a meeting of the real with thought'. 'Abstraction' accounts for the ordering of the scene, which in this work is quite overt and constraining, and includes the repetition of curves over the arches of the railway station and of the windows and entrances of the tram and the ends of the passenger island; the artful disposition of numbers down from the three arches on the station to the five or seven arches on the tram and the nine figures standing on the island; the working off each other of curved forms and rectilinear; and the placing of a row of heads along the median horizontal. In so far as the abstract design also produces, however, the withdrawal of the work towards the station entrance and its moving away to the right through the departing tram, it equally gives on to an entirely other dimension of 'thought'.

The importance of the man with a suitcase is that he introduces the viewer into the work, that he looks in the direction of the tram while turning towards the railway station (against whose blank entrance his head is silhouetted when the sculpture is seen from directly in front), that he invites one to go in either of those two

12. *London,* 1956

directions by entering in imagination, via a number of steps, into either of the two interior spaces, and that his suitcase, being placed on the ground, marks the pause, seemingly, where the two possibilities of physical and metaphysical travel are contemplated. The stress between the turn of his head and the turn of his body exhibits the strain between the horizontal pulling-across of the tram and the inward pulling-back to the far-away depth, while one sees the two mysterious entrances, to the vehicle and to the building, as if they were next to each other.

The receding space to the left of the tram, which is designed to pull 'the spectator's eye straight in' and which creates the illusion of distance mainly by the graduated diminution of size of the human figures, replaces the disturbing emptiness of *Place Saint-Germain-des-Prés* by a deepening field whose every moment is accounted for and filled with presence. Yet to reach that remote and rigorously ordered obscurity one would need to mount a long series of steps, rather as if one were climbing the scale of perfection to a beyond within human experience, where the suggestion is of departure and where the tiny and almost invisible farthest figures also suggest a far unknown within humanity.

I might not have ventured such a literary reading of a single area of a 'realist' sculpture were it not for the way Mason himself refers to the other axis of the work. Of the tram, as of other conveyances in his works of

the 1950s, he remarks that an artist who concerns himself with '*the* great subject — the world which moves around him', cannot avoid treating modern forms of transport; that such conveyances add sculptural interest by placing people on different levels; and that trams, along with buses and motor-cars, were 'a major part' of his childhood in Birmingham. Here is already a considerable depth of motivation, but he also writes of the 'almost ritualistic' arrival of the trams before the 'solemn, sunlit grandeur' of the railway station, and he indicates above all that, alongside the concern with reality at its strongest, 'there was an attempt to suggest that the people depicted were being carried away to their destiny'. He adds that he 'even placed the window-bars before the driver in the form of a cross.'

The move from 'reality' to 'suggestion' is visible, in fact, on the tram itself, which bears a fair resemblance, one can assume, to a Barcelona tram, and yet which has no wheels. The leaping woman, the most conspicuous diagonal in the work and the figure who stands out from the others owing to her dramatic movement, is on the point of boarding this miraculous vehicle. For all its quotidian presence, the sculpture withdraws from its sunlit surface (enhanced by the warm brown of the bronze and the brick colour of its recesses) into an otherworldliness of repose and shadow, where a simple tram becomes a vehicle of destiny, a transitory 'house of the soul' for passengers about to be transported elsewhere by a Christ or a Charon with a peaked cap. As well as the 'somnambulism' of a great Mediterranean city, one enters a form of dream, inside the human figures and inside the work, where nothing specifically Christian or even dogmatically religious is to be concluded from the cross — which is no more than an available symbol, and a feature of the actual trams — but where some unnameable and other-than-human force seems nonetheless to be abroad.

A vehicle floats away in full view, as it were, of the spectator. It moves to the right, away from what Latin calls the 'sinister' left. Behind it, a stairway rises in a quite other direction, towards a far distance and further departures. The simple greatness of *Barcelona Tram* is that both its horizontal and its withdrawing axes, which give to the sculpture a strong form and the energy of tension, also convey its inner meaning, its transformation of a daily scene into deliberately unresolved suggestions of being conveyed or of mounting. The work moves perfectly between the seen and the unseen, between the joy of the here and now, of a presence made present more vividly and eloquently than in the previous reliefs, and the intimation of possibility, of elsewhere. And there is a final character who seems to comment on this. The only person between the station and the tram is a woman, partly hidden, who looks at the viewer from between the man with the suitcase and the woman leaping. She is a look appearing from the depth of the work, which the viewer no doubt takes time to discover, and which maybe questions precisely the work's depth, and asks quite what it is that one would find, if one climbed the steps to the square of darkness or entrusted oneself to the conductor of souls.

The plaster of *Barcelona Tram* was presented in Mason's first one-man exhibition, which was held — remarkably, since he had been out of the country for almost eight years — at Helen Lessore's Beaux Arts Gallery in London, in February-March 1954. Mason was one of a number of as yet unknown artists, most of them painters and all of them figurative, including Frank Auerbach, Leon Kossoff and Michael Andrews, to be given early showing by the most discerning Mrs Lessore. (The first appearance of a bronze would be at the Galerie Claude Bernard in Paris in 1965.) The exhibition also included *The House of the Soul* and, among other plaster and terracotta reliefs and drawings, a low relief of Paris, also executed in 1953, which is one of many panoramic works of the period to which we shall return in a later chapter. The exhibition was important for attracting reviews by Robert Melville, whom Mason had known through his artist brother, John, while still in Birmingham,[9] and by David Sylvester. Writing in *The Times*, Sylvester referred to the 'quite haunting sense

of reality' achieved in *Barcelona Tram* (despite 'the crudity with which the figures are realised') by its 'disposition of forms and masterly use of illusionistic perspective', and declared roundly: 'Of all the young British sculptors who have lately emerged into the public eye, none has confronted us with a more individual artistic personality'.[10]

Barcelona Tram was also associated with a series of important meetings with other artists. Mason, who had encountered Picasso in 1952, went to see him at Golfe Juan in the south of France in the summer of 1954, while recovering from the first of a number of operations that he has had to undergo during his life, on this occasion for peritonitis. He hoped for an introduction to a ceramist with a view to producing terracottas, which were all that his strength would allow. In the course of a lunch at a crowded table, Picasso picked out the *Tram* from photographs of Mason's work (the subject itself attracting his attention, since when he had travelled regularly from Barcelona to Paris in his youth he had climbed up to the station in the work, the Estación de Francia), and 'praised it highly, saying that it wasn't compilation art but something personal'. He admired it sufficiently to suggest presenting Mason to his dealer, Kahnweiler, though the offer was not taken up. He also called Mason an 'English' artist, on the basis, as he revealed, of a thorough knowledge of English art from Hogarth onwards. That Englishness is a dimension of Mason's work which we shall indeed want to consider.

Two further meetings were the beginnings of lifelong friendships. Francis Bacon asked to meet Mason on seeing *Barcelona Tram* at the Beaux Arts Gallery exhibition. (He was himself associated with the Gallery, having exhibited there in 1953.) A dinner party was arranged by Helen Lessore, which also included David Sylvester. Balthus was encountered in the spring of 1955 during an evening with Carmen Baron whose first husband had been Pierre Colle, Balthus' dealer, and who held regular gatherings in her Paris flat for artists, writers and musicians, including Man Ray, Max Ernst, César, Jacques Prévert, Jacques Lacan, Georges Auric and Francis Poulenc. Balthus accompanied Mason back to his studio, where he saw *Barcelona Tram* and also *The Idyll*. He returned the following day to examine them again.

Picasso, Balthus and to a lesser extent Bacon all have a bearing on Mason's work. Marcel Duchamp represents precisely what Mason rejects in modern art, and yet was responsible for obtaining for Mason the only prize that anyone has thought to award him. He visited Mason's tiny studio on place de la Sorbonne with a view to sitting for a portrait by Mason's first wife, and saw, like Picasso, the photograph of *Barcelona Tram*. In 1962 he met with the other directors of the William and Noma

Copley Foundation in Chicago (Max Ernst, Man Ray, Sir Herbert Read and Darius Milhaud) to confer the Foundation's annual prize. Copley himself had seen the *Tram*, along with other works, at an exhibition in Paris in 1960, and mentioned Mason among the promising artists encountered in Europe. Duchamp said 'It's him', and Mason received the prize, which consisted of the useful sum of two thousand dollars.

Mason's living quarters at the time consisted of a cramped single-room studio with a further cupboard-like space reached by a ladder. He had managed to construct *The House of the Soul* in the 'cupboard', and had made *Man in a Street* at a moment when he had the studio to himself. *Place Saint-Germain-des-Prés*, on the other hand, was made in the studio of his friend Joseph Erhardy; *Barcelona Tram* was begun there and finished in the flat of another friend. Shortly after completing it, however, in mid-1953, he took possession of a large studio in another street of the Latin Quarter, on the other side of the boulevard St Michel and close to the Luxembourg Gardens, where most of his subsequent work has been done. Rue Monsieur-le-Prince is an ancient street where, only a few doors away, at the end

of the 1650s Pascal had famously solved some of the problems of the cycloid, having been attracted for a time, in his own way, by a figure that was attracting Mason, the spiral.

Much of 1955 and 1956 was taken up with two very different sculptures, *The Idyll* and *Les Epouvantées*, to be considered in the next chapter, and with another panoramic relief, this time of London. The next street relief, *Place de l'Opéra*, dates from 1957, though it was preceded in 1955 by a particularly fine ink drawing. It is even larger, nearly six feet wide and over four feet high, yet returns to low relief and contrives to represent, almost as a virtuoso performance, a broad, perspectival, illusionistic scene — with a greatly increased profusion both of architecture and of human figures — in a depth hardly greater than that of *Man in a Street* and *Place Saint-Germain-des-Prés*. The 'sculptural forms' of the people, as well as the need to separate the prominent tramcar from the façade behind it, had led to the high relief of *Barcelona Tram*. Low relief is still appropriate to the largely pictorial concerns of *Place de l'Opéra*, as it will remain appropriate to similar concerns of the work that follows, *Boulevard Saint-Germain*.

13. Study for *Place de l'Opéra,* 1955

29

It is no doubt a sign of increasing confidence that, as Mason enlarges his frame, so he produces his first true crowd, whose members, more numerous than in the previous work, hasten with mainly unrelated purposes over a wide city square. The animation is created by the gestures of many of the figures, the diagonals which traverse them, and above all the deep cutting which moves and energizes the surface. The effect is to remove all echo of the empty cityscapes of de Chirico, and to suggest, not anxiety before the crowd as in one

14. *Place de l'Opéra,* 1957

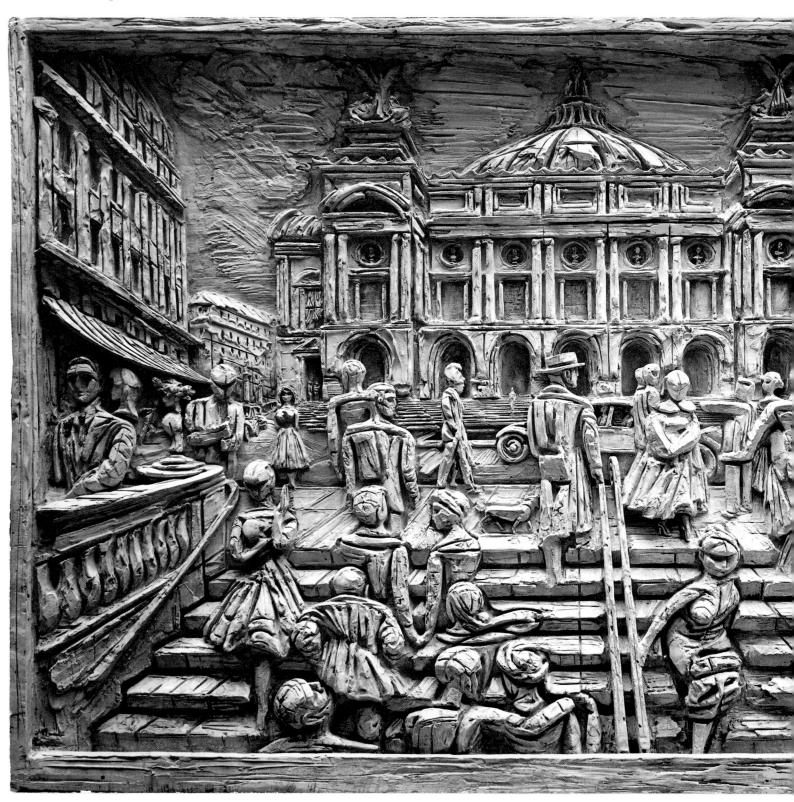

of the darker myths of our time but, on the contrary, a delight in 'men in the street', in people outside among human buildings and under the sun. The delight is certainly spontaneous, though it is also stayed on a belief (which is not of our time but which Mason makes one reconsider): that a crowd is an appearing of humanity, of 'my fellow men'.

The human crowd is what is celebrated initially in this most convivial work, which also dispels the unquiet of the first two reliefs with completeness and panache. The work descends to a Metro entrance in the foreground, which stretches across the full width of the base and seemingly opens beneath the viewer as if it might engulf both him and the whole scene. The view shows no more than what happens to be there, and a purely sculptural reason for the artist to choose this unusual standpoint is that steps, even more than buses and trams, add interest to the human figures by placing them on different levels. The suggestion of a descent underground is nevertheless impossible to avoid, but is also accompanied by the realisation that most of the figures are coming up rather than going down, and that the work can also be seen as rising from this underside of place or of self, by steps and then through the gradations of a steep perspective, until further steps lead to the climbing façade of the Opera House. Three of the four figures who do descend are young women. These Persephones or Eurydices clearly have nothing to fear from the underworld, and Orpheus is for once successful, since two pairs of lovers are returning to the light and the Orpheus who has just appeared can safely look. The final person to emerge, moreover, of whom one sees only the shoulders and the tilted-back head, has his eyes fixed on the top of the Opera House, where what he is looking at, on the pediment beyond the dome, is no less than a statue of Orpheus himself, now raised to the highest point in the work and presiding over it.

Whatever it is into which one might descend has been jubilantly freed of threat. Mason's childhood also seems to appear, but without design or disquiet. Of the dog in the scene Mason has said in conversation that he placed it there so as to fill a gap, and so that the curve of its tail (reminiscent of Seurat's *Sunday Afternoon on the Island of La Grande Jatte*) would respond to the circle of the car wheel beyond. Yet the conjunction of dog and car, returning from *Place Saint-Germain-des-Prés*, is itself suggestive. The dog is even looking at the car, whose windows are now perfectly transparent. The siting of the wheel just above the dog, in a central but not immediately eye-catching area of the work, suggests an untroubled situating of the memories of a faraway childhood within a sculpture exuberantly enacting the present.

The sculpture also situates and removes the certain anxiety of another previous work, a white terracotta relief made in 1953 immediately after *Place Saint-Germain-des-Prés*, which represents a number of men queueing at the entrance on the left of the Opera House.

(The relief was shown, along with a preparatory drawing, at the Beaux Arts exhibition of 1954, and was sold from there.) As the queue climbs away from the viewer over some steps and into a dwarfing doorway, surmounted by a classical pediment, which is merely the blank at the rear of the work, one wonders into quite what futurity those backs are rising and disappearing, and one sees the last person in the queue turning to gaze at the viewer as if asking the same question. The two works are unconnected for the artist, yet the effect for the viewer is to spot the location of the earlier work in a small part of the later work and to see its mood dissipated.

One emerges from the underground and into a crowded reality, and one does so, as it were, with the hatted man turning at the top of the steps who, like the cyclist of *Place Saint-Germain-des-Prés* and the man with a suitcase in *Barcelona Tram*, guides one's entry into the work. Although his head, too, is silhouetted against a recess, that of the central doorway to the Opera House, he leads one's imagination not towards otherness — 'destiny' and the mystery of departure — but into a quotidian and familiar world, across whose wide spaces he casts his look. The perfection of composition of these early reliefs shows, here, in the fact that, while in the drawing a woman rises for no particular reason to the penultimate step, the man rises precisely to the final step, and arrives on customary ground. He surfaces from below to greet the plenitude of the visible. He is the moment of waking from sleep or from somnambulism into the clear daylight. He is the artist issuing from an inner world into the outer world to which he is dedicated. With one foot raised, moreover, and his head turning, he seems to pause, so that the viewer also enters through a pause, which causes everything else to pause around him.

For if the work moves, it is also stilled: by the repetitions over the façade of the Opera House, where the to-and-fro of answering forms merges with the immobility of matter and of design; by the stationary man on the left leaning on the balustrade and sending a tranquil gaze beyond us, and by the woman on the right who has also stopped, who looks steadily in the opposite direction, and whose hand is resting on stone. She, too, is observing the Opera House, for the motive in this momentary pause within movement is, first, to call attention to a further celebration, that of art. *Place de l'Opéra* celebrates the urbanism of Haussmann (who in a drawing of the same year[11] is seen surveying the excavation of the Avenue de l'Opéra with the Opera House visible in the distance), by recreating the potent geometries, the liberating order, of a radiating square. It celebrates sculpture, in the statues on the roof of the Opera House and in the horizontal row of busts along the façade, which relate compositionally to the busts of passengers in the omnibus facing into the work. It celebrates architecture, in the Second-Empire-baroque masterpiece of Garnier on which the whole work focuses. It celebrates music, and above all the artistic and human fullness of opera, the art whose ambition is to be complete.

As the viewer pauses on the threshold of the sculpture, with a figure whose head is placed close to the midpoint, he discovers that the whole world has become, for the moment, a work of art. Hence the importance of Orpheus, on whom the very handrails of Hades converge. For the dynamic of the work enacts, with perfect objectivity, the emergence of the artist from a depth of privacy to the world and the life around, and to a unification of the demands both of the visible and of art — of 'reality at its strongest' and of sculpture at its most robust — where the figure of Orpheus stands for the high ideal, for the great masters to whom one might aspire. He is the culminating point of the work which he irradiates with his distant presence.

One pauses also for a celebration of place. For the *Place* is a centre, radiating through side streets and most emphatically through the buildings which flank it. No figure need advance to meet the viewer since the work itself advances, in the rapid expansion of façades whose perspectives derive from the Opera House and of which Mason has said in conversation that they amplify the imagined music by their trumpet calls. The viewer is drawn in by what also rushes towards him. And equally, Mason remarked that when working on this relief he felt he was depicting the centre of the world. This is not hyperbole, for a square filled with the crowd and pervaded by art has become an omphalos, the convergence of all places in one, a single place so vividly entered that it changes into Place itself, where all the ways begin. The time of the work is the moment of realising this, as one of its figures takes the last step into consciousness, of the world and of its resounding presence.

In his exploration of place and of human meaning in relation to place, Mason moved, in *Barcelona Tram*, from sunlight to suggestive obscurities. Four years later, he makes of *Place de l'Opéra* a celebration of the Here, of the Now, in an astonishingly shallow low relief where all the depth is in the vivid surface. The anxious underside of experience is dismissed with an ease which surprises in the light of so much of the art and the writing of the century, but then the work does follow *Les Epouvantées*, 'the terrified', of the previous year.

15. *Passers-by,* 1958

Raymond Mason, avril 1958

16. *Boulevard Saint-Germain,* 1958

So much is achieved, in a period often thought to have been dominated by abstraction, through the unashamedly figurative representation of an over-familiar site. On the evening after Mason had done the drawing, a figure not unknown in the world of art remarked to him that earlier in the day he had seen from a distance *un pauvre type* ('some poor fool') drawing the Opera House. Mason enquired the time and admitted the offence.

By studying not human figures only but people in streets, he explores essentially, during this phase of his work, the human meaning of place. It is the human situation that concerns him, in an outdoor world charged with form and with suggestive direction by the strong geometries of the city. The next low relief, *Boulevard Saint-Germain*, advances the exploration by returning to a 'portrait' format and squeezing the sides together so as to produce a new sense of height. It is also, however, the work where Mason for the first time closes exactly with his central subject, by describing a crowd in a street (rather than a square), and achieves the particular depth of focus which this permits.

The work approaches the viewer through the warmly feminine advance of a young woman whose foot is poised on the base of the frame. She is Mason's first representation of 'la Parisienne', who will return in *Carrefour de l'Odéon* and *The Crowd*: of a type of woman, that is, whom he sees as belonging perfectly, in her person and in her dress, to a city where, for over a decade and until the end of the 1950s, everything was thoroughly and bracingly 'Parisian'. The façade along which she walks seems to approach with her, or else it withdraws into the distance of the work, along with the row of gradually diminishing pedestrians which the eye follows down a long gap. This, too, is a productive innovation, the first of many 'tunnelling' effects by which Mason penetrates a visible world and involves the viewer.

The work moves, in fact, between the near and the far, between considerable presence in the foreground and a background into which people and buildings, treated in perspective, will 'vanish'. The opening in the crowd equally leads the eye upwards, to the first trees to appear in a street relief and thence to the sky, which is animated by the first clouds.[12] The façade rising narrowly also suggests the vertical intention of a sculpture unusually high for its width, where the sky itself begins well below half-way. *Boulevard Saint-Germain* is not a mysterious work, but the upright stiffness of the figures and the immobility of most of them (which is not annulled by their reacting against each other as the viewer passes across the front) lends strangeness to the movements inward and upward. The vertical and the receding axes of perception are, potentially at least, axes of otherness. They derive their suggestive power from our situation on an earth above which there exists an infinite height of space and whose surface, even, always disappears eventually below the horizon. The vertical goes to what is over our heads, to the inexplicable proliferation of the real, to the unknown of the sky, and maybe to the intimation of infinitely superior divinity. The receding goes to what is beyond us, to the recesses of the real, to the unknown of our own planet, and maybe to an intimation, within our proper domain, of the sacred, of divinity impinging, albeit at a great distance, on the here and now.

The feeling of rising in the work, which differs entirely from the enclosed and fanning-out verticality of the exuberantly mundane *Place de l'Opéra*, is new in Mason, and confirms his ambition, in a series of reliefs which might have been variations on a theme, always to produce something different and unique. And it matters greatly that both the way up and the way in start from a cluster of people and objects close to the viewer. Mere height and distance rarely occur in Mason, since they are usually associated with, and take their meaning from, a feeling for what is near, a participation in a world within reach. Hence a work's propensity to advance towards the viewer across the intervening space. And hence also the horizontal axis, which traverses sight and speaks most clearly of a presence, of place and of time. Yet in this apparently straightforward work which actually examines with some care the three traditional dimensions of a spatial world, the horizontal axis is also made strange. The gaze of the woman whose head and shoulders are at the entrance

17. Study for *Carrefour de l'Odéon,* 1958

Raymond Mason 1958.

to the sculpture continues endlessly from the large intensity of her eye, and is accompanied by that of a man who is curiously doubled by a second man sitting, equally erect, on a bench and gazing with him. The looks go off to the right, with no hint of 'destiny' but with the suggestion, nevertheless, of a consciousness seen in profile, concerned elsewhere, and travelling to the side.

Perhaps because the artist's interest is in the human situation, the figures are still not individuals, the work remains in that sense impersonal, and the relief presents itself candidly as a work of art. Its graphic quality, which relates it to the drawing technique that Mason considers to be the origin of his sculpture, is shown in the multiplicity of corresponding diagonals crossing and re-crossing the work, and in the active and decisive strokes of the knife. Mason is a great incisor of plaster. He applies and shapes it with the flat and the point of a triangular trowel and also cuts into it with a penknife, which he sees as replacing the pencil in drawing. Most significantly, the figure closest to the viewer is treated, in Mason's own words, 'like a medallion'. Since the eye is led into the distance of the street and up to the sky by the empty pavement seen above her head, and since she traverses the work from side to side, the scene and the dimensions of the scene are set off for the viewer by a small piece of art, by a medallion which exemplifies relief sculpture.

This is very subtly done. For the danger of an art which draws attention to itself blatantly, especially in a period when art has become, for many, the only surviving value in a world without further belief, is that it withdraw attention from the world outside art in which one is obliged, each day, to choose and to act. Mason is particularly well placed to know this, and he has expressed the scarcely possible equilibrium simply and powerfully when declaring of Giacometti, in his essay of 1987, that he concentrated on 'the essential problem, the meeting-point of aesthetics and life, each at its most intense'. The conflict has to be equal and unremitting, for the more intensely the two demands are met and the two desires satisfied, the more they rouse each other to a pitch. Should art at any time predominate, the simplest recourse is no doubt the most effective. Mason also recounts how Giacometti, having in mind a sculpture similar to *The Palace at 4 a.m.* but including the head of his brother, wondered why, instead of struggling with the work, he should not ask his brother to come in and pose. 'Once Diego was sitting on the chair,' Mason continues, 'Alberto had a sombre revelation. This, he remembered, was precisely the problem he had never succeeded in facing at art school and which he had shirked by slipping into modern art.' (The last phrase

says a great deal.) Mason never works with a model, but Paris was his model at the time, and because *Place de l'Opéra* was perhaps 'too aesthetic' he returned to what needed to be represented by confronting the Carrefour de l'Odéon, looking in the same direction as in *Boulevard Saint-Germain* from a short distance back along the same street, for the purpose of producing what he has described to me as 'a slice of life'.

And there is a deeper motive for this redressing of the balance. In the text on Anne Harvey from which I have already quoted, he also says of the 'meeting of the real with thought' that it is a 'dramatic meeting,

where one sees the creator, devoted to his own forms, overwhelmed in the same instant by a world more genial than himself.' This is the first of Mason's several references to Goethe's dictum, which perfectly voices his own acknowledgment that the world is larger than the self and reality greater than art. It is a dictum of which it might be thought that we have some need, in a period rightly critical of the concepts 'world' and 'reality' yet inclined to exploit a philosophical and linguistic problem as a means of avoiding the recognition of an otherness to be understood and adhered to. The particular delight in being thus overwhelmed simply by walking into the street — a delight which all the urban reliefs of the 1950s seek to express — is then described in 'La Foule', a piece of lyrical prose written in French in 1965 as a reflection on *The Crowd* itself, their culmination: 'It begins when I step out of my door. Immediately I am bathed in light. Has anything ever been said of this astonishing moment? I straighten my back, I forget myself so as to wear this mantle of light. Outside, above all, we are part of the celestial'.[13] Stepping into the street is an entry into myth and meaning, provided one leaves one's self behind, according to a double movement, out of the house and out of the ego, which English cannot

18. *Carrefour de l'Odéon,* 1958–59

translate. For the French begins: 'ça commence quand je sors de chez moi', and ends: 'Mais d'abord il faut sortir de chez soi.'

This is absolute Mason, the point of his art. And once outside, it is the art which finds. The shot of a Paris street scene, with a large number of Parisians relaxing in a variety of ways, does indeed discipline the art, so that one is less aware of it, but it also intensifies the art by making it more inward and more searching. *Carrefour de l'Odéon* is a return to high relief, which enables Mason to draw the eye of the viewer deeply into the work 'by the grouping of all the windows and doors' of the boulevard St Germain in 'a multiplication of fine stigmats',[14] and to detach, from the middle-ground façades, the bus moving off to the right and the man moving in from the left. But it also combines with this man a central figure walking towards the viewer, while the man himself, unlike the 'medallion' woman, is about to traverse the whole of the sculpture. No previous relief has exactly this satisfying geometry, because the configuration of streets which allows a wide movement across, together with a movement both approaching and withdrawing and situated in the centre of vision, is of course a *carrefour*, a crossroads.

Mason had noted this perfect dynamic of the two bisecting axes in Seurat, a painter of some importance to him in his willingness to concentrate on a few masterpieces (along with Manet and as opposed to Monet, Degas, Cézanne), and in his rendering of contemporary life. Mason's interest is not in Seurat's *pointillisme* and his engagement with colour and with theories of colour but in his superb composition, which is Mason's own overriding concern and explains many of his other unfashionable enthusiasms, for David, or Joseph Wright of Derby, or Ford Madox Brown. (It is indeed painters who mostly attract him.) A study of his work even enables one to read a Seurat painting with renewed clarity. In *La Grande Jatte* the woman with an umbrella comes towards one from the middle of the scene, while the couple on the right — statuesque in their pose and rendered immense by the long perspective and by the smallness of other figures in their vicinity, especially the further couple seen in the distance beyond their profiles but also immediately in front of them — are about to process across a foreground dominated by their gaze. A similar charging of space is produced in *The Circus Parade* by the looming trombone player and the ring-master, who sends another fixed gaze across the picture plane; but *La Grande Jatte* is clearly of particular interest for also being the most impressive crowd scene, where a large number of apparently random figures are organised with consummate science into a single whole. The crowd scene of *Carrefour de l'Odéon* is also per-

fectly composed, and articulated by the crossing of the approaching woman, another version of 'la Parisienne', and the traversing man, whose entry from the left rather than the right corresponds to Mason's sympathy for rightward movement. By distinguishing the two halves of the horizontal plane he also creates a new division of the work into three sections: the café, the street, the bus, and without undue emphasis alludes to a triptych. The central 'panel' is the two-way motion of a crowd advancing and withdrawing along a narrow passage pressed between rapidly receding façades, that on the left being an excellent example of Mason's skill in moulding the complex surface of an architectural perspective. Even the single figure walking across the centre has been drawn into the force field of this 'procession' (the word is Yves Bonnefoy's, in the finest of all essays on Mason's work),[15] where an approaching humanity is combined with a receding of the human into a distance which is both source and end, and which is indicated sculpturally by the locating of the vanishing point just above the heads. A nearness of human presence is accompanied by a remoteness not foreign to appearance, but within it; by a possible mystery behind but also within the real; by an invisible which happily preserves the visible from being a mere simulacrum.

On the left a second crowd sits at ease with leaning, diagonal poses, along the terrace of a café which is itself a diagonal. Its members are spectators of the scene and themselves most clearly a 'slice of life'. The man on the left, however, who rises to the middle of the work and seems to absorb it all through his long gaze, is strangely alone, his separation emphasised by the removal from the preparatory ink drawing of 1958 (which is now in the Musée national d'art moderne in the Centre Georges Pompidou) of all figures between him and the café. His movement contrasts with the immobility of two other figures seated at separate tables and facing ahead, which both combines the two perpendicular axes of the work as soon as one begins to 'read' it, from left to right, and increases the unfamiliarity of a simple pedestrian.

His movement is accentuated by that of the bus, in which a third crowd is being carried away to the right. The ordinary is opened once again to the suggestion of the other-than-ordinary, of being borne elsewhere, just as the more shadowy architectural forms on this side of the work seem to vanish into the enclosing box of the relief. The importance of the bus is confirmed by its having been added later to the original drawing, where a concentration on the turning of the café means that there is no movement off to the right, and where the absence of a second receding façade invites one to consider less a withdrawing into distance than a jostling of human presence. It is the relief which explores the meaning of a *carrefour*, and the need for the bus shows clearly in the fact that, through its being imposed on the drawing, rather too many people are crossing the road immediately after its passage.

Carrefour de l'Odéon is Mason's homage to 'the great subject — the world which moves around' him, where his own aesthetic demands continue to persuade place to disclose its meanings. For the crossroads in the work joins and carries to a conclusion the other urban shapes in these reliefs, where the coordinates of the city become coordinates of being. A square may be an omphalos, the calling down of a centre, the image of what it is to be here in a world which is everywhere. A street continues into the city the idea of a path, of a way; a boulevard, which stretches perhaps as far as one can see, opens to distance and maybe to infinite withdrawal. A crossroads, however, is a concurrence of all that, a meeting of ways and distances in another form of square, a *here* both more demanding and more revealing, where choice is pressed and possibilities cross. So it is appropriate that *Carrefour de l'Odéon* should be the last of these works, in view also of its combining of the procession of *Boulevard Saint-Germain* with the rightward movement and moving vehicle of *Barcelona Tram*; its perfect association of a visible world both receding and passing across one's view with a daily randomness of experience better provided for than in the *Tram*; and its intimation nevertheless, in that long travelling to the right and in the absorbed erectness of its figures — which Mason may have noted in Seurat and also in Balthus — of the ungraspable nature of what is simply there, of the unexplained which makes of the discovered world, at a passing moment of time, something more than a vacant surface.

An art which, like Mason's, acknowledges the world at a sufficient depth may change it, by a change more secret than distortion. In all these reliefs of the street, a human place, named and situated in the world of others, becomes newly visible and invites the viewer, in the sameness-and-otherness of its representation, to cross a threshold. In its final act of mastery and of being mastered, *Carrefour de l'Odéon* brings to a close this phase of Mason's work (he was thirty-seven when he completed it), prior to his turn from the meaningful geometries of the human city, in an understandable but nonetheless quantum leap, to the larger art of *The Crowd*.

Notes on Chapter II

[1] 'Responses', in Arts Council 1982, p. 13.

[2] This part of the interview does not appear in the translation in Claude Bernard 1977.

[3] For example, in an essay on 'La Foule' of 1965, published in Centre Georges Pompidou 1985, p. 66.

[4] Mason's own example (as are the Giacometti busts), in the interview in Claude Bernard 1977.

[5] Arts Council 1982, p. 22.

[6] See Chapter 10 of Samuel Johnson's *History of Rasselas*.

[7] Letter of Mason of 6 April 1986, quoted in *The Tate Gallery 1982–84, Illustrated Catalogue of Acquisitions*, 1986, p. 272.

[8] *Ibid*. I continue to quote from Mason's comments in the Tate Gallery's *Catalogue of Acquisitions* for the discussion of *Barcelona Tram* unless otherwise stated.

[9] Robert Melville, 'Exhibitions, Painting', *Architectural Review*, vol. 115, no. 689, London, May 1954, pp. 342–3.

[10] David Sylvester, 'A New Sculptor', *The Times*, London, 15 February 1954.

[11] Reproduced in *Encounter*, London, April 1957, p. 31.

[12] There are also clouds in *Boul' Mich*, a small box-less low relief shown at Mason's exhibition in the Pierre Matisse Gallery, New York, in 1968, and illustrated in the catalogue.

[13] 'La Foule', in Centre Georges Pompidou 1985, p. 66.

[14] In *The Tate Gallery 1982–84, Illustrated Catalogue of Acquisitions*, 1986, p. 274.

[15] Yves Bonnefoy, 'La liberté de l'esprit', in Centre Georges Pompidou 1985, p. 13.

19. *Carrefour de l'Odéon* (detail)

III

AN ART OF EXPRESSION

In a two-sentence description of *Carrefour de l'Odéon* for his Arts Council retrospective of 1982, Mason indicates that the doorway to the left of the café terrace would show the scene of Balthus's *Passage du Commerce Saint-André*.[1] By 1958 Balthus was an important presence for Mason, who has described their encounter of three years earlier as the second of his most crucial meetings with an artist, the first being with Giacometti in 1948.[2] On seeing together the paintings which Balthus was preparing for his first retrospective, in 1956, he had been convinced by the breadth of the work and by the 'giant canvases composed with calm mastery' that Balthus was 'the other pillar with Giacometti on which could be built a new art of the figure and the figurative world'.[3] Giacometti had confirmed his need for figuration and given the example of an ascetic dedication to art, but it was Balthus who confirmed his need for composition, and also for a certain size. By causing him, moreover, to look again at Piero della Francesca and thence at Italian fresco in general, Balthus also prepared the way for the later polychrome works. In saluting *Le Passage du Commerce Saint-André*, which is also a work of the 1950s and dates from 1952-54, and which shows a number of diverse human figures in a named Parisian location, Mason was no doubt aligning his own art with an art responding, in its different way, to contemporary life, and with a 'realism' of which he will write much later that it was the means whereby even the rather private Balthus reached the public, since 'realism . . . is the language of everybody', and that, while being for Balthus 'the point of departure, his direct purchase on the world surrounding him', it was also perfectly compatible with the most exacting aesthetic demands.[4] Mason was interested in particular in the theatrical element in Balthus, in the underlined gestures of many of his figures, and this may have entered the motivation for that other series of very different works of the 1950s to which I now turn.

For the 1950s were a rich decade for Mason, in which he produced not only reliefs and drawings of the street and of the city viewed as a panorama, but also the Birmingham watercolours and oil painting of 1958, and the three works which concern us here: *The Idyll* (1955-56), *Les Epouvantées* ('the affrighted') (1956) and the designs of the stage set and costumes for *Phèdre* (1959). Though unrelated, the works form a sequence, and by their theatrical and expressive art, which distinguishes them sharply from the works we have considered so far, they return to an art already stirring in *Belsen Head* and again coming into view in *Barcelona Tram* (which they follow chronologically and whose high relief they adopt), the only street relief to seize a moment and to include other than largely impassive gestures. Above all they reach forward, beyond even *The Crowd*, to the emphatically expressive nature of nearly all the works from *The Departure of Fruit and Vegetables* onwards to the monument for Birmingham, completed in 1991. They are forward-looking also in closing with a subject and narrating an event.

The Idyll even looks like a stage set, with the lovers' bench centre front and the two rows of trees retreating symmetrically to the rear, while the all-absorbing round arch of the upper branches and the foliage spiralling backwards above the lovers are repeated, with surprising closeness, in the actual set for *Phèdre* — where the spiralling depth corresponds to images in the play but also seems to have been ready for use in Mason's imagination. When invited in 1988 to comment on his experience with theatre, Mason declared: 'I am surprised that I haven't had more' — *Phèdre* is his only stage design — 'because I have got a theatrical streak in me. I think that's to be seen in my works. They have a declamatory sort of quality'.[5] It may be that the hostile reviews of his designs for *Phèdre* deprived us of further works for the stage where his art would have been at home. Though maybe not: he had also described the theatre in 1985 as 'a sort of Oriental market' and as 'most seductive' for the artist, who would do better not to 'succumb', while to the remark: 'You obviously prefer to be your own man in the studio', he had replied: 'Yes, I do'.[6] It was probably best that his gift for theatre should express itself in his own works.

The Idyll and *Les Epouvantées* are expressive and, indeed, expressionist in their extreme rendering of love or terror. They were the major items in Mason's 1956 exhibition of *Drawings and Sculptures* at the Beaux Arts Gallery, his last exhibition in England before 1982, which also included, as well as drawings and two lithographs (a panorama of Paris and a view of the Place de l'Opéra resembling the relief), a third sculpture in plaster which represented 'a nude girl behind a glazed window where the shadow of the window-bars emphasized the curves of the body. All this in a box approximately $110 \times 70 \times 40$ cms'.[7] The sculpture was destroyed in a friend's house, though there are drawings. *The Idyll* also no longer exists. Mason modified it for a later exhibition in 1960 at his own gallery in Paris, perhaps because of the treatment it had received in London and certainly through fear that the sentimental nature of the figures would be disparaged by the Parisian public. He removed the figures and the front row of trees and put a sheet of glass in their place. The work was finally abandoned at the Bruni foundry in Rome, with considerable anguish and with Mason suffering greatly from overwork, because his dealer of the time was unwilling, and he was himself unable, to pay for a bronze.

The Idyll is Mason's first figurative treatment of trees and, indeed, of nature, and looks forward to the works of the Luberon. The relation between the natural decor and the lovers, however, is unresolved. As the viewer observes the scene on the stage (almost as if peering into a peep-show), he may read the high rising of the work and its deep withdrawing, along with the suggestion of the wood's continuation to the sides in the additional tree-trunks, as the sign of the larger reality of which the small lovers are a part, especially since the strict alignment of the trees seems to represent the independence of the world outside which not even the self-absorption of passion can ignore. Or this may be a study of the way a world becomes immense at the onset of irresistible emotion, and seems to expand around oneself as centre. The 'tunnel' of trees suggests the recession of the relationship, the unending unknown which might be travelled. The receding horizontal marks on the forest floor resemble a sexual stairway, and they lead to a flagrantly female form which is also a serpentine line — the first to be placed at the centre of a work, many years before the same compositional device is used again in *The Departure*. The female foliage, even, makes the trunks male. An apparently pastoral 'idyll' is exploring, in fact, the erotic implications, the secret images, of the kiss, while all around, the trees are also columns, the branches are a vault, and the forest is a rather overpowering temple of delight.

Yet the whole scene could also be the inner world of the lovers. A work which Mason saw in retrospect as representing his meeting with his second wife, Janine Hao, and whose setting is the Jardin du Luxembourg, seems out of touch with those substantial truths. The Luxembourg Gardens have been abstracted from the city and transposed into the forest of love. The bench is real enough, and might have served to ground a classical idyll in the everyday world of lovers on park benches yet, in the boughs especially, nature seems to bend literally and rather too elegantly to the lovers' will. Relief sculpture, as opposed to most forms of sculpture in the round, allows the artist to place human figures within a non-human reality, but reality in *The Idyll* is little more than the lovers' idea of an appropriate backdrop. Always, with Mason, 'il faut sortir de chez soi', but here, for once, there is nowhere to go.

The trees bend also to the artist's will. The boughs assume romanesque shapes because, when modelling them, Mason seems attentive to the lovers whereas when modelling, say, the vines of *The Grape-Pickers*, he is attentive to vines. The most searching criticisms of *The Idyll* are made possible, in fact, by the values and achievements of his own art, where the real is neither inertly foreign nor an object appropriated by self, but is met by the human mind.

Whatever its deficiencies, *The Idyll* introduces (or re-introduces) into Mason's art the expression of emotion and the modelling of figures who are individuals — in this case, lovers — rather than merely people in the street. *Les Epouvantées*, which is even more gestural, could be read as another invasion of an outer world by an inner, as a collective nightmare in which terror rather than love has acquired the power to take possession of surroundings and to impel them not into order but into disorder. Mason was surprised to discover, much later, a similarity between the opening door at the back of the scene and the half-open shutter in the same position in Arturo Martini's relief sculpture actually called *Il Sogno* ('the dream'). The women themselves can also be seen, however, as possessed by a suddenly irruptive reality. In either case the work is almost unique in Mason's oeuvre in representing an interior. The viewer is no longer outside in the street but inside a violently agitated room or even the stricken psyche of the characters.

For the work is a concentrated study in emotion and its expression. The deep cutting into the plaster, as well as activating the surface suggests, almost mimetically, the terror inside. The curtain (which was reworked in 1960, the new date being added to the sculpture, then later removed) has sufficient likeness to a curtain shaken by a strong gust of wind to be a figurative representation, yet is also the sign of an emotion, a writhing

20. *The Idyll,* 1956

21. *Les Epouvantées,* 1956–60

without a name. The facial expressions — the first after *Belsen Head* and the very first according to Mason's new, realist aesthetic — are heightened by the angles of the heads, and by the equally angular positions of hands and arms which actually cover the faces in part. One might have thought that Mason had found his own solution to the problem identified by Lessing in chapter 3 of the *Laocoön*, that to show the paroxysm of an emotion is to leave nothing to the imagination of the viewer: yet the wide-open mouths, loud imagined cries and immoderate gestures ride over any thought of classical restraint in works like *The Aggression* or the *Monument for Guadeloupe*. The woman rushing forward in *A Tragedy in the North* covers her mouth in preparatory drawings but not in the sculpture itself. Emotion in Mason will be 'hot', overt, operatic, and the half-concealing of themselves by the women serves rather to emphasize the inward nature of the work and the inward direction of their panic. Even the woman who dominates the work and who turns in the direction of the viewer does not in fact face him.

Whatever the discomposure of the women and of the room, the work itself is thoroughly composed, as it needs to be for the emotion to tell. The curtain blows in from the 'sinister' left, a door opens behind, and there is no escape on the right. The forms of the women repeat variously from one to another, while three hands appear as a row. The arms of the central woman form a spiral, closely resembling that of *The Idyll* and placed, as there, at the centre of the work. But what exactly is this 'épouvante', and what is it doing in a Mason sculpture? Has something been released into the work which the viewer cannot quite grasp because the sculptor himself is only half-aware of it? Is the terror that of the artist as artist, the wind that of an inspiration unknown and perhaps unwanted, the presence of women, in Mason's first and only peopled sculpture without a male figure, a disguise for the absence of the sculptor? This is, of course, pure speculation and the only other evidence would be a drawing of the same year or the next, which shows a dog howling by night apparently in terror at something unseen, accompanied by a curtain billowing through a window.[8] Perhaps it is wiser to think that Mason has chosen an extreme emotion capable of inciting him to a comparable extremity of means. He had admired the power of the painted frieze in the Villa of the Mysteries at Pompeii, which he had seen in 1951, and what seems to be the bridal alarm in that recounting of a Dionysiac initiation may even suggest that the terror here is sexual.

Yet it remains puzzling that the emotion he has decided to explore leads to an inversion of his sense of place, and of the sense of life which this implies. In the instant suddenness of the work (which in this too is at the far extreme from *The Idyll*, where the lovers make time stand still), a new dis-ease with place turns the rear and the side of the sculpture not into a mysterious and inviting elsewhere but into a darkly inhabited region of menace from which the here and now is unprotected. Figures in the street scenes walk out into the celestial; the women of *Les Epouvantées* are entered by the demonic. The work is invaded by a primitive terror, and the women themselves, being three in number, recall numerous primitive and classical divinities. *The Idyll* and *Les Epouvantées* both portray human figures caught up into something much larger than themselves, for good or ill, but it is the latter which seems to prepare, with extraordinary precision and yet through a sheer coincidence, Mason's involvement just three years later with *Phèdre*.

This was no ordinary commission. *Phèdre*, Racine's dramatic version of the story of Phaedra and Hippolytus, is no doubt the greatest French tragedy, while the person who invited Mason to design for it was Marie Bell, a foremost interpreter of Racine and a celebrated *grande dame* of the French stage. It was her own company that was to present the play in two gala performances, on 15 and 22 October 1959, at a Paris 'boulevard' theatre, the Théâtre du Gymnase on the boulevard Bonne-Nouvelle, with herself in the title role, Paul Guers as Hippolyte, Jacques Dacqmine as Thésée, Jean Chevrier as Théramène, Henriette Barreau as Oenone and Colette Teissèdre as Aricie. The expectation was that the director would be Jean Cocteau, though in the event and after some delay the person appointed was Raymond Gérôme. Music was provided, at Mason's suggestion, by Pierre Schaeffer, who devised punctual moments of *musique concrète* — when the form which he had invented was still relatively novel, and in the year of *Etudes aux objets* — including at the beginning, as the figure of Venus was illuminated on the stage curtain in the suddenly darkened theatre, a treatment of Marie Bell's voice saying over and over again one of the play's most famous lines: 'C'est Vénus toute entière à sa proie attachée.'

Here was a very public opportunity for Mason to acquire some recognition in a city where his last exhibition had been at the Hôtel Crystal in 1950 and where none of his works since *Man in a Street* had been shown. The play's première was attended by 'le Tout-Paris', with André Malraux, De Gaulle's recently appointed Minister of Culture, in the official box. The public applauded the design, and Malraux was overheard (by Mason himself, jostled against him in the crush after the final curtain) enquiring about the designer and commenting: 'Eh bien, il sait sortir quelque chose d'une boîte', 'He can certainly conjure things out of a box'.[9] Mason was intrigued to realise that he had been doing so almost literally in the animated boxes of his recent high reliefs. Malraux, whose own writings Mason had been reading at the time of *Les Epouvantées* and whose interpretation of the difference between relief sculpture and sculpture in the round Mason will often quote, was to confirm his admiration for Mason's work ten years later by purchasing *The Crowd* for the French State. The play was also to go on to London and Athens, yet theatre reviewers, accustomed to something else, failed to admire, and Mason's set was not discussed, and indeed has never been discussed, as the important and extraordinary work that it undoubtedly is.

22. *Les Epouvantées II,* 1963

It is true that theatrical design can be an ephemeral art, and that Mason's work for *Phèdre* in a sense no longer exists. What remains are the numerous official black-and-white photographs of the performance, along with Mason's drawings and sketchbook, and above all a painted maquette which was exhibited in his 1985 retrospective at the Centre Georges Pompidou. It is equally true that his designs take their meaning from his perception of the meanings of the play. One is not looking simply at a work by Mason but at a collaborative work where the interest, for anyone concerned with Mason or with Racine, will be the effect that each has on the other — or, more pointedly, that the Other has on each.

Mason's designs are a revelation through being totally at variance with the prevailing understanding of how to stage Racine. They reach down into the play's images and render them visible, rather than allowing all that is physical and metaphysical — the labyrinth of the Minotaur, Venus, the sea, the sun; the reverberations of myth and the unconscious — to appear in the characters' language. Jean-Louis Barrault, in a famous study of *Phèdre* published in 1946, the year of Mason's arrival in Paris, had based his decorative scheme on the assumption that *Phèdre* is a 'classical work' demanding 'economy' of means, without any 'ornament or accessory external to the action'. Since all of the play is in the characters, 'the rest should be invisible' and, indeed, the 'difficulty for the designer is precisely there: how to make the setting invisible'.[10] His suggestion of 'walls, vaults, columns, in clear tones, or even white, opaque, pallid' has support from the laconic description of the stage for early productions of the play at the Hôtel de Bourgogne: 'Stage is a vaulted palace. A chair at the beginning.' Designs which propose, on the contrary, a majestic luxury, like those which Mason's friend A. M. Cassandre conceived, also in 1959, for a *Phèdre* at the Comédie-Française, recall performances before the court at Versailles. Neither minimalism nor archeology, however, was concerned to show the reality of the play in the appearance of the stage.

In Mason's designs, ulterior meanings of the work are present in the set and even on the stage curtain, which was covered with a diagonal and foreshortened representation of Venus — the goddess who is the cause or else the guilty projection of the play's tragic passion — ending in an immense and threatening hand, the fingers splayed for 'fastening', as in the words treated by Schaeffer, on their 'prey' (line 306). When the curtain was raised, the hand remained visible on the set, to suggest the goddess's manipulation of the events. The sketchbook shows that Mason had originally thought of placing a statue of Venus on the stage itself, to which Phaedra would have addressed her protestations.

The labyrinth, into which Theseus has descended so as to kill the Minotaur and into which Phaedra imagines herself going down to damnation with Hippolytus, her stepson and the object of a love which is considered incestuous, was exposed to view in a series of diminishing arches centre-stage, picked out in black against the natural colour of hessian, which withdrew, turned and disappeared. It is true that the only part of the stage on which Mason could build deeply was the centre, since *Phèdre* was to be given during the Thursday breaks of another play (Félicien Marceau's comedy *La bonne soupe*, in which Marie Bell was performing alongside Jeanne Moreau), for which the stage had already been constructed. That the central, receding axis should be a spiralling labyrinth, however, is a creative transformation of constraint into opportunity, so as to manifest on the stage this image of a terrified descent into the psyche which is likewise a sexual form, and which Mason also refers to as 'entrails'. It was even Mason's own first thought, since it figures on the opening page of his sketchbook, where one also sees, from later sketches, that this spiral which so belongs to him had to assert itself against the claims of a more orthodox recession of columns under a flat ceiling.

Mason wished only Phaedra to enter through the labyrinth (Barrault, too, had labelled a corridor facing the audience 'the Phaedra way'),[11] and at her first appearance a red light pursuing her seemed to turn the spiral until she finally emerged into the full sunlight of the stage. The circling of the arches is then displayed again in the *oeil-de-boeuf* placed immediately above their entrance, which also figures the Sun himself, the mythological ancestor of Phaedra, who 'dazzles' (line 155) and oppresses her with his relentless illumination. Because of its black centre and black rays against the ochre of the hessian, Mason also sees it as recalling the splendour of Racine's century and of the Sun King, Louis XIV, but by a process of inversion. A black sun — the *soleil noir*, perhaps, of melancholy — is indeed the perfect emblem of a tragic theatre suffused with the glory of an age and of human possibility yet steeped at the same time in the darkness of human desire.

The nearby sea — which is the lair of another monster, a bull-like creature reminiscent of the Minotaur, who will eventually emerge to kill Hippolytus — is present in wave-like forms writhing inwards from the left and recalling the curtain of *Les Epouvantées*. With touches of sea-blue and green yet predominantly yellow, they also suggest a passion whose 'flames' and 'fire' progressively invade the language of the play and devour the characters.

Mason himself painted the set and even the curtain which, being the size of a tennis court, required brooms rather than brushes. Much of the set was black, as if projected from the 'black flame' of Phaedra's love (line 310) and the 'blackness' of her action (line 1645), while the costumes included areas of black designed to blend with the scenery so as to suggest 'distance in space and time', in perfect keeping with Racine's view of the otherness of the heroes of tragedy. The women's costumes — dark reds for Phaedra, purple for Oenone, white for Aricia — would seem to have contributed to this distancing by draping them into the form of Greek columns; the costumes of the men — gold for Theseus and silver for Hippolytus — were modelled according to the musculature of the naked body and were intended to recall statues of the gods. (Barrault had also written of Hippolytus that 'his muscles are his costume',[12] though he was considering the physique of the actor.) Marie Bell eventually had the costumes made by a dressmaker not of Mason's choice, and those for the men were cruder than intended. She also disturbed the visual coherence of the work by choosing to wear the dress in which she had appeared as Phèdre before at the Comédie-Française.

Although the curled hair of the men was another reminder of Racine's own period, it is in the 'distant mythology' of the classical world that Mason situates the action. That mythology is evoked for us, he writes, 'artistically speaking, by the statues and bas-reliefs of Greek sculpture', and if the statues are visible in the actors (in the sketchbook, Mason drew the main lines of the musculature on a photograph of the Piombino Apollo in the Louvre), bas-reliefs and the pediments on which they figure are visible in the disposition of actors across the shape of the stage, with its powerful centre and its passages off to the right and to the left. (Mason had even supplied the director with drawings which described the movements of all the actors in every scene, though these were, not unnaturally, ignored.) *Phèdre* is the important occasion, in fact, for the entry into Mason's work, through a prompting from outside, of Greek sculpture, which also serves to govern within

the severities of order the otherwise flamboyant, baroque excess of the designs.

Order and excess are wholly attuned, in fact, to the play, where the savagery of myth, the rage of the psychic and the elemental, are delivered in a dramaturgy and a prosody consummately disciplined into consonance. Mason even writes, in a phrase full of interest for a poet, that 'the taut and chiselled alexandrines of Racine were perfectly suited to a sculptor'. The steps leading into the labyrinth were also intended to reproduce for the eye the succession of regular and end-stopped lines, while in the stones of the arch one can see the twelve syllables of the alexandrine, divided by a firm caesura. Mason's real sympathy for Racine can also be gauged from a drawing he made so as to calculate how to utilise the already existing stage. It shows Phaedra caught in a moment of extreme emotion which runs through all the upper part of her body, and yet placed among carefully measured distances, her right foot posed, for instance, so as to rise 15 centimetres.

But what of Racine's impact on Mason? During the delay in the appointment of a director, Mason, suffering from sciatica, seized the opportunity of studying Racine thoroughly. It was 'one of the most enthralling and fruitful periods of my artistic life', he writes, and it is true that for an Englishman, Racine is likely to be either a very foreign enigma to esteem within limits, or the slowly astonishing revelation of a different art, of a whole, French world, of another way of perceiving and naming experience. He certainly encouraged in Mason that expression of extreme emotion upon which he had entered already in *The Idyll* and *Les Epouvantées*, although it was many years, strangely, before Mason returned to such dramatic art. Racine also drew from him a colourful and spectacular art like nothing that he had produced before, which also remained for a long while in abeyance. And he gave him the occasion to reuse and to re-examine his own ways of plotting space.

23. *Phèdre Act V,* 1959

For the whole set resembles a Mason relief, and most particularly *Carrefour de l'Odéon* — which was completed in the same year — with its similar three-fold division into a long and foreshortened movement in the centre both towards and away from the viewer, and two dissimilar sides providing a wide lateral movement. If one also recognises, however, in the retreating columns under a round arch, the architectural suggestion of the archway of trees in *The Idyll*, the withdrawing axis here is the index not of sexual pleasure but of erotic self-horror. It leads not to the inviting otherness of place but to the retreat of the monstrous; the eye of the spectator is drawn in as usual, but to a place that is alien. The spiral of *The Idyll* also returns but has been demonised, the sign of life inverted into the sign of death. There is again 'destiny' to the side, but the waves on the 'sinister' left speak of a Neptune who will answer Theseus's rash cursing of his son by having Hippolytus slain. Even the vertical axis, as represented on

the stage curtain, is not a rising to 'the celestial' but a swooping down of the destructive goddess and her grasping hand. The hand will become a potent symbol for Mason, a meeting of the sculpture and the viewer, an offering of fraternity by the artist to the public, yet it too, despite the fact that it appears here for the first time, has become fiendish.

All three dimensions of a spatial world lead, in fact, to the memory of the Minotaur behind, to a sea beast on the left, and to an avenging goddess above. None of these monstrous axes is indicated in Racine's text, and yet the surrounded, untenable stage is thoroughly Racinian. It may be that Mason was lending baleful connotations to his own forms in the service of a tragic and 'religious' world-view which was not his own and to which, as a designer for someone else, he had no need to commit himself. Yet the existence three years earlier of *Les Epouvantées* suggests that Mason was responding more nearly to something in the play, where the word

Le rideau de scène, "Phèdre."

24. *Phèdre, the Curtain,* 1959

'épouvante' actually occurs (lines 224, 1305, 1524) and where all of the characters are invaded by a horror larger than life. His humanism may have confronted, with whatever degree of consciousness in the creative act, the conceivability of other frontiers to human place and other forces at work in the human psyche. Even more than *Les Epouvantées,* the design for *Phèdre* is the dark side of his oeuvre. Mason chose neither the play nor the playwright, yet *Phèdre* seems almost to have chosen him. This is no doubt why, as in the other collaborative art of translation, the result is so persuasive and original.

The celebratory, life-affirming nature of his own art, however, is enacted in the aesthetic exuberance of the design, and even discloses a similar affirmation in the play itself. His reading of the ending in particular is a happy collaboration between his own humanist optimism and what one might think of as the tragic optimism of Racine. One sign of this is actually an effect

he had not entirely anticipated: the gold glowing of the back-lit set during Theramenes's recital, in the penultimate scene, of the death of Hippolytus. The gold is a final showing of the Sun and of the age of the Sun King, and is appropriate also since, in defiance of Euripides and Seneca, Racine has Hippolytus dispatch the monster who kills him, and thereby complete the purifying work of his father and the labours, even, of Hercules. The clearest sign is in a series of small ink drawings on a single sheet arranged, act by act, in five rows and depicting key moments in almost every scene. Each drawing is accompanied by words pronounced by the characters. Detached at the base of the work is a drawing of the entrance and of the labyrinth itself ablaze with light. Characters stand in the same light on either side, while above, the dark sun of the *oeil-de-boeuf* has been transformed into a real sun unmistakably shining. Only Phaedra is a black shape lying on the steps. The emergent yet still tragic ending is perfectly realised by the

49

verse lines on each side of the scene: Phaedra perceiving that death, by withdrawing brightness from her eyes, 'restores to the light they sullied all its purity'; Theseus bearing with him into the renewed light the memory of a 'dark' action, and preparing to mourn his son. Mason's sudden and final radiance, tempered by all that precedes it as the eye travels over the page or the mind over the play, is a more just reading of the *dénouement* of Racinian tragedy than that of many critics determined to circumscribe Racine within knowing and more contemporary negations.

Mason writes of the surprising choice of an Englishman, born in Shakespeare's county, to work on a play so decidedly French and neoclassical. It is true that his approach leaves little scope for the spectator to call on his own resources, whereas the force of the more customary French staging is to allow the images of the play and its gradual evocation of a large geography and of an immense cosmology, at once celestial, terrestrial and infernal, to strike the mind without the intervention of the eye. One can at least understand the critical disapproval of his designs and of their unwonted outrightness. Yet I am sure he was justified in claiming to have come very close to the 'sentiment vrai', the true sense, of *Phèdre*, while in the history of Racinian staging his contribution is evidently unique.

To judge from the surviving evidence, he is also right to consider his *Phèdre* to be one of his major achievements. And yet one can still be surprised by his enthusiasm for a writer who works by a choice and eliminating intensity. His own art, refusing the simplifying of Matisse, the concentration and focus of Giacometti, exists through abundance, through repetitions across multiplicity, through openness to any expressive means however far from the canon. In the sequence of works in which I have placed it, the design for *Phèdre* is nevertheless intelligible. In his first attempts at creating individual figures expressing emotion in a dramatic scene, he chooses only two for *The Idyll* and then three for *Les Epouvantées*. In *Phèdre* — by chance and rather neatly — he was dealing with four principal characters. His confidence having gathered strength, as it were, through these works and also through by now quite crowded reliefs of the street, he was about to produce, with a sudden eruption of certainty and ambition and following a single hand and a three-fold torso, no less than ninety-nine figures of *The Crowd*. Appropriately, and as the perfect sign of where his origins really lie, the work following *The Crowd*, the first large composition in which the figures are individualized and united by an emotion, will be *The Departure of Fruit and Vegetables from the Heart of Paris*, a mainly Northern work whose human drama is not Racinian at all, but Shakespearean.

Notes on Chapter III

[1] Arts Council 1982, p. 28.

[2] In Centre Georges Pompidou 1985, p. 146.

[3] 'Responses', in Arts Council 1982, p. 13.

[4] In 'Balthus', a text written for a French radio broadcast in December 1983 on Balthus' exhibition at the Centre Georges Pompidou, published in Centre Georges Pompidou 1985, p. 83.

[5] From an unpublished interview given to Jane Farrington.

[6] In 'The Torrent of Life', in Birmingham 1989, p. 37.

[7] In Mason's letter to the Tate Gallery of 6 April 1986, quoted in *The Tate Gallery 1982–84, Illustrated Catalogue of Acquisitions*, 1986, p. 277.

[8] The drawing is reproduced in *Encounter*, London, May 1957, p. 48. Another version of the drawing, without the flapping curtain, is reproduced in *La Délirante*, Paris, Summer 1982, p. 176.

[9] Mason himself refers to the incident in an unpublished note, 'Marie Bell et *Phèdre*', from which I shall continue to quote.

[10] 'Phèdre' de Jean Racine: mise en scène et commentaires de Jean-Louis Barrault*, Editions du Seuil, Paris, 1946, pp. 37, 38.

[11] *Ibid.*, p. 74.

[12] *Ibid.*, p. 73.

25. Right: ink drawings for *Phèdre*, 1959

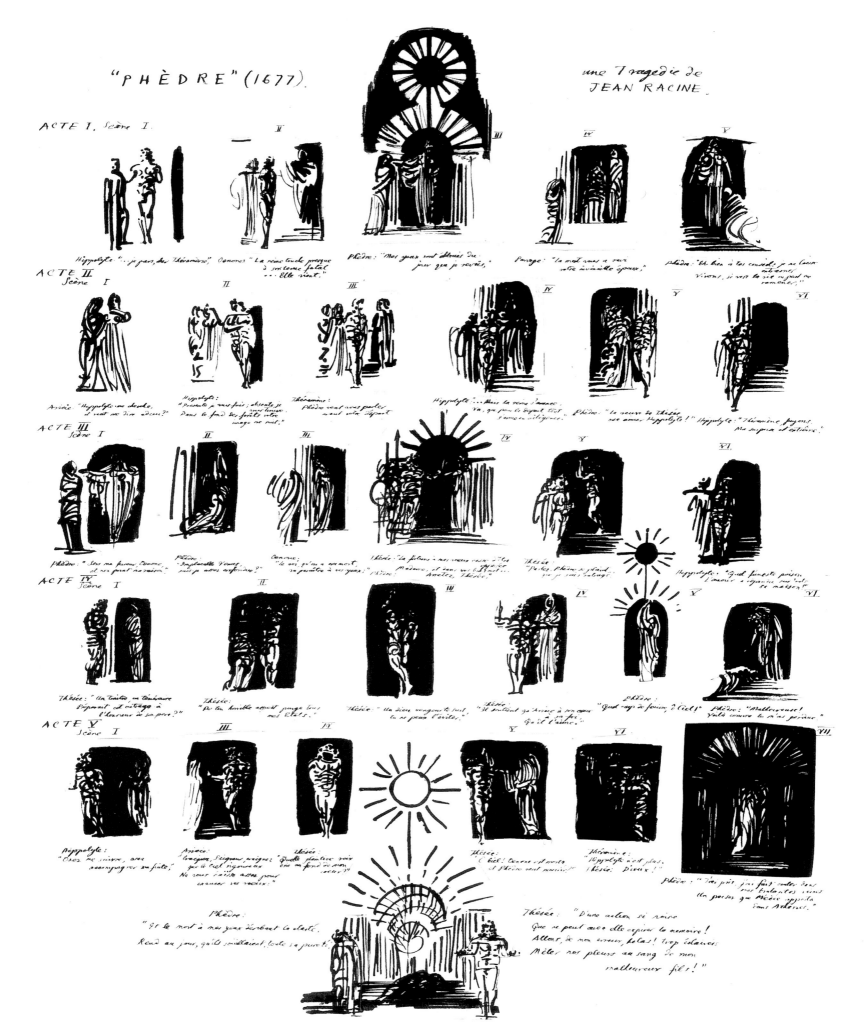

26. *Birmingham. In Memoriam, 1958*

IV

PAINTING THE END AND THE BEGINNING

Those works of the later 1950s develop an art quite different from that of the continuing series of urban reliefs and drawings. The works of a third group, depicting Birmingham, deepen the relation to place, introduce both the emotion of the artist and the themes of history and of the passage of time, and, perhaps because they return Mason to his own beginning, return him also to his beginnings as a painter, and hence to colour. Mason went back to Birmingham in 1958 on the death of his mother, for the first long stay since his departure for France in 1946. He lived for a while in his old home, to sell the furniture and close up the house, and out of this experience of recovery and loss came a number of watercolours of the street and its environs, executed on the spot, and, on his return to France, a panoramic oil painting of the city itself. The most important of the water-colours is a naming of his street: *Wheeleys Lane, Birmingham*, a realist work which nevertheless personalises in a new way the angle of gaze. The oil painting, which names his city, *Birmingham. In Memoriam*, is a quite separate, visionary work which stands alone among his very few paintings in oil and which announces the visionary dimension of later realist sculptures.

In that emotionally charged moment, Mason encountered once again, after the quiet and civil luminosity of Paris, the reds which had filled his eyes as a child. And those red bricks, which had created in the nineteenth century a unified urban whole and had spread the weatherable depths of their colour, in farms and great houses, over the sodden greens of the surrounding countryside, were also a hearth of images, with the redness of warmth and of human life-blood. The bricks of the house in Wheeleys Lane 'kept me warm', Mason writes, 'during my childhood', at a time when even the red-brick factory on the other side of the road was a 'peaceful giant', and shared in that world of story which in childhood enters and animates the real.[1] So in *Wheeleys Lane* 'I wanted to paint every brick', he has said, 'because every brick meant something to me.'

The reviving of meaning leads to his painting the rich brickwork of the houses not in fact in watercolour but in red sepia mixed with water, with the lines of certain areas marked in ink. Emotion seems to permeate, brick by brick, the black-stained or white-stained façades, as also the rain-soaked road, and chimneys reaching up into the sky. The character Imlac in Johnson's *Rasselas*, whom I quoted earlier as claiming that the poet 'does not number the streaks of the tulip', continues: 'or describe the different shades in the verdure of the forest.' Mason is an artist for whom numbering the bricks of the wall is the index of a true participation in place, and for whom the many different shades in the redness of a façade — where the smoke of a manufacturing city has entered variously into the bricks and the mortar and where decay and neglect have randomly blanched or roughened the surface — sustain one day by day in one's local inhabiting of a significant world. The endless changes from each small area to the next create for the artist and for the viewer an inexhaustible texture to observe, and also elicit emotion for every thing itself as represented: for those peeling door-surrounds, that window with the neat lace half-curtain, that other window where a brown curtain has been pulled open at an angle.

Of the recurring bricks, the recurring chimneys and, indeed, the recurring houses, each with a door and three windows (for three rooms) one above the other, all are alike yet none is identical. We may be at the origin here of something quite fundamental to Mason's work, a proliferating repetition which nonetheless avoids mere sameness. It will return most visibly in certain of the large sculptures, to take hold of paving-stones or vine leaves, and we shall need to consider its meanings. In *Wheeleys Lane* it seems to rise to its source, in a working-class childhood where Mason found himself nevertheless in a world of copiousness, whose properties repeated themselves on all sides with an almost infinite power of variation.

He was unaware at the time of his visit that only a few years later the street would be partly demolished, but he did realise that he was bidding it goodbye. It is

Cregroe Street. Birmingham 1958.
pour Sam.

Raymond Mason

27. *Cregroe Street. Birmingham,* 1958

the emotion of this departure, along with the usual generous and ingenious attentiveness of looking, which guides his hand, and which views the scene on a slant. The work neither spreads horizontally across the visual plane nor approaches and recedes directly. It draws the viewer in down diagonals retreating to the left, past a side road which, like the Lane itself, curves and disappears to the right, or else the street advances and moves past the viewer, the Lane becoming a two-fold Way, the joining of a vanished past and a future largely unknown. For time determines, now, the angle of vision. Is Mason painting the scene in front of him, or the scene as it was some thirty years previously? He has chosen (like Wordsworth, like Proust) both of those moments, so that a past reappears in a present to enrich it with an unforgotten hinterland of returning experience. He observes his childhood indirectly, both across and along his street, as if intruding, as indeed he is, from elsewhere, and places in the real and fictive scene a little girl at a corner — facing away and rather ghostly in the pallor of her dress, hovering forever between a memory of her and her own vanishing — who

used to wait regularly outside that pub for her parents to come out, and also himself as a boy, bending over and stroking the neighbours' dog, in touch with the emotion of another life. And he regards that earlier self from an even more hidden angle, from the side but also from behind. The perspective on self is both intimate and remote and is most clear in the words written on the painting, under the title: 'en souvenir de moi-même'. They announce several carefully chosen later titles which have a literary function through their opening an imaginative door on to a work, since the use of French on a watercolour of Birmingham suggests a geographic as well as temporal distance and causes even 'myself' to become foreign.

By moving from 'man in a street', from works in which the artist looks about him with a great but largely impersonal pleasure at human and architectural forms in the light, to 'boy in a street', where the boy is his own recovered, absent yet present, past, Mason finds a way — or simply comes on it — of suffusing a work with a personal emotion, not free-floating and all-consuming as in *The Idyll*, and not simply nostalgia, but one that responds accurately to a visible and remembered whole and that lodges with particularity in the details of the seen. The details are known through long acquaintance, and through the action of time on memory, on the successive configurations of experience and relationship that we call 'I'. And we are certainly, here, at the origin of Mason's act of seeing. As a child he had only too much opportunity to gaze at this scene, because his asthma prevented him from going to school in the morning. Day after day, in the downstairs room of the house towards whose door the boy in the painting is turned as if he would re-enter it, he looked out at the same street, the same factory, the same brewery cart and horses, and what must have seemed the same few cars. That slowing of attention, that repeating and deepening of the work of perception, is the founding possibility of an art which is everywhere an unceasing act of acknowledging the seen, of deferring to a world

irremovably there. This child is most evidently father of the man, and here is how Mason himself describes the relation of inner to outer: 'I . . . would sit in an armchair', he writes, 'taking in not only the asthma powder burning on the arm of the chair but also the street's little activity which I could see through the withdrawn window-curtain.' The syllepsis, the change of sense between 'taking in' powder and 'taking in' a scene, concisely enacts the drama of self in Mason, where what is occurring here, and even within one's body, is shown by a humorous comparison to be of less importance than what is occurring out there. He had recounted in a similar way the origin of *St Mark's Place, East Village, New York City*, where he was actually seated at a café window and looking at the happenings along a street: 'he gobbled up the astonishing characters who passed before his gaze more than he did the meal on the table'.[2] That early scene, of the sickly child obliged to gaze out

28. *Wheeleys Lane. Birmingham,* 1958

on a small piece of world, is the unlikely beginning; and the many spectators in Mason's work, some of whom also look out so that the viewer may in turn look in at them, and who celebrate by their looks the act of seeing, would seem also to be a way of dealing pleasurably with the no doubt extremely unpleasant illness which had made of the young Mason himself a captive spectator.

One is drawn into the work, towards the far curve of the street, the faraway and hardly present adults, the lighter distance where one might have expected a darkening of the mood, and more deeply into suggested spaces and reflections. In a world thick with time, the façade of the buildings is full of entrances, of doors and windows and passageways leading into the secret of backyards, and is mirrored in the drenched roadway, which mirrors in turn, literally and also by the intenser colours of its similar triangular shape, the sky above. Deep with presence and coherent in its responding forms and substances, the scene has been revived and, in the reviving, finally created. It will not, now, disappear, and the suggestion of its permanence was perfected by Mason's removal of the original left-hand edge of the work. In the year of *Boulevard Saint-Germain*, this had shown the façade of the factory on the near side of the road in a rapidly diminishing perspective. The shape of the whole was satisfying and the 'peaceful giant' was faithfully and successfully rendered — so much so that Mason has recently framed it as a work in its own right. It was removed so as to focus interest on 'me' and 'my house'. The result is a more mysterious work, where the median horizontal exits to the left with the rooftop of the final house, and where, crucially, the median vertical descends through the door of the painter's house itself. A threshold to the past, an entrance to the room from which the child looked out at the world, the door sustains the whole, in a force field which includes the boy and his dog, rather as the post of Odysseus's bed sustained his palace.

As an origin, *Wheeleys Lane* also includes, in the claw-like form of some of the chimney-pots, a possible source for Mason's dramatic and quite violent sculptor's sense of the way objects and their outlines strike against the ambient space. In his description of *St Mark's Place*, for example, he writes of the 'turreted roof' and the 'battlemented fixity' of a police car, and claims of the jostling figures in the scene that 'their crenellation claws and stirs the air around'.[3]

As an art of the real, the painting intensifies the scene so as to entice the imagination. From the water of the roadway one passes to the fired earth of the brick façades and thence to the air of the sky. An entirely urban view, with not even a tree, opens all the same to a kind of elemental life. The water on the road, moreover, is actual water ('That week was *rainy*', Mason has written, 'but I managed to make several very complete watercolours of the street, the factory and its surroundings'),[4] and the removal of the factory means that the viewer has to cross water before reaching childhood. A similar effect is obtained in another of this group of works, *Factory and Cemetery, Birmingham*, where, beyond the gleaming reflections on the rainy surface of a railway bridge is a scene rising to the right with a cemetery occupying a small hollow to the left. The cemetery seems to be in the midst; the only trees are growing within it. One crosses the water to houses, to Mason's 'own' factory seen from the other side and to the church of his own school — to the properties, in fact, of a town — and, down beneath, to the quiet signs of death and of life. In *Wheeleys Lane* too, a vision of the real slowly brims in the features of the visible.

The power of *Birmingham. In Memoriam. September 1958*, on the other hand, comes from the immediately visionary reading of a scene, and from an emotion that has become large and impersonal. When actually present in the streets of his boyhood, Mason recovers and exposes origin. When back in Paris, with the not yet completed *Carrefour de l'Odéon* waiting for him in his studio, he employs the emotions deriving from departure and dispossession to create a new kind of elegy. The work is still autobiographical, and begins in a thoroughly personal emotion, in which, indeed, more than Birmingham is involved. He made the painting, he writes, 'in memory of my mother and my city', for 'my mother was dead and clearly the city I knew was dying.' The return to beginning coincides with its loss; an emotion of attachment to the place and to the giver of birth is both called out and thwarted, and memorialised at the moment of Mason's definitive leave-taking of Birmingham and England for Paris and France. He witnessed the demolition, in fact, and was naturally most sensitive to its effect on him: 'Around me the bulldozer had cleared away the houses I had known . . . Gone the pub of my grandfather, gone my past.' But he also saw the destruction of a whole, and has often recounted his last night in the city and the haunting image which came to mind: 'All day it had rained but now the clouds rolled away and suddenly a great sunset lit up the red-brick city. With emotion I realised that when that sun sank, the moon of modern times would rise and all would be white concrete.' An attention which goes out to what is beyond the concerns of self works through metaphor to transform a personal into an impersonal emotion, and to raise the indispensable individual interest to a vision of historical change. A painting dedicated, moreover, not to the memory of 'myself'

29. *Factory and Cemetery,* 1958

but to the memory of Birmingham, is unsigned.

So the art of elegy here in no way consists of painting brick by brick; it aims for something other than loving detail, and for a different kind of likeness. Houses are dim black marks for doors and windows — whose edges, even on the closer façades, are blurred by distance but especially by the darkening or lurid light — and warm red walls whose colour seems to emanate from within. These painted houses resemble actual houses, but they represent more nearly a feeling for the real presence of a house, and for the real presence of humans behind the soft apertures in the slowly burning façades. A glow of emotion for the threatened city seems to emerge from these hearths, and to spread over the whole of the foreground in the browns which represent nothing more than open terrain, the wide and featureless waste ground of the present from which to observe the city disappearing, in all its sun-struck intensity, in the far distance.

The two levels of the work materialise the elegiac perspective and create a new relation of the spectator to place. The panorama is not seen from some high building but from the street itself; the painting enters the viewer's space and begins, as it were, at his feet. Even this immediacy, however, is not solid ground: it extends uncomfortably beyond the sides of the work, and lurches between the descending house-fronts on the right

and the considerably lower terraces on the left, which seem to rise. As the whole view finally plunges away from him towards the distant conflagration, the viewer may experience a kind of vertigo, in this first and only Mason work where the composition serves to unsettle one by the disparate levels and conflicting inclines of a place not under control.

For what is menaced in the faraway vision is nothing less than beauty itself. The city which the rest of the world cited as the epitome of ugliness even appeared, to the eyes of the twenty-year-old artist, 'a painter's dream, it was so beautiful'. It may come as a surprise to anyone who has been there that Birmingham could be considered aesthetically pleasing, yet the surviving examples of carefully designed and decorated redbrick buildings suggest that his judgment was correct, and that to enter into his way of looking, where one is not asked merely to admire Siena, say, or Geneva, is an education for one's own eyes. It is true that he is also thinking, beyond the forms and colours of the town, of its clarity of social purpose, of citizens 'solidly present, performing significant, useful tasks' in 'decisively shaped buildings encompassing the human act'. An unwillingness to separate the aesthetic from other human concerns will be the ground-bass of many of his judgments, against abstraction, against the notion of 'painting' and 'sculpture' as free-floating and autonomous activities, and it is important to note that the origin of this holistic view is to be found, in Mason's case, in the experience of a manufacturing city of the European north. The beauty which the painting pursues is nevertheless exceptional and indeed unique. Interviewed for the *Independent* when his other and much later work for Birmingham, the monumental sculpture *Forward*, was installed in Centenary Square, he claimed that Birmingham had been 'a perfect city in red brick' and that this was 'a very particular red' that he had not seen anywhere else.[5] Although he avoids the singularity of the definite article, this can hardly fail to remind one of classical and renaissance utopias, and perhaps in particular of the *Ideal City* of Piero della Francesca or his entourage. The perfect city for Mason is not a supreme combination of geometrical forms, whose end would be to gather the earth and human lives into the scene of Number and the shadow of heaven; nor is it, indeed, ideal. Birmingham belongs among the perfect cities through being the world's first manufacturing town and the first red-brick metropolis, with a colour peculiarly its own.

It is this sense of a beauty special in history and intimately lived in through childhood — of a beauty lost and irreplaceable — that accounts for the extraordinary ardour in the distance. What one sees there is the beauty of a city taken to the extreme, to the verge of disappearing from the world of ordinary visibility: a beauty on fire, red bricks become red coals. The city is almost unreal in the enhancement of its reality. Even its forms are vivid strokes of paint. Industrial chimneys rise up like secular spires. A factory in that blaze is like the fiery analogon of some great cathedral. One enters further and further, in fact, into the visionary nature of the painting, which is quite without precedent in Mason's works and which represents the city according to the image through which he actually saw it on that last night. For he has also said of the sunset: 'It was a flaming vision'.[6] To gaze into the incandescent distance, where the sun does not so much light the city as heat it, is like gazing into a furnace — the furnace, maybe, of a Birmingham factory, the heart of the city from which warmth was diffused, the core of creation in the vision and the emotion of the artist. One looks from the street and from houses, from the world as known, down and over into the unknown depth of place, of person, and of art.

All the city, moreover, has entered vision. Chimney-stacks on the roofs to the right disappear in their mystery into the blues of the heavy sky. A path winding back is more the image of a path, its edges delimited by thick lines as in children's art or a Fauve painting. If the embers of the fire glow red in the distance prior to their extinguishing, coals and soot are still visible in the combustion near by. The masterly transitions from colour to colour also gather the whole scene into a single activity, and focus it eventually on a sign of possible meaning which comes into view exactly at the meeting of the near and the far. For the middle ground is in fact indicated by a black line crossing the work. It resembles a path yet its trace encroaches on a descending path and road in a way that implies less a fidelity to observation than the stress of vision. It passes the foot of a tall and conspicuous post across which another thin black line seems to be drawn, though this is in reality the roof-line of terraced houses further away. The cross is only present for the eye, at this place of the painting marked by simple black strokes, but once seen it stands clear in the centre of the view. To its left the forms of a church are prominent, picked out strikingly and graphically in black, while the steeple rises high into the clouds. The church is the frontier between the two zones of the city, joining houses to factories as if it intends to be the crucible of meaning for both home and work.

In also joining the earth to the sky, it leads one to a further unity. The painter, in a work to the memory of a city and of a mother, has filled a good half of the canvas with sky and has so lowered the horizon that the sky reaches down to below half-way. The city also reaches into the sky, its browns, mauves and reds being repeated in the clouds and in the airs beyond them, while the blues of the sky descend into the depiction of the urban distances, where blue patches on the far-away plain read like reflections of the sky above. The city is caught up into imagination and infringed on by the heavenly, as if the artist is seeking an irradiating significance in that vehement and departing immensity. In a world where he is convinced of the demise of Christianity, the sky performs its work above a church invested with the emotion of someone who attended a church school and was happy there, and above a fragile cross which is only present if one cares to see it.

The sky is shaped in such a way, moreover, as to lead beyond even Birmingham imagined over in the distance, to a further and invisible City behind the terraced houses on the right. A frail, yellowish cloud — set apart from the mass of brown, orange and red cloud seemingly moving in from the left, as a sign of hope, a small token of new and innocent light to survive the intervention of the moon and darkness — is equally a door to this ulterior region of the work, to the scene unseen, to a concealed district of the city which, as so often in Mason, curves away to the right and draws the eye after it. Although only mysterious through not being visible, according to perception and its ordinary laws, this is nevertheless the domain of possibility, where the sun itself is to be found, the origin of the work's ardency

as of 'celestial' light. Owing to the intelligence of the composition, moreover, what is in every sense farthest away from the viewer occurs just behind what is closest, a row of familiar houses.

That *Birmingham. In Memoriam* should be a visionary painting is explained by the image in which Mason had viewed the city and, surprisingly, by the terms in which he always imagines it. On another occasion when he rebuts the charge that Birmingham was ugly, he calls it not beautiful but 'marvellous and transcendental',[7] and he warms to Dickens's figural description of Birmingham or 'Coketown' in the fifth chapter of *Hard Times*: 'It was a town of red brick, or of brick that would have been red if the smoke and ashes had allowed it; but as matters stood it was a town of unnatural red and black like the painted face of a savage.' It is interesting that Mason has lifted what he calls in a letter this 'prodigious description' quite out of Dickens's stream of disapproval, and even more significant that when translating the passage into French he defines the savage more strikingly as a 'Sioux' and alters 'unnatural' to 'supernatural', thereby transposing Dickens's disparagement into another vision of the city's transcendence.[8] For a painter to see the colours of a city as beyond nature and to agree that its accurate description might require the remote simile of a Redskin in warpaint is to accept that an exclusively figurative art could fall short of the truth, and that realism would need to be intensified from within so as to attain such reality.

While moving beyond the visible in search of invisible meaning, however, the painting nowhere abandons the actual townscape, and presents Birmingham in September 1958 as viewed at sunset from Lee Bank Hill. Its art is at once oneiric and figurative, and if the grime over the façades in *Wheeleys Lane* is the print of time, which makes things not merely more old but more real, black smudges and sharp streaks in *Birmingham. In Memoriam*, however supernatural, also affirm the truth of that kerb, of the edge of that wall. Hence the slightly

curving black line bordered with mauve and parting the concave brown surfaces in the right-hand foreground. It is mimetic in that it seems to represent a depression in the road, but it also intrudes as a line scored on the work to the base of the canvas, in the area where the painter's hand would naturally be. One can read it as a wound, as the darkness of grief, or as an impress, a groove, of presence, a trace of the hand that made it and the signature of an emotional belonging. As a sign from our time, where signs can no longer simply be read and fail to give access to luminous meanings in a world of meaning, it points inwards to the work, and to its search, over the way, for a significant sky and a future.

The fineness of the work — Balthus told Mason that it was the best urban landscape of the twentieth century — comes also from its not merely portraying a view but having a subject. It represents, with *The Idyll* and *Les Epouvantées*, a turn in Mason's art, and goes beyond anything he had attempted before in that it also captures a turn in history, the disappearing of a unique city and also, as one sees with hindsight, the passing of the world of work. It announces later sculptures which arrest into permanence a historical crisis, whether May '68 in Paris, or an abortive revolution in Guadeloupe, or else — and did he see this as an answer to *Birmingham. In Memoriam*, a beginning rather than an end? — the founding of Washington, D.C. Its vision of a disappearing *there* viewed from a devastated *here* also makes of the elegy not the customary gaze backward in regret but a contemplation of the actual moment of loss. The painting depicts the event: the setting of the sun of Birmingham, as it happens, and so provides drama rather than nostalgia. It reaches, even, beyond elegy. It discovers, as the city in the cauldron of its final perfection burns like the sky, a single beauty which is augmented at its vanishing, a tragic greatness which culminates in its fall. The broken cloud and the city beyond then complete the attainment of tragedy by opening the overwhelmed present to a possible future.

Notes on Chapter IV

[1] From a letter to Marie-Laure de Noailles of 1965, quoted in Centre Georges Pompidou 1985, p. 144. Mason also refers to the 'peaceful giant' in 'My Early Artistic Life in Birmingham', in Birmingham 1989, p. 11. I continue to quote from this article unless otherwise stated.

[2] In Arts Council 1982, p. 40.

[3] 'St Mark's Place, East Village, New York City', in Birmingham 1989, pp. 94, 96.

[4] 'My Early Artistic Life in Birmingham', in Birmingham 1989, p. 15, my emphasis.

[5] In Paula Weideger, 'Larger-than-life tribute to Brum's golden age', *Independent*, 5 June 1991, p. 14.

[6] In 'The Torrent of Life', in Birmingham 1989, p. 35.

[7] From an unpublished note, in French, quoted in Centre Georges Pompidou 1985, p. 147.

[8] From his letter to Marie-Laure de Noailles of 1965, quoted in Centre Georges Pompidou 1985, p. 144.

30. *Boulevard Saint-Michel,* 1965

V

THE CROWD

The street reliefs and ink drawings of the 1950s are the foundation for Mason's work. They allowed him to advance from painterly low relief to high relief, and to explore, in a resourcefully changing physical and metaphysical perspective, his sense of space and of human place. *The Idyll, Les Epouvantées* and the designs for *Phèdre* constitute an almost alternative art, a theatrical expressionism where the forms of a world are appropriated by the inner life of the figures represented. The 1958 Birmingham works reintroduce colour and, while still depicting the urban scene, home to a subject, to history, and to time. Like the expressionist works, they release desires and reveal important possibilities which enter Mason's work slowly but comprehensively. In 1958 he had bought a house in the south of France, near Ménerbes in the Vaucluse. Although here, too, the effect appeared after some delay, a yet further and quite other dimension of his art was to be derived from that hot and colourful 'sculptor's' landscape.

Mason's great work of the 1960s is the bronze *The Crowd*, the first large composition and complex masterpiece which gathers, at a depth one could not have foreseen, the surge of humanity observed on the streets of Paris and elsewhere and *imagines* it in the light of a mythic world of sea, especially, and of sky. It is in many ways the culmination of the earlier work. It is preceded by two other bronzes, *Hand of the Artist* (1960) and *The Falling Man* (1963). The first was shown in the inaugural exhibition of the Galerie Janine Hao, which Mason and his wife opened in 1960 in rooms adjacent to his studio in rue Monsieur-le-Prince. The gallery remained open for six years, and exhibited works by Anne Harvey, Michel Charpentier, Charles Matton, Miklos Bokor, Gaston-Louis Roux, Mayou Iserantant, Pierre Bégou, Sven Blomberg, Léopold-Lévy, Cassandre and Balthus, whose drawings and watercolours were shown there for the first time. The inaugural exhibition was of Mason's own works, and led to his contract with the Galerie Claude Bernard in 1963. Pierre Matisse, Balthus's dealer in New York whom Mason met at the Balthus show in 1966, became his own dealer there the following year.

Hand of the Artist owes its origin to Mason's being confined to bed for a time, where all he could do was draw his left hand. An operation on his back, strangely, which prompted an interest in the male torso, was the occasion of *The Falling Man*. Both works were conceived when he was most weak and his sculptor's body was most ineffective; they lead, in *The Crowd*, to a work celebrating energy and life with an altogether new boundlessness and scope. *Hand of the Artist* points, furthermore, beyond *The Crowd* and is another liminal work. Mason has written admiringly of his father that he 'could make anything with his hands — which is why he had come to Birmingham',[1] and it may be right to sense here a certain qualm, that of the working-class boy from a manufacturing city who left his city and his class but continued to work, in another way, with his hands. This is why it is essential to the sculpture that the hand represented is Mason's own. The first sculpture not to be a relief since the beginning of the work which Mason acknowledges as fully his, is another act of self-questioning which goes, precisely, to the hand of the artist. *Man in a Street*, whose eyes gaze into those of the sculptor, asks the thirty-year-old Mason who, as an artist, he is. Two years after his return to Birmingham, and at the end of nearly a decade of work when Mason could well believe that he had said all that he had to say in street reliefs and felt inhabited by a larger ambition, the hand asks him what he is now to do.

This is particularly appreciable in the drawing in which the work began, and which seems to have been curiously hidden from view, as if, perhaps, too personal. (It was shown for the first time as recently as 1991, at a Marlborough exhibition in London for which Mason also prepared a front-and-back version of the sculpture, in resin on wood, with the title *My Hand II*.) For even more than in the sculpture, one is aware of the artist at work, of his right hand drawing his left: of the artist looking at himself, in fact, yet not at his face by means

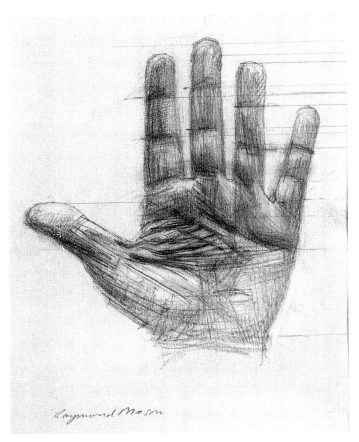

31. *Hand of the Artist* (study), 1962

of a mirror but directly at another equally expressive part of the body. The scrutiny differs entirely from that usual self-regarding of the artist and homes, with the depth of simplicity, to an origin, to the sculpting hand as transmitter and source of thought and feeling. In both of the works through which he interrogates himself and his art, Mason goes to where sculpture begins: in *Man in the Street* to the seeing eyes, in *Hand of the Artist* to the shaping hand. He even emphasises the articulations of the hand — the hand as articulate — and exhibits the opposable thumb by pulling it away from the fingers. The initial meaning of the work is the possibility of sculpture.

It represents Mason's own hand, and the representation is itself Mason's. In comparison with the hands of other sculptors it may appear at first to be simply *there*, available for inspection, in a realistic mode where a minimum sufficient form is given by a pattern of three, by the separation, from the parallel middle fingers, of the little finger as well as the thumb. Consider Rodin, however, of whose hands one might say what Henry Moore said specifically, and finely, of *The Walking Man*, that they have 'a kind of tension and a hardness and a softness, a contrast of bone, soft flesh and tense muscle'.[2] What is peculiar to Mason's hand is that he makes one see its surface, stretched, squashed, creased, cleft, weathered by time and use. Through extraordi-

nary detail, every smallest area of the hand is distinct with its own life. To place with such exactness the lines of the hand (one's 'destiny') along with the usually un-observed and paradoxical sightliness of all its puckers and nicks, is to invite attention to meaningful appearance. There is inwardness as well, of bone and tendon in particular, but the immediate look of things determines what one 'sees'.

That active and deeply cut surface, so thoroughly Mason-like, also announces later works. The motif of gullies, over the tendons on the back of the hand and over the spread-out fingers and thumb, will likewise return, most evidently in *The Grape-Pickers*, which has five 'fingers' of vine, and first of all in *The Crowd*.

With *The Hand* of Giacometti, of 1947, one seems to enter the very being of a hand, as an infinite elongation of reach, of searching through and beyond a body fragile yet at the same time densely compacted and resistant, as if sustaining the pressure of huge volumes of space. As he does gradually for the head, Mason at once finds for the hand a form of representation quite different from that of the contemporary sculptor he most admired, though *Hand of the Artist*, too, may be a resistance. It is surprising to confront this large, strong, human hand in the knowledge that only in the previous year the stage curtain for *Phèdre* had been dominated by the hand of Venus. Upheld and spread to its fullest extent, the hand could be read as the sign of a will fortified against malevolence, against the source of *épouvante*, against the monsters bred by the psyche; or simply, if that proximity in time is merely fortuitous, as a challenge to sickness, to the passivity of suffering. A feature of the original drawing is the dark shading of the palm, the strokes of deepening blackness from which the lighter areas seem to emerge. One is drawn into that central intensity as into the eyes of *Man in a Street* — to lines in the hollow of the hand which resemble lesions, moreover, as if the hand has been almost wounded in being opened and erected against adversity. Perhaps this is an inappropriate, literary response; if not, one can see here with hindsight the coming tragic works of the 1970s.

If *Man in a Street* leads, as a threshold work, to a ceaseless engagement with the head (as with the street and, indeed, with Man), *Hand of the Artist* leads primarily to an unending series of hands. Called to attention by a muscular effort which immobilises the straining thumb, the flattened palm and the straightened fingers, the hand becomes a metaphor for sculpture as Mason intends it. Opening itself to the viewer, it indicates that he should stop and draws attention both to itself as an aesthetic representation to be explored and to the shared human world that it represents. (On the original draw-

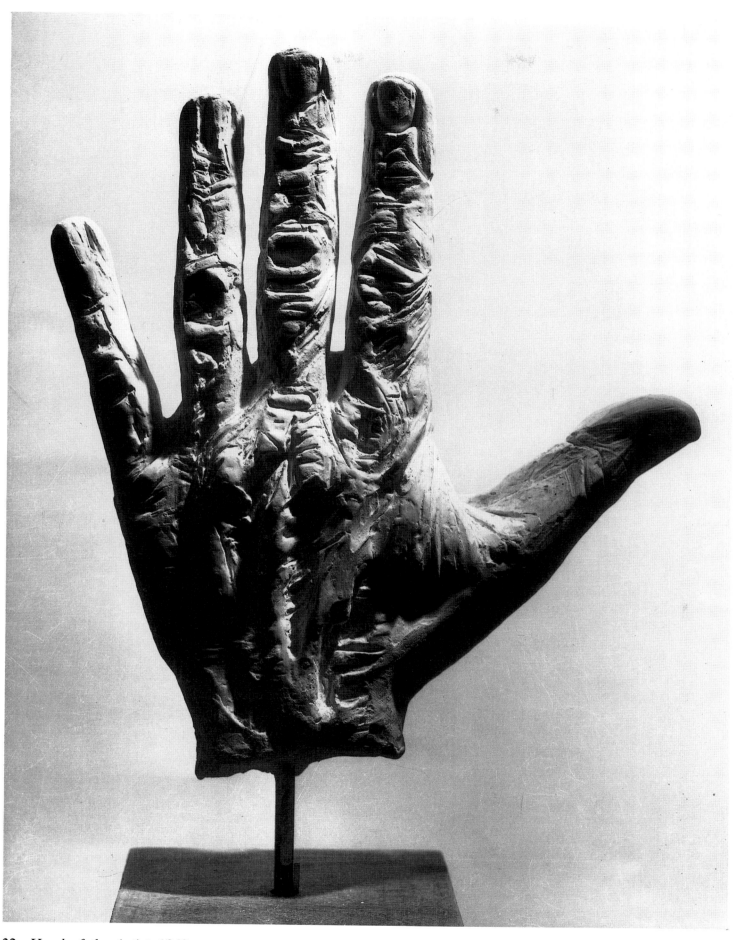

32. *Hand of the Artist,* 1960

33. *The Back,* 1963

ing, lines ruled across the paper from fingertips and joints and other junctures for measurement leave traces of a quiet deliberation on form and meaning.) Specifically as a hand, moreover, it offers itself to the viewer in the way of so many later hands. Of the drunkard's hand pressing against the window in *St Mark's Place*, Mason will write: 'The hand . . . initiates the contact with the spectator', and of the outstretched hand of the Pole in *A Tragedy in the North*: 'the hand forms a link with the viewer'.[3] An approaching or even an upraised hand is the hand of the sculpture reaching towards the viewer so as to draw him into the work; and also the hand, as it were, of the artist himself, extended to the viewer in a gesture of fraternity. *Hand of the Artist* is where this now essential and entirely original characteristic of Mason's art begins, and the fact that the first of all his hands is the baleful hand of Venus enables one to surmise that, in the constantly renewed dialogue of the hand, from *The Departure of Fruit and Vegetables* to *Forward* and beyond, a specifically human solidarity is being enacted and affirmed.

The 1960 exhibition at the Galerie Janine Hao was an appropriate gathering of Mason's previous work; *Hand of the Artist* was a new beginning. (So, as it happens, was *The Luberon*, of the same year, the first of the bronze landscape reliefs of the Midi, which will be examined later as part of another story.) In 1963 Mason produced a related work, *The Falling Man*, and also entered the Galerie Claude Bernard, at a time when it was devoted exclusively to sculpture. The major artists of the gallery were César, who had generously introduced him, Jean Ipoustéguy and Roël d'Haese, all born like Mason in the early 1920s though each practising an art, of course, quite different from his. After César's departure the others remained, with Mason, the sculptural core of the gallery, as it began to open its doors to some of the best figurative painters of the day, including Antonio López-García, Claudio Bravo and two close friends of Mason's, Sam Szafran and Fernando Botero. Although no comparisons useful to our purpose can be made with artists of such diversity, it is important to note the presence in Mason's milieu of so much figurative work, and to reflect also on the desirability of a widely based and thoroughly contemporary study of modern figuration and of the thought which sustains it. It is also necessary to think of Mason in the company of his fellow artists, not influencing or being influenced but being pushed to the limit ('each exhibition', he has written in a letter, 'had to be an eye-opener') by the corresponding ambition and unpardoning judgment of others.

The Falling Man, casts of which can be seen in the sculpture garden of the Hirshhorn Museum, Washington D.C., and before a William Louis-Dreyfus property in Miami, was Mason's largest work so far and an extraordinary successor to *Hand of the Artist*. After the hand, the body. As lying down led to the drawing and sculpting of a hand necessarily severed, a back operation led to another of the few Mason works which represent parts of the body. It is precisely the back and the upper frame it supports which interest him, along with the articulations at the shoulders and neck. For, in this series of torsos, work is even more inwardly in question. The sculpture draws on studies of workmen in the quarries at Lacoste in the south of France, which Mason visited from his house near Ménerbes, and represents, on one level, a single movement of lifting a large stone and placing it. Before the bulk of the torsos, however, it is difficult not to think of Mason's own physique (after 'my hand', almost 'my body'), and of the hours on end, day after day, that he himself has passed throughout his life as a manual worker, toiling in his studio or elsewhere, whose back has needed medical attention. A personal reading of the sculpture is particularly moving when looking at the photograph of the original plaster, where the darkness behind is no doubt intended merely to render as visibly as possible the top-lit surfaces, but where the effect is of spectral torsos moving against a background uniformly black.

The sense of ailing and, indeed, of falling is not simply a personal matter, however, and the studying of workmen indicates the other and purely sculptural origin of the work. What is most important here, in fact, is that Mason runs counter to prevailing interests by closely exploring human anatomy and taking the male torso as his subject; and, rather than merely making a statement as to where sculpture should go, that he renews contact with a long tradition and learns from it for the making of a work that is new. He returns specifically to Michelangelo himself, in whom he finds what he already knows he needs. He tells Michael Brenson in 1976 that a sculpture cannot interest him 'which is not punctuated by either drawing or indentation, where the surface is simple', because when one moves around it 'nothing happens', and because only a strongly animated surface can receive and convey the essential 'energy'.[4] Hence his distance from Brancusi and Henry Moore, and his 'very early' moving on to Michelangelo, of whom he says, memorably: 'he can take a piece of Carrara marble, which is . . . lunar white, and by the force of his drawing he can make [the] sculpture . . . black . . . If you think of Moses . . . it's hardly a white sculpture at all. There's just force and intention and energy everywhere.' In the Rodin lecture he will attribute this blackening of the marble to Michelangelo's 'drawing' and 'direct carving' and also, most powerfully, to the 'intensity of his thought'.

He is also drawn to Michelangelo's concern for the 'architecture' of the body rather than to what he calls 'the melody of muscles' in Rodin. One sees the architecture of a Michelangelo-like body in all three torsos, the central one being turned so as to display it especially, and everywhere a blackening of the work by thought. Yet Mason is not merely repeating another sculptor. The 'drawing', the decisive moulding of muscles, of armpits, of ribs and the rib cage — the latter reminiscent in particular of painted nude figures in the Sistine Chapel — presses darkness into the body, creating a surface which turns and acts, but equally encroaching on the flesh, given also the truncation, the missing limbs, the heads that are hardly heads. Incisions go further, in leaving marks which might represent, in an actual drawing, areas of reduced light, but which in sculpture make jagged scars and absences. One registers them as unlike what one might see on a real body. *Hand of the Artist* resembles a hand; the torsos resemble and do not resemble human torsos. As always with a successful combination of likeness and unlikeness, the eye is drawn through and beyond appearance.

And Mason will also say of an 'inscribed' work that it 'loses its contemplative, static nature' and becomes, of all things, a 'cry'. The rejection of still, contemplative art has its own importance in Mason's aesthetics and sense of life, and we shall consider it. 'Cry' is an appropriately energetic, indeed dramatic and expressionist word, which seems to mean, in general, that human emotion and thought — human being — are expressed in such art and call undeniably to the spectator. Of *The Falling Man* in particular one might think that it also cries out, as if in response to the artist's in-

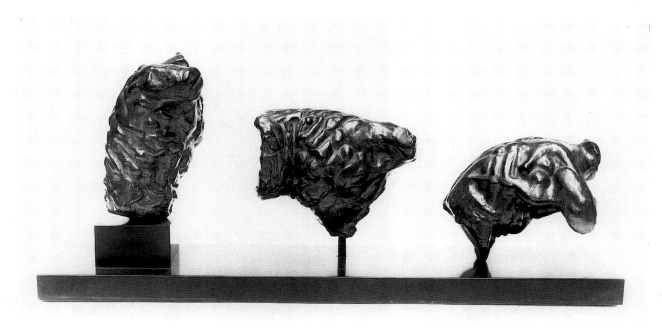

34. Study for *The Falling Man,* 1963

fringement, or to the infringement of life. It is true that Mason's language for describing the activity of the artist is often surprisingly aggressive. He writes in 'Ce que j'aime dans le dessin' ('What I like in drawing') of his preference for a 'physical attack' on the paper, such that it does not remain 'unviolated'.[5] In the course of an interview given to Frances Morris in 1988, he speaks in similar terms of the graphic nature of Paris architecture: 'the plaster buildings of the Latin Quarter [when he first arrived in the city] implied black drawing on a white ground . . . I mean the windows and doors are just so many black gashes into white façades . . . Even the Haussmannian façades now they're permanently cleaned have the same sort of stab, stab of a black into a white'.[6] One remembers the 'stigmata' of doors and windows down withdrawing streets, and when I questioned Mason about them, he wondered whether 'stigmata' was the right word and proposed 'lacerations'. He is an artist who likes to make his mark, and whose vision even of the calm, repetitive buildings of Paris is that they too live out a strangely emphatic, hyperbolic life of 'gashing' and 'stabbing'. The violence, I believe, is part of his joy in the world — it is a violence in which no one gets hurt — the violence of energy (as in Beethoven, an early and fundamental admiration) and a kind of overplus of vitality. It is part of the play of self in a creativity which is generously directed, in its origin, to the otherness of a world, and it goes towards explaining why a whole life's work dedicated to exalting an outside and to addressing the largest possible public is at the same time an autobiography.

For some ten years the work was called simply *Three Torsos*, and gave no verbal hold for interpretation. When Mason decided that it should have a proper title, however, it was the suggestive nature of the work which prompted *The Falling Man* — though even here the falling could have an exclusively sculptural significance. Although Mason was thinking neither of Rodin's *Falling Man* nor of Giacometti's *Staggering Man* of 1950, a falling man is certainly a theme for sculpture, and in conversation he has said of the workmen's movements that they allowed him to analyse the 'structure of the human torso positioning itself differently in space', and even described the work as an 'exercise in style'. The reference to space alerts one to the different angles at which the arms and heads reach out into an ambience made strongly present. A falling man, moreover, is an extreme in sculpture. Statuary in particular usually represents a body in control, exercising its muscles, holding itself still or making a deliberate and often elegant or athletic movement. It celebrates the body, and the life of intelligence which informs it. It seizes a body existing through time and, by venturing

to steady it into permanence, satisfies one of the most ancient and tenacious of hopes. To sculpt a fall is to increase the challenge, by removing control from what is being figured and placing it entirely in the figurative power of sculpture, and by sustaining in the unchanging fixity of bronze a continuing descent through time and space.

35. *The Falling Man,* 1962

The overall shape of the work, which recalls the threefold movement of *Hand of the Artist* from little finger and middle fingers towards the leaning thumb, also has a sculptural explanation. It suggests a falling wave, and is near the origin, in fact, of one of the determining motifs of Mason's work, which will culminate immediately after in *The Crowd* and will return with its present form in the front frieze of *The Departure*.

Yet the idea of falling remains persuasive. One sees the wide solidity of the frame against the weakness of the flesh and the body's rough and unlovely severing. An initial regret one might feel, that the torsos are incomplete behind, can disappear as one realises the rightness of partial presence, of the body being affirmed even

36. *Boulevard Saint-Michel,* 1960

as, fragmentary and unable to cohere into an unchanging perpetuity, it drops to the ground.

Does the man, however, simply fall? Although it stands free, the sculpture is not fully three-dimensional and needs to be viewed from the front, as a sequence advancing, as usual, from left to right. (The viewer's limited but creative-collaborative freedom of movement is shown in the photograph of the plaster, which is taken from slightly to the left so as to reveal in succession a side, a front and a back.) There is certainly a descent to the right, but it is the middle torso rather than the last which has fallen the furthest. That last torso, moreover, could as well be righting itself and be about to rise. As soon as one admits this ambiguity, the look of the work changes. The central figure may be turned this way so that Mason can represent the chest and abdomen, and that does seem sufficient reason in the two studies, but why would a man revolve with his head down and his arms wide apart if not in the execution of a cartwheel? His fall could be acrobatic; the figure on the left could be stretching upwards — raising his arm like many male figures in later sculptures — at the beginning of the jump; the figure on the right could be landing and pulling up.

If one can allow both readings, the suggestion of a willed, gymnastic fall deepens the work. A bulk of a man who is nevertheless hardly there falls headlong, yet does so as if he were springing. A torso with the heroic proportions of a Michelangelo falls heroically. The final figure is, then, both falling and rising, and his meaning lies in the doubleness of his state. He is above all facing forward, the knots of bone along the rib cage being set in a horizontal line so as to lead one out of the work on the right, as happens so often in Mason, with the suggestion of continuation and endurance.

Like *Hand of the Artist, The Falling Man* explores and resists the wounds and darknesses of our bodily condition — of our condition, that is, as lives which command but also depend on bodies. And one can read, across the sequence, the rhythm of tragedy. The first figure is large and erect and reaches into the air. The second falls, but with a tremendousness which discloses his stature. The third recovers and continues, with the knowledge at his back of all that has occurred and in the awareness that he also continues to fall. Four years after Mason's involvement with the tragic and religious vision of Racine, he produces his own tragic work, founded on the strengths and the resilience of the purely human.

It is tempting to think that he is using a Christian art form to give to his shaping of experience a large and recognisable overtone. The work resembles a triptych,

in which two very different figures on the left and right portray a man, or maybe Man, in contrasting existential poses — before and after, perhaps, or aspiring and persevering, reaching up and working with a bent back — around a central figure of perfect ambiguity, flying or falling, or both flying and falling, and who recalls the hand of the artist in being stretched to the sides, in having a focus of intensity, of sculptural drawing, in the midriff, and in turning to the viewer in a gesture of opening. The third figure is even in the same straining position as the man drawing a cart on the right of *The Departure of Fruit and Vegetables*, who visibly bears a cross, formed on his back by the straps of his overalls. This hindsight may be misleading, however, and although the work influencing Mason while he was producing his final sculptures in bronze was the biblical *Last Judgment* in the Sistine Chapel,[7] and although, in the 1988 interview with Jane Farrington, he will cite the 'first triptychs' of Francis Bacon as evidence of his greatness in that they aim to make 'a great statement', the source of *The Falling Man* as he intended it is not Christian, but Greek.

For his own major statement speaks also of art, and goes beyond Michelangelo to Michelangelo's source: hence its fragmentary nature. The sculpting of torsos, of broken statuary, is realistic in the simple sense that it imitates the fragments that one can actually find — fallen from temples, for example, and placed in a museum. To return to Greek art, however, and to render it in this way, is to declare the need for contemporary art to take its bearings from the long tradition, which is public and figurative and laden with human thought and emotion, and from which one learns that genuine newness is only achieved from the recognition that 'the fundamental problems of art remain unchanged';[8] to assert also that the source of art for us is not Sumerian, or African, or Polynesian, but Greek; and at the same time to show, by fragments which portray a falling, that the tradition is broken and must be recovered. Since Mason approves neither the aesthetics nor the metaphysics of the fragment, *The Falling Man*, though a modernist sculpture when taken in isolation, is also unique among his works, as the only one in which he required both to face and to show the challenge.

Hand of the Artist and *The Falling Man* lead, as do the street reliefs, to *The Crowd*, an even larger bronze which differs, nevertheless, from anything that had gone before. It owes its size, no doubt, to an ambition developing through *The Falling Man*, though it leaves the concern for anatomy to be continued in later works, and its response to the possibly tragic nature of our condition, in so far as this is recognised, is directly to celebrate the energy of life, and to do so in humanity at large, in a multiplicity of figures. Indeed, to advance to *The Crowd* from a single hand and a single, falling man is to repeat, in a more ample dimension, the earlier journey from *Man in a Street* to crowds in a street. For as the first of Mason's eight large compositions and, as it turned out, the only one in bronze, *The Crowd*, begun in 1963 when he was forty-one, apparently finished in 1965 but reworked and only finally cast by 1968, announced a quite new level of aspiration in his art, a willingness, after considering the working hand and the working back, by an even greater perseverance to draw long years of toil into a sculptural masterpiece. It involved the invention of what amounts to a new kind of sculpture, for a work in which he felt, for the first time, that he had a 'message'.[9] It was also his first work, after *Barcelona Tram*, to attract serious attention, being the high point of his opening exhibitions in the prestigious galleries of Claude Bernard in Paris in 1965 and Pierre Matisse in New York in 1968.[10] With its happy proliferation of preparatory small bronzes and drawings, it is the natural focus for any discussion of his central subject: the crowd and the idea of the crowd, and also the place to explore the surprising range of his figurative modes.

It is equally a work difficult to compare with any other. It clearly takes Mason quite outside the kind of art practised by Giacometti (who greatly admired *The Falling Man*), and even counters his generally small scale and his intentness towards the single figure or a few figures in tension. Mason actually told me that already by the time of *Carrefour de l'Odéon* he had come to see Giacometti, for all his fineness as a sculptor, as at root an 'aesthete', whereas the artist should 'go out of his studio' and address a public.

Following pages: 37. *The Crowd* (plaster) 1963–65

Two approaches are clearly in conflict here, which one only needs to choose between if one is a practitioner oneself. Giacometti's procedure rings true in terms of the integrity of the modern artist alone with his own devices and faithful to the thing seen and to the work in hand. Mason's recalls an earlier relation between artist and audience, which all his art is an heroic attempt to recover and to redefine.

One might have thought of Rodin, whose example could have been useful to Mason for avoiding the private intensities, perhaps, of the age. In his 1986 lecture, Mason sees him as exemplifying the evolution of the nineteenth century into the twentieth, having been, in the first half of his life, 'a sculptor of heroic groups' and in the second 'the sculptor of the single figure and even the single figure progressively shorn of arms and legs'. The current tendency is to prefer the later works,

39. *The Crowd* in Manhattan, 1989

'because the more arms and legs he saws off the more he resembles Brancusi', whereas Mason turns to the earlier period so as to rediscover there 'what we have lost'. He also notes with approval Rodin's insistence, in the opening chapter of *The Cathedrals of France*, that if the artist is to produce a masterpiece he must possess 'a soul of the crowd', and must even 'perceive through the crowd' and involve the 'ideally present' crowd in the actual elaboration of his work. Yet Mason only really became interested in Rodin when invited to give the lecture — by which time most of his own large works had been completed or conceived — and when, in particular, he saw the plaster of *The Gates of Hell* not lit by indifferent sunlight, as he had known it in the Rodin Museum in Meudon, but sharply lit in the new Musée d'Orsay. Before, he had thought of Rodin as being precisely not a relief sculptor.

The fundamental relation of *The Crowd* to Rodin, as to Giacometti, is that it is different. There is one important sign, nevertheless, of the unconscious presence of Rodin, as we shall see; and there are hints of Henry Moore. Mason has referred very little to Moore, whom he knew personally but who, although twenty-four years Mason's senior and so hardly a rival in his own generation, was nevertheless the name which sprang to mind whenever English sculpture was being considered. Mason places him among the 'landscape' artists while placing himself among the 'narrative', and this does seem a usefully large if preliminary way of distinguishing the two major English sculptors of the century. Mason was not thinking of Moore while making *The Crowd*, but he does recognise that he would probably not have run heads together without the example of the early Moore, and that the lines over heads and shoulders often resemble his contours. One also notices a Moore-like mother and child to the right of the sculpture, where a large maternal arm and shoulder protect a small child looking in our direction. For the viewer, though not for Mason himself, they link the warm humanism of a surging and crowding work to a similar humanism in Moore, whose works, on the contrary, with their often harmoniously smooth surfaces, turn slowly, like the earth they 'improve', and invite the viewer not to move through story, but to contemplate.

A photograph of Mason at work on the plaster shows him in the midst of a multiplicity of forms which seem to spread away from him in all directions. His body, itself covered in plaster, is the final, hundredth figure from which the other ninety-nine derive. His working hand is hidden within the sculpture itself, as it meditates the most enigmatic of all the figures, while in his left hand is the tiny half of a rubber ball in which the

40. *The Crowd,* Tuileries Gardens, Paris

plaster is mixed and from which the sculpture is emerging. As far as the work is concerned, the walls and ceiling windows of the studio look as provisional as its own division on the floor into its various sections, for Mason's sole concern now is with the crowd itself and with his relation to it — with how to sculpt and how to understand a crowd in the absence of decor, of the architectural geometries of line, plane and recess which frame and reverberate human emotion. As a child he had peered through the downstairs window in Wheeleys Lane, and the street reliefs also situate an urban world on the other side of an imaginary window, through which the viewer is nevertheless invited to pass. Here, Mason mingles with the crowd and the frame is left behind.

The two casts are situated, moreover, one in Paris, one in Manhattan, amid the actual crowds which they imitate and under the sky which they need and suppose.

And while the viewer continues to observe passers-by, on this first occasion when he himself is literally a passer-by — on the way no doubt to another destination beyond Madison Avenue or the Jardin des Tuileries — he is arrested before a work where, as Mason writes, the subject has 'ceased to be uniquely the street scene' and passers-by have 'started to assume their new role as members of humanity'. The work may have begun in numberless drawings made on the boulevard St Michel and then the Canebière in Marseille, yet its theme is not the street but people, and specifically 'the union of people'.[11]

The union is in part historical, to the extent that the crowd which confronts the viewer, invites him in and passes around him, is the crowd of modern times. Mason has commented during a television programme on his work on the appropriateness of its being situated in the Tuileries Gardens on the steps leading down from

75

the Jeu de Paume, since the site 'was the very epicentre of the French Revolution. The guillotine was at those doors of the gardens, and the revolutionary crowd — which is, after all, *the* great crowd of history — came and surged and went in front of the very spot where my sculpture stands today'.[12] It is not that the crowd is political. André Malraux may have been photographed expounding on the work with eloquent hands at the old Centre national d'art contemporain in the same month of May 1968 in which another crowd was taking to the nearby streets, but *The Crowd* does not describe the student demonstrations that will appear in *The Month of May in Paris* and *The Latin Quarter*, nor does it even portray, as will *The Departure*, *A Tragedy in the North*, *The Grape-Pickers* and *Forward*, the world of work. Mason needs the modern crowd *en masse*, not the individualised and purpose-laden crowds of, say, the fifteenth century, but only so that he can go beyond even Manet's crowd of spectators at the Folies-Bergère, or Hogarth's crowds in the four paintings which simply observe them at sundry *Times of Day*, in removing all intention from his figures other than that of walking in one of several directions. These people may be more than passers-by, but pass is all they do, since their meanings are beyond their activity. The power of the work comes from the fact that the crowd is not defined, from its merely being there. The first work to isolate the crowd from all surroundings also frees it of adventitious significance, by a massive act of abstraction which one understands after the event to have been the necessary first step, in preparation for the contrastingly overt meanings and specific locations in history, or at least in time, of *The Departure* and *A Tragedy*. If *Place de l'Opéra* focused so intensely on an urban scene as to make of it an image of Place itself, *The Crowd* centres so single-mindedly on human figures in their spatial and other relations that it becomes, for Mason, an image of the Human.

It begins in a human head, that of the man walking towards the viewer in the centre of the work. All of Mason, indeed, begins in a head, for he indicated, when we were standing before *The Crowd* in the Tuileries, that what he considers his 'first important work' was a large drawing of the head of Beethoven made when he was fifteen and associated in his memory with the Fifth Symphony. His continuing engagement with the head, right through to the 1992 and 1993 reliefs of rue Monsieur-le-Prince and of Stockholm, and the significance of the music for him, make of that moment upstairs in his room in Wheeleys Lane an extraordinary threshold. One recognises the head from another beginning, from *Man in a Street*, and one sees not only the giant advance in sculptural terms but also a new relation to the viewer.

The face smiles, while the relaxation of the whole man, whose hands are in his pockets, invites the viewer himself to relax, at least for the time being.

The man also walks directly towards the viewer, and to understand that approach it is useful to pause on the largest of the bronzes that accompany *The Crowd*: *The Street*, a relief in four distinct, descending parts of 1964. As with *The Falling Man* of the previous year, the freezing and then unfreezing of movements through space, whether horizontally or vertically, was partly a means for Mason of advancing from the framed and quiet animation of the later street reliefs to the tumultuous animation of *The Crowd*. The central figure in *The Street* approaches the viewer in successive stills through the changing geometries of a pavement scene until what one sees in the bottom tableau is that he is finally *there*, with all the other pedestrians seemingly placed in relation to him. That slow and unexpected appearing of someone who becomes not just another figure but, as it were, *the man*, and who confronts the viewer not with the smooth and finished features of exteriority but with an interiorised depth of gaze and uncertainty of form, is an exercise in presence. The central figure of *The Crowd* is more simply there, but he too, as the eye continually returns to him, presents himself.

As the viewer is drawn into the sculpture, moreover, by the sheer bulk of the hatted man who enters on the left and the contrasting tensile strength across the shoulders and down the arm of the man entering on the right, he is also drawn towards that central figure in particular, by a surprising mimetic process which belongs to the work's originality. The near figures are without feet or even legs, like figures in a real crowd seen close-up, and a deliberately out-of-focus modelling both imitates the facts of perception and places one immediately inside the crowd, as a participant in the action. And one sees that everything proceeds likewise from him. His head becomes a triad of heads, which recall Daumier's *Les passants* — as Mason was only later to discover — and which were based on the three giant heads of Shiva in the temple caves of Elephanta. Mason had seen these reproduced in the second volume of Malraux's *Musée imaginaire de la sculpture mondiale*, and was no doubt drawn by the number three, and by the possibility of transposing a three-fold divine head into three purely human heads signifying youth, maturity and old age, and the attachment of all humans one to another. A spiral of other heads and bodies also moves away backwards from the central head, like the hemmed and foreshortened crowd in *Carrefour de l'Odéon*, and like that very first generation of human otherness in the cyclist riding away from the facing head in *Place Saint-Germain-des-Prés*. The oceanic swirling of the work

41. In front of the Jeu de Paume, 1986.
Photo: Raymond Mason

42. Studies for *The Crowd*

begins, for the viewer, in the imagined swaying of the central figure's body, and all the other waves of the crowd are seen in relation to that central movement of which he is both the source and the end.

One can see the sculptural logic of deriving a large work from a single form and shaping the union of people around a single figure, but why, in human terms, should a crowd be so centred and, one might think, self-centred? Mason himself supplies the answer, when describing the crowd, in 'La Foule', as 'man multiplied', and more pointedly as 'myself like others, repeating myself to infinity, a part of the movement', and while adding that the movement 'must pass through me like a flame through a forest'. He suggests the existential origin of repetition, in the fact that one finds oneself a human in a world where humans repeat each other beyond the power of numbering; and also of comparison (in a humanist world dispensing with the divine), in the fact of first discovering understanding in the likeness of others to oneself. The crowd only repeats 'me'

because I am unavoidably, where I am, the centre of consciousness, and because I am the necessary conduit for that something much larger than the 'I' — that unboundable human-ness which can only be named by comparison, by likening it to a *flame* — to travel through in the ecstasy of destruction and birth. It is true that the central figure rises towards one as oneself, in the thick of the mass, and one can fantasise about one's own centrality and consequence. One only needs to step, however, to the right or to the left, to see him from the side, to perceive, as it were, the self that *is*, the third-person self that one can observe (almost) from without, and view with others' eyes as being not only here but there, and one among many.

The humanism of the work is carried in its composition, which also accounts for the work's larger human meanings. In a certain light of the mind, the figures around the central figure can seem to be staring in panic or even screaming, with an intensity of gesture reminiscent of *Les Epouvantées* and as if enacting, in a private

43. Mason in his studio, 1965. Photo: Tony Saulnier

area of the sculpture tucked away from the unconcern of the others, a scene of incongruously extreme emotion. Behind the mother and child is a woman with her hand to her mouth as if frightened. Should the light change, however, these baroque actors become pedestrians engaging in conversation, protecting their eyes from the sun, wiping their lips, breathing heavily from the heat. The open mouths serve also to fix the sculpture in space, by reaching space into the sculpture, where a smooth surface would exclude the ambient air and close the work into itself. (Or as Mason expressed it, again while looking at *The Crowd*, the figures 'snarl at or grasp the space with the open mouths.' Crenellations 'claw', mouths 'snarl': one discovers again the unexpected violence, not of the perfectly calm figures themselves but of the sculptural gesture.) Here is the impress of Rodin, in fact, as Mason realised later in his Rodin lecture, when he had produced many other major works. For according to Mason's reading of the continually changing movements of the figures in *The Burghers of Calais* as one passes around it, Rodin excelled in the 'vivid occupation of space'. 'I can see now', he adds, 'that it is my debt to him', and then, interestingly: 'I had always thought that it was my link with Giacometti.'

A quite tremendous energy is released, moreover, in the jostling of the crowd, in the looming, the leaning and the near-colliding of figures, in the pressure of form against and away from form, in the strength of the gullies that travel into the distance of the work and press the files of people apart. The whole is quickened by an ever heaving movement, the 'shiver of life' ('La Foule'), and by an exuberance and by a seemingly unending copiousness. In its execution it 'brimmed over', he has said, 'in a wide context of music and literature — Mussorgsky, Hugo, Manzoni . . . '[13] And yet one cannot forget those passing intimations of horror, and certain close-ups of 'gashed' heads, along with the possibility of a skull in the head which just appears above the central head, suggest that a work which aims for universality includes both life and our anxieties about life. It is true that Mason himself sees no gashes and no skull — only strong 'drawing' into an active surface and the capturing of space — nor any wide-eyed panic. He has stated, however, as I noted, that in working on his last bronzes, he was influenced by Michelangelo's *Last Judgment* in the Sistine Chapel.[14] This is, after all, a thronging crowd scene, and a traditional one in Western art, where the focus is always a dominant central figure who faces the viewer. No doubt the shape of the work was what counted for *The Crowd*, and I would not wish to read into the sculpture meanings furnished from elsewhere. It certainly contains no suggestion of the saved and the damned. One may think, nevertheless, that for

44. *The Birth of the Spiral,* 1963

this non-Christian and anti-apocalyptic crowd, an artist who believes the sublime and the grotesque to be present in all great works has used the bare hint from Michelangelo, with whatever degree of awareness, so as to bring into the warmth of the trivial a glimpse of the far reaches of joy and of despair. And certainly of joy, above all, overcoming despair, as the insinuations of fear are quite overridden by the teeming of the whole.

If the sculpture is humanist, however, it also explores, like the street reliefs, like *Birmingham. In Memoriam*, the edges of humanism and the possible beyond. Mason is perfectly conscious of this. The end of 'La Foule' suggests that the wider the base of a work as it stretches out to humanity as a whole, the higher the culminating point, and evokes a thought 'avid for grandeur and humanism. And for more.' As that more is approached, so the sculpture increases its movement and then, conversely, attains immobility. Its figuration deepens, its presence intensifies, and the 'I' is surpassed.

Movement is in the axes of the work. In a sculpture where there is now nothing but human figures, they bear the viewer, as always, beyond the human and beyond the work. The vortex that whirls back from the central head to create a withdrawing axis, abounding first with the densities of the here and now, culminates in a wave which gathers the whole sculpture and which finally breaks — in almost invisible figures on which Mason worked for no less than a year — to suggest the endlessness of generation, the dipping horizon of the real. Another comment in the Rodin lecture is apposite, this time on *The Gates of Hell*: 'Layer after layer of bodies and then maybe a very last one, an inch or two high, turning her back to you and disappearing into a tiny hole, a grotto . . . Instead of figures emerging from a dark background into light, here they do the contrary, deepening the relief *ad infinitum*'. Mason uses a similar device to suggest, not humans disappearing infinitely (though also with infinite vitality) into horror, but the infinite continuation of the crowd — and of all other crowds of which this is the exemplar — through space and time. The horizontal axis is similarly prolonged. Several sequences of figures lead the eye to a man leaning out on the right at a resolute angle, just behind the mother and child. Although lacking the mystery of

vehicles in the street reliefs, he nonetheless opens the work to the 'fortunate' right (as in augury), and to that intimation of infinity that awaits in any uncountable profusion, whether of persons or of stars. The vertical axis is now the upright human body, reaching into air and sky. Even if the work were installed in a gallery, the viewer would go, as it were, outside to see it, to sense the 'mantle of light' worn by its figures and 'the celestial' under which they stand. He meets the approaching, central figure with a world above him.

Movement is also in the single simile in terms of which the whole work is composed, and which likens a crowd to an ocean. The simile is perfectly traditional: Edgar Allan Poe, in his story 'The Man of the Crowd', writes of 'continuous tides of population' rushing along a London thoroughfare and of 'the tumultuous sea of human heads', while Baudelaire in an essay on Constantin Guys, 'The Painter of Modern Life' — which describes Guys as 'the lover of the crowd' and which often calls Mason to mind — claims in a famous passage that for 'the perfect *flâneur*, for the passionate observer, it is an immense pleasure to take up residence in number, in the undulating, in movement, in the fugitive and the infinite.' For Mason, the tumultuous 'waves of the ocean' ('La Foule') are a trope for seeing, for saying that copiousness in which he delights, that variety and immensity which are features both of life and of the art which responds appropriately. (He is pleased to find himself, as a Pisces, in the company of other 'oceanic' artists: Hugo, Mussorgsky, and also Michelangelo, Daumier and Bach. One sees the difference from Giacometti, whose fundamental trope might be a tree.) And just as the motion of an actual crowd is compounded by his own motion, so that even the spacing-out of doors and windows is 'set moving' by his passing down a street ('La Foule'), so the rigid bronze of *The Crowd* — a work intended to be large enough not to be grasped in a single glance — moves as the eye moves along and between its waves and as the viewer-as-pedestrian varies his point of view by walking across the front. There is a shifting abundance; a unity to the whole which makes of *The Crowd* an image — so alien to post-modernist thought yet so appealing to desire — of oneness; and also a vision of what Mason calls in 'La Foule' 'continual metamorphosis'. By turning a crowd into a sculptural

45. *The Crowd* in the Pierre Matisse Gallery, New York, 1968

representation of a crowd, Mason enables one to look again, to see further than a congeries of 'I's, to contemplate, I suppose, something like life itself. And because life is a unity, for Mason, continually proliferating and changing, in his words about the crowd he compares it over and again to something else — it is 'like a lava flow',[15] 'like a procession of clouds, the ocean waves, the diabolic dance of flames' ('La Foule') — and so opens the crowd to the terrestrial presences through which humans move, and even to the ancient elements of earth, air, water and fire.

A figuring of human bodies becomes a figuring of the ocean, whose unceasing movement is intensified by the compressed perspective, by the sharp raking of what, in the origin of the work, was the slope of the boulevard St Michel. Yet the work also stills the imagining eye, as if in the ocean depths. For if the near-realism of the modelling of the central figure becomes blurred in the others — perhaps this is the first ever sculpture not to pretend that the viewer can look everywhere at once — it yields considerably in figures which are even nearer. To pass from that central figure to the man also walking towards us in front of him is to move, in the same work, from a figurative art concerned with how the world appears, to art that feels its way (literally) behind appearance. The man's wide, deep shoulders receive the light of the visible, but his face is mined and his chest is hollowed. Having no mouth, he expresses himself otherwise. Incomplete, encroached upon and, as it were, unseen, he is nevertheless quite awesomely present, looming from within. The same is true of the leaning figure walking towards the left — one of three such, in fact, who seem to be the same figure repeated, twice hidden, once coming into view — who remains, however long we may stare at him, a fleeting vision of 'man' crossing our path.

By thus defeating appearance while sounding the limits of figuration, Mason calms the viewer's gaze, demands an increased attention (for all its open-handedness towards the public, *The Crowd* is a 'difficult' work), and sends the 'I' way down into the person. He does the same and more with shadows and with hollow eyes. According to 'La Foule', the 'ubiquitous shadow' to be seen in crowds is 'the power of the unknown in everyday reality'. That power can already be seen on the plaster, photographs of which reveal that Mason, who rarely speaks of the medium and is not at all concerned for fidelity to the material being worked, nevertheless allowed plaster, through the action of trowel and knife, to create shadows and draw them into its whiteness. The effect of light on the ceaselessly active surface of the bronze likewise carries

46. *Small Crowd*, 1963

shadow deeply into each of the figures, who also walk through the shadows standing in the crevices of the work and seemingly sustaining the humans from below. Shadows slow the work, retarding movement with the gravity of being. They suggest the invisible within the visible, the unknown through which the 'I' descends and from which collectively we arise. In many of the preparatory ink drawings, as also in *Boulevard St Michel* of 1960 and *Faces of the City* of 1962, a world actually struggles for visibility against the serried darkness of the drawing itself, which expresses the distance of the world that appears to sight, and the non-manifest from which it seeks to emerge.

The deeply moulded eyes, which serve, like the open mouths, to fix the sculpture in space, also fix themselves to the viewer. Their hollowness is the reverse of a void. It suggests, on the contrary, the dark intensity of a deeply living gaze, and gives a graphic, 'speaking' articulation to the sculpture. It is related to Mason's years of drawing in unmixed Indian ink, where the black blobs of the eyes are a capturing of life. The huge eyes of the foremost figure in the bronze *Small Crowd* of 1963 call attention to this awesome act of looking, rather than merely glancing or scanning a surface. To look into someone's eyes is as often as not to see the reflected world of which one is oneself the centre. To look at sculpted eyes is to see the resistant membrane of the visible. To look into hollowed eyes is to gaze into the mind, to travel the distances of mind, and to be gazed into with the same endlessness of look. The hollow eyes of *Man in a Street* return the viewer's and the artist's gaze, and open, it seems, to a not entirely undisturbed unconscious. The hollow eyes of *The Crowd* absorb the viewer's gaze as they are themselves absorbed, and invite him to participate in human being.

One begins with a myriad of figures, shocking like rocks in some giant's causeway, and then discovers incompletion, shadows, infinite eyes. Is this why, in the first of his large works, Mason invented a new form of sculpture — or stretched and enlarged an old form to a new limit — so as to create a backless high relief which relies on perspective yet whose nearest figures are virtually free-standing, and which partakes thereby of both relief and statuary? There is a customarily bold assertion of Malraux's which is worth considering in itself and which can come to mind when thinking of *The Crowd*. 'Statuary', he claims, 'expresses symbol as relief expresses the scene, and tends towards being as the scene tends towards action'.[16] Mason's art tends towards both, and the viewer attentive only to action, drama and narrative, will forfeit the underlying absorption in being. Perspective here tells him where to stand and prevents him, as nearly always with Mason, from

47. *The Street,* 1964

walking around the work and circumscribing it into an otherness of space, but as he looks into the work, he may realise that he is being drawn, nevertheless, way beyond motion and happening.

So one sees again the importance of the central figure, for the idea of the crowd and for its materialisation in sculpture. He is the frontier between action and being. His external figuration allows the viewer a mental hand-hold on the familiar as he sounds the more inward figuration of other forms closer to. His relatively simple presence is the measure of the deeper presence to be felt elsewhere. The relative clarity of his 'I' is the necessary counterpoise to the surpassing of the 'I' in the whole. The power of everything in the work which is not the figuration of appearance depends, in fact, on his being there. He stands like the everyday 'I' in the everyday world to which, however far we travel, we always return.

He is also Mason's address to the viewer, and the means by which the sculpture attracts the viewer into the remoter dimensions of its aesthetic. Mason's forms are quite as exploratory and as demanding as those of Giacometti. His desire to take sculpture out to where people are is accompanied by as strong a determination to sound the expressive possibilities of his art and to find sculpture that is his own. By placing at the centre of the work a man who, reassuringly, looks like a man, he orients that personal quest, and his own adventurous probing of the crowd, towards anyone who is prepared to look — towards the human crowd itself.

With *The Crowd*, Mason found the 'message' which underlay what had long been his theme and subject-matter. At the price of years rather than months of labour, and of final prostration and discouragement under the Roman sun when chasing the two casts in bronze, he produced his first great work and turned himself into a major sculptor, at once rooted and utterly original.

48. *Faces of the City,* 1962

49. *Piccadilly Circus,* 1969

Notes on Chapter V

[1] 'My Early Artistic Life in Birmingham', in Birmingham 1989, p. 13, note 2.

[2] See Alan Bowness, 'Rodin, a conversation with Henry Moore', in *Rodin: Sculpture and Drawings*, Arts Council 1970, p. 11.

[3] Centre Georges Pompidou 1985, p. 70; Birmingham 1989, p. 97.

[4] In Claude Bernard 1977.

[5] In Centre Georges Pompidou 1985, p. 77.

[6] Tate Gallery Archive, Raymond Mason collection, material concerning *The Tate Gallery 1986–88: Illustrated Catalogue of Acquisitions*.

[7] 'Responses', in Arts Council 1982, p. 13.

[8] I quote from a much later article on contemporary art, '... et pour quand?', in *Revue des deux mondes*, November 1992, p. 90.

[9] 'The Torrent of Life', in Birmingham 1989, p. 36.

[10] The plaster was originally shown in 1965 in Mason's first exhibition at the Galerie Claude Bernard in the rue des Beaux-Arts, a few hundred yards from the Carrefour de l'Odéon and a short walk from the boulevard St Michel and from Mason's studio. It was also part, in 1968, of the inaugural exhibition *Trois Sculptures*, of the Centre national d'art contemporain, rue Berryer. On the evidence of the plaster, Malraux bought the work for the French state. One of the bronze casts was placed in the then Musée d'Art Moderne, and in 1975 was moved for the summer to the Jardin des Tuileries, where it was installed permanently in 1986. In the meantime it had been installed for several months at the Part-Dieu, Lyon, in 1980 and in Vienna at the International Exhibition of the Wiener Sezession in 1981. At the time of writing, a project to return the Tuileries (almost) to their original condition threatens the sculpture with removal.

The casting was done (1967–68) at the Bruni Foundry in Rome, for the New York dealer Pierre Matisse, son of the artist. Because the casting was incomplete, the plaster was shown again at Mason's first New York exhibition, in 1968, at the Pierre Matisse Gallery. For the same reason, the frontal frieze only of one of the casts was exhibited at another inaugural show of 1968, *The Obsessive Image*, at the Institute of Contemporary Arts in London. The first showing of a complete bronze, the brown-patinated cast which now stands outside 527 Madison Avenue, New York, was in 1969, in a group exhibition, *The Crowd*, at the Arts Club of Chicago.

[11] From Mason's letter of 6 April 1986 to the Tate Gallery, quoted in *The Tate Gallery 1982–84: Illustrated Catalogue of Acquisitions*, 1986, p. 273.

[12] *Raymond Mason – A Full Meal*, directed by Catherine Collis, Central Television, 'Contrast', 14 February 1989.

[13] From an unpublished lecture at the Paris-Belleville School of Architecture, 16 December 1987: 'Le Peuple dans la Cité'.

[14] 'Responses', in Arts Council 1982, p. 13.

[15] Centre Georges Pompidou 1985, p. 148.

[16] André Malraux, *Le musée imaginaire de la sculpture mondiale*, vol. 1: *Des bas-reliefs aux grottes sacrées*, Gallimard, Paris, 1954, p. 65.

50. *Paris,* May 1968

VI

OF CROWDS AND COLOUR

Birmingham. *In Memoriam* achieves all it does because, as Mason reflected one day when we were looking at the work, he 'had something to say'. With *The Crowd*, the first great sculpture in which he defines his subject: the crowd itself, he also establishes his relation to an audience through having 'a message'. His next concern, in the two major works of the late 1960s and the 1970s, *The Departure of Fruit and Vegetables from the Heart of Paris, 28 February 1969* (1969-71) and *A Tragedy in the North. Winter, Rain and Tears* (1975-77), is to find ways of telling a story and of expressing human emotion, and to recover for himself, with these purposes in mind, the art of polychrome sculpture.

As to story, Mason has often discussed his allegiance to the 'unbroken . . . line'[1] of British narrative artists, from Hogarth through Rowlandson, Blake, Cruikshank, Samuel Palmer, Ford Madox Brown, Stanley Spencer and many others, down to his friend Francis Bacon. He reads the history of English painting, in fact, against the grain, since he relegates landscape painting, with which the English feel at home and which has undoubtedly been influential abroad, and sometimes dismisses portraiture tacitly by not mentioning it. The allegiance results from a belief that the highest art investigates human behaviour; from a turning away from contemplation towards 'motion' and 'energy'; from a vision of art as the desire 'to steal the spark of God'.[2] It is a matter of firm and reasoned choice, and also, naturally, of predilection, of the personal specifics from which any artist's work, however 'universal', must emerge. The unconcern for contemplation is shown frankly in this comment, made admittedly in connection with abstract painting: 'my idea of art is not a contemplative art . . . one has to look at a Mondrian as one looks at a sort of Japanese Garden . . . with almost a religious, zen-like quality, which isn't in my nature at all'.[3]

Mason enables one to think again about the English tradition, possibly against the grain of one's own prejudices. He is also quick to insist on the artistry of narrative art. Of Stanley Spencer, indeed, whose work

he encountered while studying at Birmingham, he says that he was the origin of what one has learnt to be quintessential in Mason: the interest in composition.[4] He is equally anxious to indicate, on the other hand, that it is not for the furtherance of Art that he does what he does, that there is nothing programmatic in his continuing of the English narrative line. If he is a narrative artist, it is because he has something to narrate, not because he has a tradition to continue. He even disclaims any art-historical purpose, pointing to the fact that he has worked outside of England, 'with no thought of national arts', and even saying of Hogarth himself: 'I never studied him, I mean I think he has never been a conscious interest of mine.' The work in hand and the viewer to be welcomed into it are what count, and if, as a result of the kind of work offered, he turns out to be part of an English tradition, 'it can only be a natural trait with me'.[5] One is continually surprised by these denials of knowledge, these disavowals of influence.

It is clear, in fact, that in developing in himself a desire to narrate, he has gone well beyond English or any other local art, and has penetrated, quite simply, to the core of all art, to the source from which the supreme works have sprung, whether in painting or sculpture. The 'greatest cycles of Western Art, the absolutes', for Mason, are the west pediment of Zeus's temple in Olympia, the Giottos in Assisi and Padua, Piero's History of the True Cross in Arezzo, and the ceiling of the Sistine Chapel — all narrative, and all large-scale.[6] No doubt there are other views, but Mason does stir an anxiety here, about the possible loss of story. In times of belief, as he has said, even single sculpted figures are part of a story known to all,[7] and it may well be the case that one is only ready to take narrative seriously — to accept it as a serious way of shaping and understanding human experience — in a society where some kind of belief is agreed on, religious or otherwise. We tell stories because we believe that the world has a story or because we desire it to have one, whereas it seems modern and certainly post-modern to conclude that we live in a story-less world. The writing of history itself has doubted story. Mason can pursue his narrative work because he still believes, on the contrary, in a variety of ways that we are examining, in Man, in something like the story of Man, and in the possibility, moment by moment, of meaningful human eventfulness.

Malraux may even be right to contend that the main characteristic of modern art is 'not to tell a story'.[8] One sees here a second reason for distrusting story, as something adventitious from which art will need protection, as from any literary, historical or psychological intrusion, if it is to explore its own nature, through that apparent purifying of attention which is behind abstract art and minimal art and many other art forms of the twentieth century. There has been a similar move in modern poetry, while even the novel has sometimes found story disconcerting. Alan Bowness, discussing Rodin with Henry Moore, commented that we now prefer the anonymous and headless *Walking Man* to *John the Baptist* with its cloud of associations. Moore agreed that this was so, but only at the price of removing from consideration dense contexts of meaning.[9] It is out of a concern for those contexts — and a fierce antagonism to pure and self-reflexive art — that Mason compounds his narrations. We may have suffered

a demise of story for serious purposes, yet writing the story of that loss is not beyond us, and it cannot be useful in the long run to renounce this prime resource of thought, this very early means of making sense. Mason reminds us, at what is a crucial moment, of the proximity of story to our humanity, and he does so in works involving different kinds of story, to explore and to deepen, on each occasion, one's sense of story, and the various relations to time which story implies.

The move towards colour was involved with a change in material, from bronze to resin, and resulted from a number of apparently disparate happenings coming together over a short period in 1969. The most momentous threshold in Mason's art was crossed almost by chance. He had already produced coloured sculptures — not unnaturally, having begun as a painter — and although the ones he had shown in London before his departure were figurative, those which he had shown in Paris, as long ago as 1947, had become abstract. A small painted car, however, exhibited at the Salon de Mai in 1966, and some small painted heads of *Les Epouvantées* in a series of shallow boxes (now lost) suggest that, not long before it occurred, he sought to apply colour to figurative works. In the summer of 1969 he

51. *First Movement of May 1968*

52. *The Month of May in Paris,* 1968

found himself painting in oils the plaster of *The Approaching Storm* (1963), which had come back in poor condition from its casting into bronze for the 1968 exhibition at the Pierre Matisse Gallery in New York. He had already discovered that, like the other three landscape bronzes shown, it was too heavy for hanging on a wall. Not long after, his friend William Chattaway, another British sculptor living in France, introduced him to Robert Haligon, whose grandfather had been Rodin's enlarger and who was now moulding synthetic resins for Jean Dubuffet. Epoxy resin was strong, light and paintable, and Mason's first thought was to use it for

his Luberon landscapes. He took a small version of *Le Roucas* up on to the hill and painted it with acrylic paint.

Bronze had already dissatisfied him, moreover, for an even weightier reason, which seems to have been prompted by the subject-matter of the early works. He found that it betrayed the out-of-doors look of the plaster and transformed scenes into objects, into pieces of metal. It lost 'the lightness and light' of the city views as he had originally sculpted them.[10] The colour which resin made possible, the acrylic paint which bonded perfectly with its support, recovered the look of things in the space about them.

53. Four studies of Les Halles Market, 1969

A coloured sculpture is also warmer, he claims, and more human than a sculpture in marble or bronze, or even plaster. It is therefore more accessible, and fulfils even more clearly Mason's other and continuing requirement, that the work address and invite the viewer.

The new material solved, as if miraculously, all his problems; but this was not a question of strategy, of conscious thought, any more, it seems, than with any decisive and creative turn. 'It is very mysterious to me, this change,' he told an interviewer, 'and I can't really tell you why it happened'.[11] The example of Claes Oldenburg, whose exhibition he saw in autumn 1969 at the New York Museum of Modern Art, was another incitement, though the full realisation that he was working in the long tradition, that sculpture from antiquity to the baroque period and often beyond had been polychrome, only came gradually. The move was very personal — and although this is always the case with Mason, it is particularly important to stress the fact here — and one sees that if, for all of us, colour is not something external to things but a means of access, along with all the other visual signs, to the visible and the invisible, it must descend for the artist (as does language for the poet) far into his customary experience, into his ways of being in the world. Mason's return to colour satisfied needs not necessarily felt by other sculptors, but sufficiently urgent to have freed and then sustained the rest of his work. We shall also find that he does not treat colour like other sculptors.

The move towards expression began more directly in a dissatisfaction not so much with bronze as with the way he had been modelling for it. He has said of *The Crowd*: 'when I had done it, I did feel that it was a crowd of faces without expressions, and without real personalities', and even that it has 'a sort of emptiness about the figures'.[12] To think that is to wish each figure to be charged to the full with humanity and for that humanity to brim into every feature, and to emphasise less 'the union of people', the oneness of the work, than the differences from which the union and the oneness are to be achieved. It is to want every part of the sculpture — and here one glimpses another fundamental of Mason's work — to bristle with vivid detail. This will require a new kind of modelling, but it is essentially colour that will work the change, by giving expression not only to human faces but to everything encountered by the eye: by giving features to every object. Or as Mason himself has written, it was in *The Departure* that he 'first used colour to detach and personalise a quantity of separate elements'.[13] We shall need to return to this idea of detaching with a view to personalising, since it takes one both to a living centre of his work and to the centre of controversy.

Narrative, colour and expression are all features of the next major work, *The Departure of Fruit and Vegetables from the Heart of Paris, 28 February 1969*, which was first shown in 1971 at the Galerie Claude Bernard in Paris and the Pierre Matisse Gallery in New York. One can see it in Georgetown, Washington D.C., at the Four Seasons Hotel whose façade also carries the upper part of Mason's later *Twin Sculptures*, and, most appropriately, in the church of St Eustache in Paris, which is represented in the work.

It was when *The Crowd* was being finished that a decision was taken to close down Les Halles, the market of central Paris, and to move its activity to the suburban town of Rungis. Mason had already contemplated the possibility of a market scene, as one of the 'happy' subjects, along with 'the journey' and 'mealtime', for which he felt a need after the tremendous effort for the bronze.[14] A sculpture of *The Journey* had been begun in 1966 but still stands unfinished, and he had also started a sculpture of a meal which he found he did not quite know how to handle. The news of the departure of Les Halles had even more effect on the Parisians and on Mason himself than the loss of Covent Garden had on Londoners; by choosing that departure, Mason both seized the occasion — indeed, in an artistic sense, redeemed the time — and focused on a depth and particularity of emotion. By renting a room in the area, drawing for long hours among the market workers, and living something of the life of that mainly nocturnal but glaringly illuminated world — which had a fabulous quality even before, as now, it was transformed by the power of memory — he prepared a real and more than real work of exact, singular and teeming detail. By concentrating on fruit and vegetables (Les Halles was also a meat and fish market) — in a way the heroes of the piece, since it is *their* departure which is memorialised — he homed in on a relation with the fruits of the earth. By sculpting the very moment of the departure, he elected narrative and assembled his human figures into a new kind of crowd: not the modern crowd of indifferent passers-by, as in *The Crowd* itself, but a crowd of individuals gathered for a purpose, of the kind he would later refer to in fifteenth-century painting.[15]

But where can one begin to discuss the work? There is so much, and not the multiplicity of objects only but their composition draws one further and further in. Mason has written of Picasso that he was 'a painter of composition, a painter of history and a painter in large dimensions,' to which he adds: 'The three go together'.[16] In *The Departure*, a work which resembles nothing by Picasso — or by anyone else, for that matter — one senses nevertheless the lesson of his achievement, since all three features are similarly present, and one realises that, while it is not possible to discuss Picasso's imprint on any particular work by Mason (except perhaps *The Costa Brava*), among all modern artists he is the one whose example is probably the most important. 'As soon as I entered the period of my large works,' Mason writes in the same note, 'my thoughts went almost exclusively to Picasso.' (Interestingly, from another angle, the critic of the New York Times opened his article on the 1971 Pierre Matisse show by declaring: 'Guernica had its Picasso, and now Les Halles has its Raymond Mason.') And one might say of Mason what he says of Picasso himself, that he is 'a compositional genius'.[17] The evidence is before one in *The Departure*, in its layer after layer of significance.

One first sees, perhaps, a profusion of humans in a riot of fruit and vegetables, which are presented, stacked, carried or carted in all the ways imaginable. They are individually 'realist' — so much like the real thing, in fact, that they enhance one's vision of the real, to the point that, after gazing at *The Departure*, one sees Mason fruit and vegetables in shops (especially when neon-lit and reflected in mirrors), just as, after certain of the Luberon works, one sees Mason clouds from the window of an aeroplane — and their abundance is an equally accurate transposition of the prodigality of the market. One is also aware, however, of the art which celebrates the beauty of that natural world, and of Mason's use of colour both to compose and on occasion to enhance the sculptural volumes. For someone who has always been concerned with multiplying the complexity of a work, colour was a clear gain since, as he has said, it 'heightens a hundredfold the spatial possibilities of recall and repetition'.[18] The eye, as it roves over this large-minded and yet meticulous work, cannot exhaust the relationships to be discovered. The figures are painted boldly in flat colours as in primitive and popular art, but visible brushstrokes also follow and perfect the swelling of a form, as in the further rounding of the apples carried by the woman at the front, and of the coat over her breasts.

One becomes aware, moreover, of the affinity between the human figures and the fruit and vegetables among which they live. That woman's breasts are painted with the same strokes as the apples which nudge and seem to repeat them, despite the clashing red and green which serve also to separate and individualise the coat and the fruit, and when Mason writes of chancing on a number of commonplace images in the process of the work — a potato nose, a cauliflower ear, an Adam's apple, a kiss suggestive of forbidden fruits[19] — the humour is surely concealing a serious purpose. We enter, here, the world of the natural, where humans — or at least these humans — are involved with the earth or with the fruits and vegetables which emerge from it. The realisation enables one to read again a work of the previous year, *The Month of May in Paris* (1968), a low relief which was enlarged, cast into epoxy resin and painted in 1974. It has a quite different story to tell, yet if our participation in the work begins, as in *Man in a Street*, with the bust of a man looking at us at eye level and from the base of the work, what rises from behind his head so as to dominate the work entirely is a tree. And not only does the tree spread out over the milling figures, which it dwarfs, as if to take them under its protection, it is also itself opened out so as to reveal at once the density and the depths of its foliage and the strength of its internal structure, the architecture of its branches. Although unconscious of the fact, the crowd has in its midst this giant and living thing, which also possesses, like them, a trunk and limbs. And one then sees that the most concentrated vision of the oneness of human and vegetable life is a work which accompanies *The Departure*: *Les Halles*, one of four small studies of the market in wood, resin and acrylic paint executed in 1969. From the middle of mountains of vegetable produce a single head appears, surrounded by the vivid leaves of the green world.

This is the exuberant layer of the work, where one also sees, in the vegetables and the fruit, a luxuriance of spiral growth, a common form which they share and which is their life. What may seem at first a jostling crowd entering into the work from several directions has also been carefully shaped into a single spiral which begins, when the sculpture is viewed as a plan, from the man in the centre raising a box of oranges over his head, and which circles anti-clockwise until it finally crosses the foreground and bears all the figures away to the right. The spiral composes the whole work and displays that composition in numerous details. But it also provides another link between the humans and the vegetables: it contains everything living in the work like some great horn of plenty, and it takes the viewer's imagination to the source of life, the law of generation.

PARIS   le 28 fev. 1969

Preceding pages: 54. *The Departure of Fruit and Vegetables from the Heart of Paris. Feb 28 1969*, 1971

Above and left: *The Departure of Fruit and Vegetables from the Heart of Paris* (details)

The crowd, in *The Crowd* itself, was a wave, a joyfully unbounded multiplicity. Here as always, it retains its copiousness, and even the suggestion of a falling wave in the figures at the front (just as *The Crowd* contains a spiral); but it is all gathered into what for Mason is another essential figure. A further layer of the work appears in that this spiral governs a procession. The market workers have formed a line because they come with offerings: a cauliflower presented like a bouquet, a spring of parsley resembling the widow's mite, a box of oranges held aloft with intent concentration at the origin of the spiral and at the centre of the work. The sculpture is a kind of secular Adoration of the Magi, in which the givers are the ordinary market folk and the gifts are the 'wonders of nature' themselves among which they have lived their lives, not on one special occasion but always, 'at night, under the stars'.[20]

Yet it is also a Carrying of the Cross. The man pulling his cart with such quiet strain and with his eyes to the ground literally bears a cross on his back formed by the straps of his overalls. The cross is immediately repeated on a lettuce displayed beyond him, which becomes not only the sign of his pleasure but of his toil. For there is toil in the sculpture as well (as there is Mason's toil), and this is accentuated on the other side by the man stooping beneath a prodigious (and spiralling) sack of potatoes, who by his angular exertion swings the procession round. What the market people offer is also their work, but one senses a darker mood beyond that offering. This is, after all, a departure, and as the man draws his cart, so he draws all the front of the sculpture with him. The falling movement across the foreground figures which leads to his bent back is a means of composition and recalls *The Falling Man*, but it serves also to link the figures and to project them forward into him. And he draws with him, of course, the whole procession, all of which one imagines leaving the work in his wake. His cart is another vehicle moving off to the right, and it recalls in particular, through the deliberate detail of the cross, the tram of *Barcelona Tram* and its equally real and yet more than real driver. There, in the radiant sunlight of Barcelona, a departing vehicle, moving away from the dark entrance to the railway station, bears its passengers into whatever may lie behind or within the sensuous and sunlit world. In the nocturnal but brightly illuminated scene of *The Departure*, the man with a cart carries all the human figures away from the dark and empty entrances of the pavilions, out of the work and out of the world. The sign on his back is the burden of sorrow and loss, as he leads 'the man of the Middle Ages' out of paradise.[21]

Hence the expressions on the faces, all absorbed, some withdrawn and meditative, others gazing and rapt. The change from *The Crowd* is total, though there is not yet a great variety of expression. What Mason needs is a similarity of emotion from person to person, a common intentness of presence, so that the union of people within an undifferentiated humanity may become a conscious communion. Every face is itself, but the art which relates them is quite as powerful as the art which gives them that lavishness of difference.

The hints taken from two recurring motifs in Christian art are thoroughly humanised, and Mason has stated categorically that 'there is nothing religious in the sculpture at all'.[22] If the forms of the church are repeated all over the work, this is in the interest of composition, though one does see that its tracery is recalled in the cabbage leaf suspended in the very centre of the work, serving as a kind of crinkly halo for the old lady; while one of the church windows, and the old lady, whose shawl is covered in the flowers of the field, both carry the emblem of the work, the 'heart' of Paris, the core of emotion of the Parisians. Mason has also written of the church, moreover, that it lent to the activities and products of the market 'a grand scale, their essential and spiritual dimension',[23] and it is difficult not to feel, at the depth of the work, a spiritual quietness. After the energy, the spiralling movement, the vivid and clashing colours, the freehanded superabundance of things, the sculpture becomes still again, and one is entered by the solemnity of the procession, by the gravity of this offering, by a knowledge too much for any individual, which has gathered the celebrants into one and enlarged the world around them. To what is the old man bowing? In what dimension more ample than ours does that woman carry her crate of apples? What meets in the lovers' kiss? In *The Departure*, more possibly than in any of his other works, Mason reaches beyond mere narrative and attains the simplicity and infinite resonance of epic or myth.

Perhaps he even suggests the non-Christian nature of the myth. In the centre of his work is an offering, an elevation, and on either side two leafless trees. In the centre again is a cabbage leaf held upright so as to resemble a tree with foliage. Are we to understand that there are three crosses, that the work is also a Crucifixion, and that in place of the Cross is a tree of life and in place of the sacrifice a tray of oranges? The religion is natural and earthly, and the person hidden in the middle of the work, holding the cabbage leaf and looking up wide-eyed beyond the offering, is a black man. One then remembers the plane tree of *The Month of May in Paris*: the tree of liberty sprouting from the man's head but also the tree of life towering above the humans and, as Mason was happy to realise much later, the pagan May-tree.

The Departure of Fruit and Vegetables from the Heart of Paris (detail)

Above and right: *The Departure of Fruit and Vegetables from the Heart of Paris* (details)

So one glimpses a larger meaning for the departure of the natural man of the Middle Ages. The joy of the work is the abundance of life and the desire to possess it. The sorrow is the knowledge of the difficulty of satisfying that desire. Les Halles and its people, on whose ceremony we intrude, are the emblem of natural joy, while the loss of the Market is the realisation of all that, in a human life incomprehensibly imperfect, militates against finding natural joy in ourselves — not merely high spirits but a joy worthy of a world more genial than us.

There is further to go. For if the work has been blessed (by no external power) into ritual, it is also enchanted into art — not so as to quit the real but, on the contrary, so as to meet a real world at its deepest and richest. We can guess this is northern art, from the celebration of the accidents of a real world however unsubmissive to canons of beauty, and from the refusal of an unmitigated sublime. Yet Mason has also described the work as a 'three-dimensional fresco in vivid colour',[24] and one sees why he has been most powerfully impressed by Italian fresco from Giotto to Tiepolo,[25] and why he refers his compositional technique to the quattrocento in particular and his use of matt paint to the effect of tempera. It is not a question, for the viewer, of merely taking note of a touch of northern here, a touch of southern there. To look hard at the work is to find one-self gazing at the art of Europe, gradually appearing and becoming one. Without in any way losing its prime intention of reconstructing an actual place and the emotions it aroused, the sculpture also leads one into a memory, an image, of art.

It also leads one through a number of particular works, not as influences or as allusions to be recognised in a spirit of connoisseurship, but as worlds to be entered and enjoyed. As one advances from, say, seventeenth-century still life (consider the naturalistic touch of the abandoned lettuce leaf and the squashed tomato which are also the last ripples of a dying wave or the final and perfect notes of a descending phrase) to Hogarth's *Morning*, perhaps, or to his practice of composition in the hand at the front repeated in the trees; to his aesthetic in the serpentine line of beauty governing the middle of the work through the upheld cabbage leaf; to Spencer's *The Dustman* or *The Lovers*; to Samuel Palmer's tiny *Coming from Evening Church*; above all to Bruegel's *Peasant Dance*, whose kissing lovers are imitated in *The Departure* in a similar region of the work — one finds that door after door is being opened.

Other doors are opened by a more literary device. One discovers that kiss, for instance, by moving to the right and following with the eyes a story of extraordinary richness, which begins with the hollow-eyed man, continues with the 'widow' and then the Negro, and culminates

104

in the lovers. As one walks across the work, not only do different perspectives come into view, as in *The Crowd*, along with jostling and ever-renewed relationships among the figures — made even more complex here through the use of colour — but numerous further narratives are there for the seeing. As a three-dimensional fresco, the sculpture can propose more stories than the one which appears on the surface, and it does so partly like a play, which places different characters together scene by scene. Mason has invented, in fact, a powerfully eloquent new form, where the stories, too, partake of the multiple. They are not made explicit, their function being essentially to allow the viewer to step from world to world, from that implied, for example, in the Negro to that of the lovers. With each move one is in a particular world and in *The Departure*, just as to remember the dancing crowd of countrymen in Bruegel is to glimpse their shades among Mason's urban peasants.

To see his lovers with Bruegel in mind is also to see two perfectly real market workers transformed into personages in a painting. And next to them is a worker who is also Bottom, with a sorrel leaf for an ass's ear, for the final door opens on to the greatest of all the other worlds in the work: Shakespeare's *A Midsummer Night's Dream*. *The Departure* is Mason's midwinter night's dream (he has said so himself, in an audio-visual presentation of the work), in which these cousins to the

'rude mechanicals' are also caught up into a world of fancy, brilliantly lit yet surrounded by the mysterious largeness of the night, where there are lovers, solemnities, magic, and transformations. Entering Dream, they are drawn together, and find themselves following each other like sleepwalkers, offering fruits to the night, bearing a cross. Pomona appears, wearing a white bobble cap.

And there is once again a small, far-off character who is partly hidden and whom one only comes upon after a while. One finds him by looking up from the hollow-eyed man in a certain perspective — this is another of the work's local narratives — and there he is, perched on a great heap of produce, completely surrounded by the market wares, looking at the viewer from the distance of the work, and smiling broadly. He is the king of fruit and vegetables, with a sack of garlic for his crown, who is not part of the procession but seems to preside over it, and although he is not Oberon one cannot avoid remembering Puck's announcement: 'The King doth keep his Revels here tonight.' Mason himself calls him the 'maraîcher en majesté', the market-gardener in majesty, so yet another Christian motif is being appropriated. He is a secular Christ in Majesty, with a halo of garlic bulbs and a mandorla of fruit and veg.

The smile and the thought of revels conduct one into the hope of the work. This may be a departure, but the

colours of the workers and of their produce are bright against the sombre buildings and the night, with a preponderance of reds and greens bursting against each other, and of other warm tones of orange and yellow. The wheel on the cart which bears them away is matched by a wheel-like rose-window in the church, where time will continue to turn. The procession leaves but the red cabbage remains, posed on its crate as the most evident offering by the artist but also as a simple vegetable itself turning in its roundness. The fruits indicate that the apparently lifeless trees will again grow leaves (one of the many accompanying drawings shows a wintry tree ascending from a positive rifeness of produce), while the falling rhythm across the front nevertheless leads to a cart whose upward angle suggests a rise.

The Departure is a vision of the world's plenty, of the cornucopia of the earth in the night sky. The hesitation, however, the anxiety concerning the possible departure of that reign of plenty, returns, or so it seems, in the man with the hollow eyes so strangely full of humanity. As one approaches the work, he commands its centre, its axes and its rightward movement. As one moves across the work he associates in various narratives with a host of other figures, including the lofted oranges, and in each case he is the question mark in the sentence. By his reaching-out eyes he joins the sculpture to the space on this side of it; he draws us into the work, by removing the distance which would have enabled us to look it over as an art object; and as he looks far into us he invites us to look far into him. The dream of the work is in his eyes, or in his head, and his hand is placed next to his head as if he were the sculptor. His mouth is stopped because he expresses the work by his gaze, or because the final meaning of the work is not expressed but remains a question. As one glances from him to the oranges especially and to the festive king, his gaze becomes more and more interrogative, as if the work's unconscious speaks through him. As so often with Mason, there is a final moment when the work opens to another depth, which is not an answer or a final truth, but the silence of life.

In this crowd by night which follows a crowd in daylight, Mason has created a sculpture which takes the viewer further and further in and which, like some great theatrical work — like *A Midsummer Night's Dream* itself — opens to level after level of significance, to world upon world. It explores the processes of the imagination, which always, as it seeks to understand the world, whether in sculpture, or poetry, or mathematics, leads one progressively deeper until the world itself becomes imagination, becomes art, becomes the possibility of repetition, of order, of oneness. But

Above: *The Departure of Fruit and Vegetables from the Heart of Paris* (detail)

unless one is to remain in the dream, in the *cosa mentale*, one has to return to the everyday real, and so one remembers the exact date in the title of the work, one realises that the light there is not only the light of dream but a precise imitation of the light of the market projectors against darkness, and one sees again that the emotion of the work goes to the actual market workers and to the 'very heart' of every single fruit and vegetable — to 'each cauliflower cluster, each artichoke leaf' and even 'each window on the streets of Montmartre and Montorgueil'.[26] It is the great paradox of any art which is true to a perceived reality and true to itself that both the world and the work are primary, and that, if all goes well, the more the work is aesthetically achieved, the more the world beyond the work is enhanced. As Mason said in a 1975 slide lecture on polychrome sculpture, the work of co-ordinating 'each form with every other' is for him 'all-important', so that the 'spheres of the oranges, for instance, not only have to group together in significant fashion but also make a counterpoint in form and colour with the rectangles of the windows' in the street, and one sees at the same time that oranges and windows are things that matter. Part of the lesson one learns from Mason's art is that if it expands with such inexhaustible power, this is because it takes root in what one might have considered the opposite of the

imagination: not only an everyday world and his emotion before it, but a delight in seeing and rendering that world down to its smallest prosaic detail. He can transform the real so persuasively because his concern for the work coincides exactly with his concern for what the work is about.

This large, grave sculpture has a small and comic tail-piece, *St Mark's Place, East Village, New York City*, of 1972. The original drawing was done in November 1971 when Mason, in New York for the showing of *The Departure* and seated at a café with paper and a drawing-board luckily beside him, witnessed the irresistible scene through the window. He planned the sculpture back in Paris as a 'light relief' while finishing and painting the remaining copies of the heavy relief of *The Departure,*[27] and first showed it in New York, in his exhibition at the Pierre Matisse Gallery of 1974. One of the copies is owned by the Tate Gallery in London.

   Although *St Mark's Place* is not narrative and returns to the earlier street scenes, the even greater individuality of its figures, and especially the explosive variety of their expressions, make of it another turning-point in Mason's work. Its imaginary size is created by the milling of the crowd before the evident geometries which counter and thereby augment it, by its further milling

55. *St Mark's Place, East Village, New York City,* 1972

the unlike — Arab and Irish cop, the 'convulsed face' of a drunk and the 'pacified grimace' of a pot-smoker — likewise opens large distances and permits a long journey through space and time.[29] After *The Departure of Fruit and Vegetables, St Mark's Place* is an image of human plenty. And we may note that it is not an art of suggestion, or of visionary expanses, which produces this immensity, but a realism of likeness. The more he could make a chimney like a chimney, Mason writes, and a curtain like a curtain — 'the more, in short, that they showed likeness to themselves' — the more they would differ and move apart, to a degree minute, immeasurable, 'so therefore why not infinite'?[30]

as the viewer moves, and by the full range of Mason's seemingly infallible science of composition — a deepening of field, for example, by the axis which plunges from the head of the beatific 'cyclist' via the heads of the black woman and the strolling girl to the minute salt-cellar, and a stretching of the whole towards the viewer by the arm and hand of the drunk, whose fingertips flattened against the window also mark, for once, the limit of the work, and spin the observer dizzily from the suggestion of a small restaurant fish-tank in which he is a clumsy lobster[28] to the suggestion of a large street. A fictive immensity is created, however, by a new science of expression. Certain works of the 1950s had been expressive and even expressionist, but here a multiplicity of characters spring apart in their singularity through a new inventiveness in the modelling and through a use of colour which is garish, fast-changing and compositionally exact. The controlled heterogeneity of the colours follows through in the diversity of sentiment and of racial or social type, where the juxtaposition of

This page and left: *St Marks Place, East Village, New York City* (details)

By making each thing vividly itself, he turns his little peepshow into a view of the world. He is an artist who can put 2 and 2 together and get 22.

So what of the charge of vulgarity, of producing ugly fairground or comic-strip figures in ghastly colours, which has pursued Mason through much of his career? The charge is as crazy as anyone in *St Mark's Place*, but one can always learn from folly. Mason's offence is that he wishes to include everything — everything of the *there is* which constitutes reality as it insists on appearing — and that he exaggerates. The exaggeration does not produce caricature, for which Mason has neither the gift nor the inclination.[31] Even less does it produce satire: his figures do not finally resemble Daumier's gallery of political portraits in painted clay. It produces life. The vivid particularity of each form, each colour, charges the work, to bursting point, with a sun-like energy, with the exuberance, no doubt, of the artist himself, whose gift to sculpture is the gift of life. Exaggeration is the resource, after all, of much great art, since it belongs to the heightening, the magnification, which is one of the reasons for art. The overplus

here is partly the irrepressible 'madness' which exudes from the word 'PAZZA' in the very centre of the work, finds its emblem in the helmeted man carrying some sort of palm-branch (*St Mark's Place* also has its Fool), and lights up all along the street many of the other implausible but authentic words. It is a place which counts 'Iggy' among its denizens, and where a hotel for 'transients' aptly describes these *transientes*, these people who walk across in one direction and then the other, and who have nowhere else to go since, as number 4 nonchalantly informs them, they are in 'Limbo'. Hence the fact that the person looking at us from the work is a hippie, and hence, perhaps, the uniquely closed eyes of the drunk, for whom the whole work is a giddy dream.

Vulgarity is smaller than life, this is larger than life. And maybe it is also too close to the truth for comfort, so that to call it vulgar is to defend one's good taste and to call it caricature, to defend one's good looks. There is a passage in Dickens (a writer in whom the absence of overtly intellectual topics, compared to George Eliot, say, or Proust, can prevent one from seeing that

111

56. *Rocas Planas, Costa Brava,* 1967

he has a huge mind) where, as an apparently irrelevant aside spoken when the real subject of a conversation is elsewhere, a character suggests of a portrait that it is 'so like as to be almost a caricature?'[32] The comment — a suggestion, perhaps, about Dickens's own art, dropped into the text with remarkable aplomb — proposes, against all expectation, that the closer the artist gets to the real the more he will seem to be giving it undue emphasis. The world for Mason, as for Dickens, *is* emphatic, because of the energy with which, in his

art, he lives it. Each thing in Mason, as in the very British philosophy of Duns Scotus, is emphatically itself, and has as its purpose to brim with selfhood.

The same is true of his works. Each one is elaborated until it shows a perfect 'likeness to itself' and so differs from any other. The *this-ness* of *St Mark's Place* is that it manifests Mason's comic zest, and concentrates, in its very smallness, the desire, throughout his whole *oeuvre*, for abundance, continual metamorphosis, infinity.

Notes on Chapter VI

[1] 'Responses', in Arts Council 1982, p. 15.

[2] Interview in Claude Bernard 1977.

[3] *Ibid.*

[4] 'My Early Artistic Life in Birmingham', in Birmingham 1989, p. 13, note 5.

[5] Interview in Marlborough 1985.

[6] From an unpublished reply to a talk on narrative sculpture, Birmingham, 3 June 1989.

[7] *Ibid.*

[8] *Le musée imaginaire*, Chapter 2, revised edition, Gallimard, Paris, 1963.

[9] *Rodin: Sculpture and Drawings*, Arts Council 1970, p. 11.

[10] Interview in Marlborough 1985.

[11] 'The Torrent of Life', in Birmingham 1989, p. 36.

[12] *Ibid.*

[13] 'St Mark's Place, East Village, New York City', in Birmingham 1989, p. 96.

[14] Interview in Marlborough 1985.

[15] Interview in Claude Bernard 1977.

[16] 'La Dation Picasso', in *Cahiers du Musée national d'art moderne*, no. 3, Centre Georges Pompidou, Paris, 1980.

[17] 'Responses', in Arts Council 1982, p. 13.

[18] *Ibid.*, p. 14.

[19] 'The Departure of Fruit and Vegetables from the Heart of Paris, 28 February 1969', in Birmingham 1989, p. 90.

[20] *Ibid.*

[21] *Ibid.*

[22] 'The Torrent of Life', p. 33.

[23] 'The Departure of Fruit and Vegetables . . . ', in Birmingham 1989, p. 90.

[24] 'Responses', in Arts Council 1982, p. 14.

[25] *Ibid.*, p. 13.

[26] 'The Departure of Fruit and Vegetables . . . ', in Birmingham 1989, p. 90.

[27] 'St Mark's Place, East Village, New York City', in Birmingham 1989, p. 94.

[28] *Ibid.*

[29] *Ibid.*, p. 96.

[30] *Ibid.*

[31] His disclaimer is in an unpublished interview with Jane Farrington quoted in Birmingham 1989, p. 41.

[32] *Our Mutual Friend*, Book 2, Chapter 16.

57. *The Costa Brava,* 1966–83

58. *A Tragedy in the North. Winter, Rain and Tears* (detail), 1977

Right: *The Tragedy of Liévin* (below) with a contemporary photograph

VII

TRAGEDY

The next long moment in Mason's work, after *The Crowd* and after *The Departure*, is expressed in a sequence of three sculptures: *Monument for Guadeloupe* (1976), *The Aggression at 48 Rue Monsieur-le-Prince on 23 June 1975* (1976) and *A Tragedy in the North. Winter, Rain and Tears* (1975–77), whose origins are diverse and unconnected but whose roots in his thinking about the human condition are the same. Their relation to those two previous large sculptures is the essential one, as also to the painted sculptures and gouaches of the Luberon of 1974. To come to their violence specifically from *St Mark's Place*, however, and from its racy comedy of manners, is to make, from work to work, the same typically large journey that one makes, inside the works, from figure to figure or colour to colour, and to realise that individual works too spring apart in their singularity and enlarge the whole.

A Tragedy in the North was first exhibited in Paris at the Galerie Claude Bernard in 1977 and at the Pierre Matisse Gallery in New York in 1980, and also at the Musée des Beaux-Arts of Mons in Belgium in 1979. One of the casts is owned, appropriately, by the Birmingham City Museum and Art Gallery. In 1976 Mason and his wife would move from their flat in rue du Cardinal Lemoine to a considerably enlarged flat adjoining his studio in rue Monsieur-le-Prince, but it was in their house in Ménerbes in the south of France that, at the end of 1974, *A Tragedy in the North* had its remarkably charged beginning. Shortly after Christmas Mason read in a local newspaper about a mining disaster in Liévin, a small town in the Pas-de-Calais, and saw in the accompanying photograph an 'anxious milling crowd' in front of brick buildings and on cobble-stones 'agleam with rain' which spoke to him, suddenly and imperiously, of his own 'North'.[1] The familiar summons outwards from where he was — 'I . . . at once felt nearer to this painful scene in the North than the near-idyllic one of the festive Provençal interior in which I was sitting' — is the most tremendous that he had experienced, since he was called from festivity to grief, from the south

to the north, from self to others, and also from the maturity of his fifty-two years to a Birmingham childhood and youth. He began a small plaster relief the same day and, when he had painted it, wrote along the base (in French): 'The Tragedy of Liévin. 27 Dec. 1974. The North, winter, rain, tears. Love of one's own. REALITY. R.M. Ménerbes (Vaucluse)'.

All of his great works begin in the pulling power of an emotion, but here one senses the overwhelming immediacy of a revelation, the epiphany of what is truly and finally real: human tragedy — human immersion in a vast non-human world of geography, seasons and weather, to which we nevertheless belong since its rain resembles our tears — and not universal love but particular human loves. Hence his faithfulness to the buildings, reproduced exactly as they appear in the newspaper photograph. Hence the indication of the place where the work was made, since the movement out and away is essential to its meaning. And hence, perhaps, the restriction of his name to his initials.

For those words have the intensity of a mystical utterance ('REALITY' is not so far from Pascal's 'Fire . . . Certainty, certainty . . . '), yet the very strength of what Mason had seen seems to have caused a kind of resistance to the work which had to be done. The

coloured drawing of the mine buildings, *Liévin, la Fosse 3*, executed the following February when Mason found himself driving in the Pas-de-Calais and decided to visit the site of the accident, suggests once again an irresistible attraction, as the rising and narrowing perspective of the road draws the eye in to the lovingly detailed red bricks, or else the widening road draws forward to where one is standing the whole remembered world of which they are the effectual sign. The road even resembles that of *Birmingham. In Memoriam*, the arrowed colouring of its cobble-stones replacing, as an incitement to the viewer, the vertiginous descent. Despite having resolved at the time to abandon decor, Mason did decide to undertake a large sculpture out of fidelity to that suddenly present past, yet, as he recounts in the catalogue for the 1977 exhibition in Paris, once he had built the decor against the wall of his studio he stopped work, 'as if the buildings alone had answered my need.' His experience had been in part a haunting by an image, by the redbrick factory at which he had stared as a child, out of his asthmatic affliction, from a window in Wheeleys Lane. He had already realised while doing bronzes that one day his art 'would have to pass that way',[2] and even after completing the buildings in *A Tragedy* he seems to have known that the

59. *Study,* 1976

factory would still be waiting for him. (It returns in *Forward*). It is true that the Guadeloupe proposal had also arrived in February 1975, and that a bout of sciatica would restrict him for a time to the making of the small-scale *Aggression*. It was nevertheless a full year after abandoning the work that Mason went back to it; as soon, one may think, as the largeness of the emotion could be faced, so that a return to the deeps of childhood and to 'the poor edge of stately Edgbaston'[3] could issue in a homage to the working classes, and as soon as the demands of a fully seen Truth could be met.

For if *The Departure* amplifies a scene in Les Halles to become a waking dream-vision of the world's plenty and the possibility of loss, *A Tragedy in the North* (and what a strong, classic title that is) replaces the pit-shafts with an ominous slag-heap — and for once suppresses the date — so as to maintain the centre of gravity in the people below and amplify a specifically mining catastrophe into a tragic reading of the human condition. The crowd no longer walks or processes but resembles the random disposition of an actual crowd, yet at the same time, in this most turbulent of Mason's works so far, the waiting and passive crowd of the press photograph has been invaded by a single emotion, which causes dramatic gestures, tilts many bodies and limbs at vigorous diagonals, and sends people running in various directions, like the woman far away on the left who seems to rush towards the viewer with open arms. The bursts of activity are all the more remarkable for being sporadic, in a scene where most of the characters simply stand. The sculpture even seizes a moment, and suspends a number of feet above the ground.

The drama is in the movements and the moment, in the disarray of the crowd against the strict geometries of buildings and cobble-stones. The tragedy is in the overall structure, and first in a recurring compositional pattern to which Mason himself refers and which tells the 'story' of the work. The repeated slopes of the slag-heap, like the many angles of *The Departure*, are part of the 'abstract' dimension of the sculpture and clarify the scene into order, but they also bind into meaning the people, the street and the buildings, and this 'enigmatic, symbolical pyramid'[4] which menaces from above and bears down on the whole work. They descend through the gables and the kerbstones to the arms and features of the woman at the front, and reappear to the side in a white handkerchief. Their inverted V passes in its descent through the beauty of a simple architecture and the warm bricks which associate work with dwelling and are the first home of emotion.

60. *Pit no. 3* (or *Liévin, la fosse 3*), 1975

61. Following pages: *A Tragedy in the North. Winter, Rain and Tears,* 1977

It passes down the road, itself brimming with emotion in the wound-like colours of its cobble-stones, in the seemingly endless repetition of their form and the inexhaustible differentiation of their colouring. It turns the road — which attracts the viewer in like a perspective triangle while also impelling the emotion towards him, to the rhythmic accompaniment of the fence — into a road of life, on which the reverberation of death is being felt by the human figures. (One may recall, though it is not necessary to do so, the similarly raked perspective of Uccello's *The Flood*). It reaches finally the fleeing woman (the clearest change from the newspaper photograph, added immediately in the small relief), who is the familiar central figure facing the viewer, and who here runs from the work with all the emotions of the work and carries all its meanings into the viewer's own world. It then returns, however, with the woman in the architectural raincoat standing stolidly on the left. Her bulk resembles that of the man in a similar position in *The Crowd*, but she not only takes the viewer into the work, she stills him, amid all the movement, into a recognition of grief, and into a realisation that, if her handkerchief is a sign of the tears produced by the 'pyramid', which symbolically covers the dead, its whiteness is a perfect inversion of that black and a small centre of resistance. One then sees that if all these recurring shapes press downwards, they also point upwards, and that the whole sculpture descends into grief so as to rise through it.

The structure of the work only becomes fully visible, however, with the miner, who appears for the first time, like the slag-heap, in the final sculpture. We see him down to his working hands, and above all, according to a deliberate and significant denial of the facts of modern mining, we see coal on his face. The mark of the slag-heap is on all three characters at the front, but he is the one who bears its colour. By exiting where he does, he also completes the overall movement of the work, not up to the right but for once down to the right, and although the blue of his coat belongs to its cold coloration, he is not part of the action, but someone who steps forward to tell the viewer.

Is he not the messenger, who walks out of the work but who also comes from its distance, and who emerges, indeed, from the earth underneath? His wide-open staring eyes are an equivalent, in polychrome sculpture, of the intensity of look achieved in the bronzes by the moulding of shadows in the eye sockets, while his mouth is closed because his message is what he has seen and because we, too, are to see into the work with the eye of the mind, or the eye of the heart. And if he is the messenger, we are assuredly witnessing a tragedy. The 'enigmatic' slag-heap looms from behind, in the manner, say, of the Trojan War. On and about the real and symbolic road a drama is being enacted of pitiable loss and terrible expectancy, peopled in part by Trojan mothers and widows. In front of the work is the messenger. The structure once seen is powerful in its simplicity, and may possibly have been prompted by Mason's study of *Phaedra*, since there too the goddess Venus descends to pursue the characters, and Theramenes finally comes forward to tell the tale. The difference between the labyrinth and the roadway suffices to show, nevertheless, the dissimilar worlds which the two tragedies imply.

The most conspicuous figure, therefore: the Pole with outstretched arm, who is within the action, who relates to the drama since he restrains the fleeing woman, who is central to the sculpture since his arm reacts to every movement of the spectator, and who is the principal link with the spectator through his advancing hand, is rather like the dramatist in the midst of his play, or the sculptor in the midst of his sculpture, offering, once again, his sculptor's hand. He is not a representation of Mason, any more than is the central figure of *The Crowd*, but unlike that figure he is the focus of compassion, of a reaching towards the other, and expresses in the worked furrows of his brow and in the far-seeing gaze of his deep-set eyes something of the overmastering emotion at the origin of the work and now at its centre.

Between the slag-heap, which will remain, and the miner whose eyes speak of the 'winter, rain and tears' which are part of the human condition and also seem to ask their meaning, is the scene of knowledge and of triumph. For 'tragedy' here is thoroughly humanist and leads to a quite traditional hope, the power and beauty of which are in the manner and the depth of the rediscovery. Out of the catastrophe comes a victory of good in the realisation, across this scattered crowd, of community. In his text on the work, Mason refers to Malraux as suggesting that low-relief or high-relief sculptures allow the representation of people who do not know each other, whereas in sculpture in the round people do know each other or are directly in contact, and adds that in 'a scene of tragedy, the unwilling actors recognise each other in their suffering'. The French version of the text is more telling, since it passes from characters who 'se connaissent' or 'ne se connaissent pas' to tragic characters who 'se reconnaissent'.[5] It is this recognition, this re-cognition of each other, that creates the specific community of *A Tragedy in the North*. The otherwise indifferent passers-by of *The Crowd* are made one in the oceanic wave of the human. The individually absorbed members of the procession in *The Departure* are united in their shared mood and their collective offering. Here the crowd *becomes a* community in the awareness of a common involvement in the winter of life and an acknowledgment in the other of a fellowship of suffering.

The recognition has a sculptural dimension, since it is shown by the looks which cross the space and which add further axes to the composition. Those which converge on the woman running out at the front, and which serve to hold her within the work, form yet another triangle (of imaginary dotted lines, for Mason, as in comic strips),[6] and include the turning look of the woman with the handkerchief, whose tears, one sees, are not only for herself. In one of very few works where the characters look at each other, Mason has taken a fundamental of his art: the gaze, which has usually meant the human gaze at and into a visible world or the mutual gaze of the viewer and the sculpture, and has turned it into both a new compositional device and a means of bonding characters into a scene of recognition. The device is another link with Florentine painting, of which he will remark in a later unpublished note, of 1989, that it emphasises the placing of the figures 'by rhythmic accents governing even the direction of glances just like a play being enacted on the stage'. The recognition, the *anagnorisis*, is appropriately the end of the tragedy, where the characters recognise who they are and the world in which they live.

The truth of the work is in the artist's own warm recognition of each character, and each object, in the enactment of compassion and the sense of fellowship. The 'art' of the work is directed with the usual relish towards the beauty of the overall 'imitation' — towards the composition, that is, in which the work's idea will be made

A Tragedy in the North. Winter, Rain and Tears (details)

to reside — but it homes in even more than usually on the reality, as in the actual world, of the thing imitated, in which there are no ideas but simply the possibility of contact from one existence to another, in the experience of silent meaning. Although it certainly opens to the memory of theatre and to tragic form, *A Tragedy in the North*, unlike *The Departure* or *Place de l'Opéra*, is reticent about celebrating art. It declines flights of the imagination, and if Mason relies on the cobblestones to participate in the underlying geometry by 'counting out space' beneath the drama and the grief 'like the lozenged pavements of early perspectives',[7] this further link with the quattrocento, while it may enable one to view the work more clearly, serves mainly to reveal the difference between smooth and measured forms which declare the presence of art, and these rough and infinitely variegated rain-soaked stones.

Mason's approach to the equally rough and variegated human figures is likewise to meet them so fully that he can express as vividly as possible who they are. This explains an aspect of the work, here as elsewhere, which it is easy to misunderstand. So as to attain that maximum of expressivity, he needs once again to avoid the smooth, and to find attitudes which are awkward (like the turning towards each other of the Pole's feet), forms which are unbeautiful (like the woman on the left, with her twisted belt), and faces full of contrasting lines

and volumes. So here too one might hear a charge of ugliness and caricature, and it is true that, even if one does catch immediately the beauty of the whole, one probably has to learn how to appreciate the details. Dickens's comment quoted in the previous chapter ('so like as to be almost a caricature?') can again help one to see, and one can place alongside it this comment by Mason himself, in reply to an unfortunately phrased question about the kinship of his works to 'things like *The Beggar's Opera* and penny dreadfuls': 'No, I think people have forgotten life as it is. Fellini did it marvellously, of course, years ago. His extraordinary distortion is much nearer actual life'.[8] It is indeed, and if there is distortion in Mason, moreover, it is rather an added emphasis, a painted stressing of the lines, say, that mould a face and externalise emotion. No doubt everyone begins by thinking that his faces in particular are not like actual faces, and yet a patient acquaintance with them changes the way one looks at other people and no doubt at oneself. As with fruit and vegetables, after a while one begins to see Mason faces everywhere.

It is in his colouring of the work, in fact, that Mason's nearness to humans and to things is especially enacted. It is also here that much of the work's originality lies. For, even more than in *The Departure*, he paints not like a sculptor but, in certain respects, like a painter. He paints atmospherically, as in the earlier work, moving from a brightly lit night scene, where the vivid and clashing colours on the stage (as it were) are surrounded by the sombre colours of the buildings and the blackness above, to a daytime scene dully lit and washed by rain. The many blues, and other colours containing blue, suggest a winter in the north and a cold tragedy. He also composes by colour, since the blues, which descend from the roofs in the background via the cobble-stones, among other things, to the clothing and shadows in the foreground, gather the work into a whole. There is also composition by a more sculptural use of colour, familiar from *The Departure* and from *St Mark's Place* (and to which Mason himself refers in the French version of his essay on the work), in the further triangle formed by the contrasting green, orange and yellow raincoats of three of the women.

The advance from *The Departure* is seen in the splashes of rain, or reflections of rainy light, not only on the roofs and the cobble-stones but everywhere on the hair and skin and clothing of the human figures, and in the shading which moulds and works their features and their clothes, and sends blues, for example, into the coat of the woman fleeing towards us. The reflections of the figures on the wet cobbles are particularly important, and seem to announce the thrown shadows of later works, and to serve a similar function. A thrown shadow, Mason will write, 'makes one believe in the existence of the thing painted', and reinforces, in a narrative composition, 'the capture of the spectator and his dragooning into the action'.[9]

If those reflections are provocatively new, since they contravene the spectator's movements across the front of the sculpture, and yet necessary also in showing the belonging to each other of people and place, the reflections over their bodies are part of what counts greatly in the work: the detailed closeness of presence of the characters. On one occasion at least the closeness is an effect of contrast. Before the only smile, a forced one, on the face of the old man who attempts to comfort her, the bright colours and fashionable flares of the little girl — one of two children looking up to adults as if for an explanation of a world in which catastrophe exists — are reminders of the ordinary gaieties of a life which continues, while her jaunty hat and scarf, which signify the Lens football team, also lead out from the work to other activities of the mining community. (The stiffness of her scarf in the wind may also recall the ribbon of the woman's bonnet in Ford Madox Brown's *The Last of England*, much admired by Mason, and thereby intimate loss, England, and indeed Birmingham, in whose gallery the painting hangs.) Everywhere else, however, the homage to the working classes — or simply, the homage to the real — is in the dense local variegation of the painting, which makes every hand, every cheek, every shoe or lapel, come alive with its own life. The passage from tone to tone, from stroke to stroke of the brush, is another means of animating the surface, so that even the back of a coat shivers with existence. To concentrate on any small area of the work is to discover exigencies and felicities of painting, which carry the pathos of the work and which are the viewer's contact with its inner sense.

So one is not surprised to find Mason saying that what interests him above all in colour is 'expressivity', and that he associates this with 'communication'.[10] One understands also why for a long time he was not able to accept help in painting his sculptures, and has devoted much of his time as an artist to the painting of the several casts of each — though in recent years his stepdaughter Iris Hao has helped him considerably in this work. His enjoyment of faces that have been weathered by life suggests another interpretation of the gashes and other intrusions into the heads of *The Crowd*. They too are expressive, a denial of the smooth, and although they do not correspond, unlike the penetrative modelling of *A Tragedy in the North*, to actual features, they also seem to reach into the person so as to increase the impression of his or her existence.

A Tragedy in the North. Winter, Rain and Tears (detail)

In *A Tragedy in the North* one does not discover world after world of significance as in *The Departure*. Yet here too, after slowly learning the structure of the work and the roles of its characters, one probably comes late to the realisation of its depth, to the meeting with a profound human solidarity within a tragic world in a modelling of forms which might have seemed caricatural, but are not, and a way of painting which might have looked over-emphatic or unsculptural. To use analogies of Mason's own, because of the complexity and finish of the composition, everything finally falls into place as with the puzzle in a detective story, and because of the complexity and finish of the thought, the meaning is only revealed, as in a play, in the last act.[11]

While *The Departure* has been more popular with the public, moreover, *A Tragedy in the North*, which created wide international interest when presented at the Venice Biennale of 1982, has appealed more to artists and writers and is often considered Mason's finest work. At the very moment he finished the sculpture, and walked, exceptionally, through the courtyard to the street-door 'to breathe in deeply the outer world', Francis Bacon happened to be walking along the pavement. His first comment on being ushered into the studio was, 'Oh Raymond. A real sculpture! Not a steel girder making a right angle and painted orange.' (This was in 1977.) The next day he returned with the writer and ethnologist Michel Leiris. Jean Dubuffet, who also saw *A Tragedy* in the studio, along with the recent coloured landscapes, and who astonished Mason by the rapidity with which he recognised the essentials of a work so different from his own, concluded his visit with a statement which is both right as it concerns Mason's art and singularly revealing of Dubuffet's: 'you have succeeded in putting into your sculpture something I have tried in vain to include in mine — the popular element.'

What matters in both *The Departure* and *A Tragedy in the North* is that Mason found subjects of universal scope capable of speaking to everyone (hence his admiration, of course, for a work such as Picasso's *Guernica*, and his many reticences about other artists); that as they differ from *The Crowd*, so they differ from each other, and bring one to realise that each of his crowds is humanity seen in a different perspective; and that they are both extremely ambitious. In recovering the great art of polychrome figurative sculpture they also transform it. They stretch high relief to the point where it changes with each step as the viewer moves across it, yet still retains the steep climb-up of perspective which pulls the viewer in. They invent three-dimensional frescoes which combine colour with a sculptural occupation of space. They devise ways of painting sculpture which are quite new.

With *St Mark's Place* and *A Tragedy* Mason becomes thoroughly what he has always set out to be: the sculptor of modern life. In the bronze reliefs the figures are contemporary but lack expression, and even *The Departure*, despite its modernity, is in many ways a threatened pastoral, with a Black in the centre who is the Negro of imagination and who differs entirely from the *Tragedy's* realistic black mine-worker. Mason will later describe his aim by quoting Ruskin on Giotto (where Ruskin himself is remembering Vasari): 'It was not by greater learning . . . that he became the head of the progressive schools of Italy. It was simply by being interested in what was going on around him, by substituting the gestures of living men for conventional attitudes, and portraits of living men for conventional faces, and incidents from every-day life for conventional circumstances'.[12] Mason adds Caravaggio and Manet as other origins of 'vivifying moments' in European art through their 'imperative need to move closer to their fellow-men and set down what they saw', and in connection with *A Tragedy* one could also instance Courbet, whom Mason salutes in an essay on Balthus[13] and whose *Burial at Ornans* is particularly close.

The modernity of his art is reinforced in *The Aggression*, which interrupted work on *A Tragedy* and was completed before it, and which owes its scale partly to the fact that Mason, suffering from sciatica, needed to model it sitting down. It was first shown by Claude Bernard in 1977 and by Pierre Matisse in 1980; one of the casts is in the Manchester Art Gallery. The work is important because it contributes in its own way to Mason's thinking during this period, about death and grief, about different forms of violence against humanity, and about how sculpture might respond to this dimension of pity and terror in the human condition and might rise, specifically as sculpture, through and above it. After the elegies of *Birmingham. In Memoriam* and *The Departure* come the tragic dramas of *A Tragedy*, *The Aggression* and the *Monument for Guadeloupe*.

The Aggression, too, is based on a real incident, which occurred a few doors from Mason's flat. He saw a crowd gathered but, being at the wheel of his car, asked his friend Michael Brenson to go and see what was happening. An ophthalmologist well known in the neighbourhood had been stabbed and left for dead, and his distorted and bloodstained face when he was brought out on a stretcher was like 'a red drawing on a blue ground'.[14] It is no doubt because of an artist's total responsibility — to the realities of life and also to the claims of form and colour, to 'the woman smiling in the metro but also [to] the green light of the train bearing her away'[15] — that an image which one might have been inclined to consider trivialising and 'aesthetic'

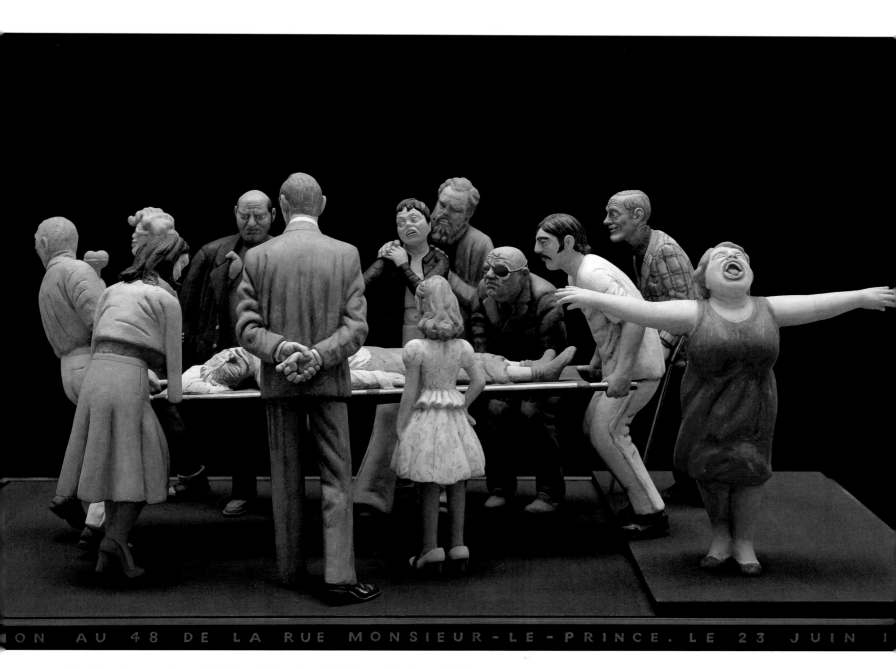

62. *The Aggression at 48 Rue Monsieur-le-Prince,* 23 June 1975

seems to have been as much a stimulus to the work as the more obviously weighty business of murder. And indeed, the aesthetic and the existential quickly merge. Blue becomes the dominant colour in this scene of cold aggression, while red is the colour of life and of the protest of life against death.

Like *A Tragedy*, *The Aggression* occurs after the event and enacts a moment of recognition. Its characters, however, do not recognise each other within a community of suffering but, in a work dealing not with inhuman but with human violence, they recognise aggression and death in their midst. In another work where the looking of the sculptor and his education of the spectator's own looking are represented and dramatised, the gazes go not from one character to another but almost exclusively to the unseeing face of the man dead or dying. This is presumably one of the reasons for the work being in the round. With no perspective to draw us in, we look at the crowd of onlookers and participate in the scene as they do, by seeing with their eyes. The absence of small figures in the distance increases the intent focus on the inert form.

That the victim had been an eye specialist and, like the artist, a curer of sight, is pure coincidence, yet Mason seizes the opportunity to have as his only stooping and most intently peering character a man wearing an eyepatch, and so draws attention both to seeing and to the difficulty of seeing. (The man on crutches also has his

125

63. Model for *Monument for Guadeloupe,* 1976

right eye askew.) More even than in *Barcelona Tram* the characters are spectators and a spectacle, yet what they see is even more clearly not the answer of the work but its question. The person turned in our direction, moreover, the doctor's wife, does not look hard out of gouged or wide eyes but screams with her eyes closed. She cries beyond the work and its questioning gaze, partly in the direction of the viewer and partly upwards.

For the sculpture takes meaning from its relation to a Deposition or an Entombment. In the unique leftward movement, in the bearing of a horizontal inert body, and in the converging on the face not only of looks but of various lines descending through rows of heads, one sees any number of versions of those deliberately ritualised Images. Here, as elsewhere, Mason seems clearly to return to Christian archetypes (there may also be the hint of a Golgotha in *A Tragedy in the North*) as part of his recovery of an art of large meaningfulness, of signs which, far from being empty or self-referential, signify beyond themselves — though, strangely, he denies any such intention. Certainly the archetypes, if present, are turned entirely to his own use. Here, he increases the number of the wounded, adding to the doctor (a saviour of bodies) the man with an eye-patch (possibly a patient and therefore a kind of disciple), the man supported between metal crutches which he grips as the bearers grip the stretcher, and even, metaphorically, the woman whose empty sleeve hanging next to the streaks of blood suggests a missing arm. All the characters are left exposed, in fact, by the lack of decor. He then gathers this wounded and appalled humanity into the wife's cry, which is both highly expressive sculpturally, since all the roundnesses of her body meet in her round and fully expanded lips while her backward-pushing hands seem to force the cry out of the depth of her person, and mimetically inarticulate, with that lolling tongue.

She is also cruciform. The horizontal movement of the here and now becomes the movement of human life through time while, in the absence of any distance to the work, the new movement downwards of her heavy body and of the dead weight of her husband, along with the descending looks, is the way of death. Her cry, with her husband's lidded gaze, is the sole movement upwards and, given the suggestion of the Cross, can only be a truly unbelieving 'Why hast thou . . . ?' addressed, from this small sculpture totally surrounded by space, to the nothing outside.

But the work is not only a cry. If it is stretched dynamically away from the passive centre by the extended arms at one extreme and by the turning-away and leaning-out of the ambulance man at the other, its mood stretches all the way from a woman's cry to the indiffer-

ent smile of a girl walking away on the left with her strawberry and pistachio ice cream. Her smile, like that of the old man in *A Tragedy in the North*, sets off the rest of the work by its contrast, and seems to make her the Judas among the twelve figures grouped around the victim. Mason himself describes her, however, as simply 'unwitting',[16] and with her glasses which suggest the sun, her blond hair which reflects it, the bright colours of her ice cream and the relaxed turnups of her jeans, she is surely life that goes on, and that accompanies and counteracts the bearing away of a dying man to the 'sinister' left. It may be then that one notices, at the very middle of a sculpture showing the urgent and emotional aftermath of a lethal aggression, a woman's bare navel, which is visible next to the only child. It is the sign and origin of life, in its circle of living flesh.

It was while working on *The Aggression* that Mason said in an interview: 'I can't think of one thing without thinking immediately of its contrary',[17] and he will also say: 'It would be very unlike me to do an entirely all-despairing work or vice-versa'.[18] In full cognisance of the physical ills, the grief and the horror by which human life is undermined, and convinced of the silence into which the human protest vanishes, he contrives nevertheless in *The Aggression* to celebrate life. There is even something in the work of *St Mark's Place* (to which Mason links it more than to *A Tragedy in the North*), in the comic incongruities, in the description of casual passers-by unprepared for drama. And the work is also a triumph of art. The figure through whose back and slightly turned head we enter the work (as in *Barcelona Tram* and *Place de l'Opéra*) has his arms behind him so that we can see his large hands. Their red shadows recall the trickles of blood on the mugged man's nearby face, while his suit carries the leading colour of the whole work. As we move to the side we discover a gaze compassionate like that of the Pole in *A Tragedy* but harder and more aghast, beneath the heavily worked eyebrows, in keeping with the harsher mood of *The Aggression*. He seems to be once again a representation of 'the sculptor' — by no means of Mason personally but of the human involvement and artistic activity from which the work emerges — who by his successive acts of seeing brings reality into relation with art. (I say 'seems' because it may not be the case: as far as intention is concerned, Mason has stated that, the whole of his art going towards others, nothing could be more uncharacteristic than to place himself, even symbolically, in a sculpture.) The details which inevitably send even the theoretically most sophisticated viewer out from the sculpture into the circumstances which it narrates — the little girl seems to have come down to look at the spectacle in her mother's shoes, for

64. Project for Pointe-à-Pitre, Guadeloupe, 1976

instance, and the man with an eye-patch, in his slippers — are more insistent even than those of *A Tragedy*, but the work of sculpting and painting is to gather everything into a single composition and into the network of recalls and contrasts by which the composition is amplified and made dense. Before a sculpture which one might be tempted to see as a piece of naïve figuration, it is as well to note Mason's hostility to the purely figurative as much as to the purely abstract.[19] The more a real world enters and fills a work, the more his art is free to pursue its ends, to transform real time (often, as here, exactly dated) into sculptural time and a passing moment into a moment of truth. In a work where the representation of death is unusually stark, the composing of the reactions to death — in the three women, for example, at the ends and in the middle — is customarily precise. The artist cannot change the facts of life and of death, but he can bring his peculiar gift. His victory, as artist, over the ills of the human condition portrayed, is in the art itself and, to use one of those apparently outmoded words to which Mason's directness and clear-sightedness restore the plenitude of meaning, in its beauty.

The Aggression seizes an event at a moment of extremity. It is properly 'popular' in that, like *A Tragedy in the North*, it begins in stark and simple emotions which it modifies and raises, through the activity of sculptural thought, to the level of the aesthetic and the serious. And it retains something of melodrama, which Mason does not disparage,[20] in keeping with this comment in his essay on *A Tragedy*: 'if emotions are to be examined, they should be sharp and simple like a botanical section.' Or as he put it with customary gusto during the unpublished interview with Jane Farrington from which I have already quoted, if the artist is to bring the world to the viewer, 'it has to be served hot'.

The other work in the period, the maquette of the *Monument for Guadeloupe*, was the first to be made and is even more extreme. Had the work been completed, it could have been quite simply the most radically different and astonishing of all Mason's works and, indeed, one of the most sculpturally interesting of all sculptures, totally original and a reference point for the study of the art. The fact that the commission for the work miscarried is typical of the continuing frustration of Mason's career. This was also the period which saw a growing recognition of his importance. Already in 1972 a programme on his work had been presented on French radio by Jean Paget, and in 1976 a video of his work was shown at the Musée national d'art moderne. In 1975 he gave a slide lecture at the Musée on polychrome sculpture and, most significantly, *The Crowd* was installed for the summer in the Tuileries Gardens, next to the Jeu de Paume and not far from its present site, while *The Departure* was installed in the church of St Eustache. The clergy of the church had asked for a Christmas crèche, and on being told that Mason was working on something too urgent to interrupt, had asked to exhibit as a crèche, the new work itself. It was placed below the organ and, after some contention between the church and the municipal authorities, was permanently located in the not entirely inappropriate side-chapel of St Joseph. (During Midnight Mass in 1976, slides of the work were projected on three giant screens to the accompaniment of the organist Jean Guillou and of the priest's reading of Mason's text.) In the year in which both of his big sculptures were on public display, he also received his first large-scale commission, the one for Guadeloupe, while in 1976 came the commission for Georgetown, Washington D.C., which led eventually to the *Twin Sculptures* of 1988. In 1978, shortly after the first showing of *A Tragedy in the North*, he was decorated by the French state as a Chevalier de l'Ordre des Arts et Lettres. Despite all this, however, along with

the continuing admiration of his peers, Mason had not achieved fame.

The commission for *Monument for Guadeloupe* was for a sculpture to stand at the entrance of a Centre for Popular Arts which was to be built near the Town Hall of Pointe-à-Pitre, the chief city of Guadeloupe. The mayor, Monsieur Henri Bangou, wished the sculpture to depict the final moment of the island's resistance against French troops dispatched by Napoleon to impose his reintroduction of slavery. The resistance was led by a mulatto, Louis Delgrès, whose final gesture, during an assault by overwhelming numbers, was to blow up the hideout in which he was besieged. Over three hundred men, women and children were killed in the explosion, along with the avant-garde of the French assailants. Mason had already decided that his sculpture would represent that 'pathetic instant' of the battle, the explosion and the 'apotheosis' of Delgrès,[21] when the same suggestion was made in a letter from André Schwartz-Bart, the novelist and author of a book on the young mulatto woman Solitude who also figures in the story, on grounds which had equally appealed to Mason, namely that this is one of the most striking images of the collective heroism of slaves struggling for their freedom.

The sculpture, in painted polyester resin, would have risen to a height of over six metres through the awning in front of the Arts Centre, projecting Delgrès and his

65. Project for Pointe-à-Pitre, Guadeloupe, 1976

129

cry of 'Vive la liberté!' on to the first-floor terrace which is a continuation of the exhibition rooms. The work would have been visible along the main axes of the town and from the glazed halls on the ground floor, while Delgrès, illuminated at night, would also have been visible from the sea. Even in terms of spectacle a great opportunity was lost when the commission was withdrawn, through no fault of Mason's, and to appreciate the loss to sculpture one need only consider the maquette in painted plaster, completed in a mere two weeks and shown in the 1977 exhibition at the Galerie Claude Bernard along with *A Tragedy* and *The Aggression*, and reflect on the length of time Mason would have allowed for making the final work both stronger and more subtle.

In his essay on *A Tragedy*, which was written after the making of the Guadeloupe maquette and which picks up a phrase from the audio-visual presentation of that work, Mason surmises that 'if one could portray extreme emotion, it might attain an extremity in sculpture itself.' His interest in 'extreme emotion', which reaches a paroxysm in the *Monument for Guadeloupe*, is a search at once for extreme life and for extreme art, and one realises of his work as a whole that what some critics have read as a handling of lurid sentiments and as a return to crude forms of realism is, on the contrary, a continual exploratory pushing of sculpture to the limit. Here the limit is absolute, since he sculpts an explosion. There is usually in sculpture a tension between the immobility of the work and the change of form which would have to follow in the real world; the tension is particularly strong in a sculptor alive to the motion in the streets and many of whose works represent moving crowds. Already in *The Falling Man* Mason had taken a further step by suggesting a movement uncontrolled by the subject represented and so arrested only by art. The explosion of *Monument for Guadeloupe* is the final step, the stilling of a moment that cannot hold, the sculpting of forms on the edge of not being, the conceiving of an extreme in sculpture beyond which it is impossible to go.

The challenge of the work is to gather yet another crowd, this time an exploding and vertical one, into a single, satisfying and meaningful composition, while the opportunity, in Mason's first work to face in all directions, is to guide the moving eye not across but progressively around the work (as in certain narrative capitals), to depict bodies in any position imaginable, and to exploit to the full the many contrasts provoked by the violence. The contrasts of colour take in the shocks of reds and yellows in the explosion itself and the diversity of skins, not only of blacks and of whites but of mulattos and of the African 'blue Negroes' fighting with the

French, while Mason writes of the heterogeneous emotions, too, as 'colouring' the faces. That Mason's 'first thought' should have been for the hand-to-hand fighting, for the luxuriant green grass saturated with red blood, means another return to the colours of childhood, to the bricks of Birmingham and the country outside, and to the learning then of what would become his fundamental colour contrast. He has often said that he paints like a sculptor, not harmonising his colours as a painter might but using colours which fight and separate, and he writes in one instance: 'Red and green. There's an explosion and a space is created between the two'.[22] One hears again the violence in Mason's seeing of the world and dealing with it artistically, which is a violence of energy, of superior vitality. In the real violence of *Monument for Guadeloupe* there is an explosion indeed, and those homefelt colours sink into their existential connotations, into the red of life and of the shedding of life and into the green of the earth.

One might remember Van Gogh, for the intense expressivity of his colour and in particular for the 'red and green' by means of which he 'tried to express the terrible passions of humanity'.[23] Mason has not discussed his colour — it is the draughtsmanship which he praises, that of 'one of the greatest draughtsmen in all world art'[24] — and it is unlikely that he was actually thinking of him when making the maquette. It is useful to bear Van Gogh in mind, nevertheless, since Mason's enthusiasm dates from his student days, when the paintings of factories and of people working showed him how he might 'exalt the industrial city around' him.[25] Van Gogh's presence can be felt in *A Tragedy in the North*, the architectural background of which was against the wall of his studio while the *Monument for Guadeloupe* was being created. The use of colour in the latter is certainly Mason's own, and is masterly to the point that any close view of the painting of this quite small maquette is a feast for the eyes, and suggests something of the impact which the completed monument would have had — it would have been Mason's only fully polychrome open-air sculpture — in its dazzling variety and in the local subtleties of tone and touch.

The monument is also the most extreme and triumphant of this group of works exploring tragedy. The violence, the death and the dying actually occur in the work, the lower part of which is full of shooting and stabbing, of bodies falling and slumping, among them a headless corpse, and of the emotions which breed and are bred by racial conflict and such intimate slaughter; yet Delgrès himself, in a sudden élan which is also a powerful sculptural idea, rises more victoriously than anything in the other two works, in what Mason calls an apotheosis and which could equally be an entirely

66. Model for *Monument for Guadeloupe* (detail), 1976

67. Louis Delgrès, *Monument for Guadeloupe* (detail)

secular Transfiguration, on that higher plane, or Resurrection, or Ascension in clouds, or even another appearance in glory, his mandorla being the swirling fiery smoke in which he stands. Mason makes the triumph possible by choosing the very moment of the explosion, and just as *A Tragedy in the North* is his only movement down to the right and *The Aggression* his only movement to the left, so the *Monument for Guadeloupe* is his only movement upwards.

The triumph is completed by Solitude, who belongs to the lower part of the sculpture and is facing in the other direction. In the explosion she was only wounded, but she was later executed, after being delivered of the child she was carrying, who belonged to her owner. Facing the town, with her naked breasts and her naked and swollen belly she suggests 'the eternal future of the country' and also, as against the heroic and emblematic life-out-of-death of the man Delgrès, a natural and female fecundity which survives and continues, as in some archaic and staring Venus.

Her living belly is the perfect symbol of life amid all that death. By choosing to depict the explosion, Mason creates at once his most violent work and his most resurrectional, a vision of disintegration which is also the peak of vitality. Delgrès mounts to his death through a living spiral of forms; he takes with him both his wound and his violin; his raised arm replies, according to a motif which is at once sculptural, narrative and conceptual, to the down-stretched arm of the man falling backwards below him.

One sees the variety of these works, in their approach to meaning, which is based in each case, of course, on the subject that offered itself but which is not determined by it. The natural violence of *A Tragedy in the North* issues in a tragic humanism of solidarity, in recognition of the other. The human violence of *The Aggression* leads to tragic humanism in a second and grimmer form, to the human cry of agony into the silence, and also to a simple affirmation of human life, to the colourful gaieties that continue. The acme of human violence and war in the *Monument for Guadeloupe* produces a corresponding acme of tragic heroism and a deeper and more primitive vision of life that insists on surviving. In a relatively short period, Mason explored three fundamental perspectives, in the tragic mode, on to his essential theme, which is of course, as he says often and with no protective irony, Man.

That violin, moreover, is a fact of Delgrès's story on which Mason seizes so as to take art as well into his apotheosis. While proclaiming freedom, Delgrès also seems to rise to a great high note as in some fierce, impassioned opera. A sculpture which reconciles in itself the antagonism of the members of different races — the explosion hurls them, Mason writes, 'into the same space' and 'the same defeat' — also gathers everything present into the domain of art, since the explosion hurls them also 'into the same enchantment of flames'.

Coming from another kind of artist it could have been irresponsible, 'aesthetic', to see the flames which will annihilate soldiers and civilians alike, including a black woman and her child, as a visually pleasing act of artistic sorcery. From Mason it means the power of art, not to gloss over the horror of oppression and warfare but, in representing them as consummately as possible, to raise them to beauty: to that beauty, indeed, which is a part itself of human hope.

And so, to return to something I suggested in connection with *The Departure* and to which we shall need to return, Mason goes once more beyond narrative, and on this occasion quite explicitly. Below is the narrative of the battle and the literal explosion. Above is the symbol, 'the explosion of truth', the joy of resistance, self-sacrifice, music, figuration, colour, form, in a 'crater of fire'.

68. Solitude, *Monument for Guadeloupe* (detail)

Notes on Chapter VII

¹ 'A Tragedy in the North. Winter, Rain and Tears', in Birmingham 1989, pp. 96–8.

² 'My Early Artistic Life in Birmingham', in Birmingham 1989, p. 11, referring to a letter to Marie-Laure de Noailles of 1965.

³ *Ibid.*

⁴ 'A Tragedy in the North . . . ', in Birmingham 1989.

⁵ 'Une Tragédie dans le Nord. L'hiver, la pluie, les larmes', in Centre Georges Pompidou 1985, pp. 72–3.

⁶ 'A Tragedy in the North . . . ', in Birmingham 1989.

⁷ *Ibid.*

⁸ Interview in Marlborough 1985.

⁹ 'Sur la lumière', an undated note in French, Centre Georges Pompidou 1985, p. 78.

¹⁰ Interview in Claude Bernard 1977.

¹¹ *Ibid.*

¹² *Giotto and his Works in Padua*, section 12, quoted as a note to the preface in Marlborough 1991.

¹³ 'Balthus', in Centre Georges Pompidou 1985, pp. 81–3.

¹⁴ Arts Council 1982, p. 44.

¹⁵ 'Les mains éblouies', in Centre Georges Pompidou 1985, pp. 75-6.

¹⁶ Arts Council 1982, p. 44.

¹⁷ Interview in Claude Bernard 1977.

¹⁸ Interview in Marlborough 1985.

¹⁹ Interview in Claude Bernard 1977.

²⁰ 'If you are going to deal with the world, the world means the motion, the drama, the melodrama and the humour . . . ', 'The Torrent of Life', in Birmingham 1989, p. 38.

²¹ From the unpublished text for an audio-visual presentation of the work, dated August 1975. I continue to quote from this text.

²² 'My Early Artistic Life in Birmingham', in Birmingham 1989, pp. 11–15.

²³ See the letter to Theo of 8 September 1888. The comment is made in connection with *The Night Café*.

²⁴ From 'Rodin. An occasion to discuss sculpture', 1986.

²⁵ From 'Le Peuple dans la Cité', 1987.

69. *Monument for Guadeloupe* (details)

70. *The Grape-Pickers* (detail), 1982

VIII

PEOPLE IN A LANDSCAPE

This is the moment to consider Mason's landscapes. They are not narrative, and they represent a kind of work which Mason opposes to the narrative tradition; yet, as one sees in retrospect, they prepare *The Grape-Pickers*, his only large sculpture set in the country, where he finds a new relation to narrative. *The Grape-Pickers* does not so much go beyond story as exist already on its farther side. As works whose actual subject is natural beauty, and whose concern is not loss or tragedy but the evidence of the earth in sunlight, they also prepare a harvest in the south which is the converse of *A Tragedy in the North*.

The works are important in themselves, moreover, and they recall 1958, which is the year both of *Birmingham. In Memoriam*, Mason's farewell to his boyhood city, and of the purchase, partly for health reasons, of the house near Ménerbes. The contrast could hardly be sharper between the English manufacturing city and the Provençal countryside, where the house, surrounded by vineyards, stands on a hill facing the northern slopes of the Petit Luberon. Mason has written, in fact, that as a city-dweller he needed some two years to realise how exceptional were the views surrounding him, and how right they were for a sculptor. 'When the mistral wind blows', he says, 'every tree and rock of the mountain opposite springs into such relief that I feel that I can stretch out my hand and touch it'.[1] He began by doing drawings from the terrace of the house, 'just turning my chair' (there was so much, and it was all available), and eventually took plaster and 'modelled directly from the landscape, the white paper of my drawings swelling, as it were, to become the plaster forms of my relief, whose crevices replaced the black ink-lines.' One sees again, precisely described, the origin of his sculpture in drawing; this is, after all, 1960, a year only after the completion of *Carrefour de l'Odéon*. The first landscape reliefs, made one each year from 1960 to 1963 and cast into bronze for his first exhibition at the Pierre Matisse Gallery in 1968, span the period, in fact, between the street reliefs and city panoramas and *The*

Crowd. They will lead us forward to the painted reliefs and the gouaches of the 1970s and to *The Grape-Pickers* of 1981-82, but it is illuminating also to see how their apparently quite different preoccupations relate to the previous works, and even to *The Crowd* itself.

Like the earlier works, they respond to what Mason happens to see because of where he is, and to what compels his attention. There seems to have been no reluctance about doing landscapes, and no need for invoking, say, the many landscapes among the paintings of Balthus, whom he had met five years previously. As so often with Mason, for whom the place of art is essentially *here*, the landscapes have their origin in 'the raising of [his] eyes.' And their interest is in part that they explore the kind of going out to a world which is represented, in the works of the 1950s, not by the street reliefs, where the viewer enters by fictively walking in, but by the panoramas, where he enters by the eye alone. The first, *The Luberon* (or *Big Mountain Landscape*) of 1960, even presents the flat valley stretching out below with something of the formal features of the bronze *Paris* of 1953. The views are not on our level or in our scale, and face the artist simply with themselves.

It is of course, and for the first time, the earth which confronts him, not a human city. And he sees the earth not as an object of contemplation but as an otherness of movement and of energy. Even the rocks 'spring' into relief. So the ravines and rounded folds of the Luberon, as soon as he represents them in a sculpture, become the waves of some turbulent ocean, their apparent surging across the work highlighted by places where rising cliffs seem about to roll over like breakers. In *The Approaching Storm* of 1963 a turmoil in the clouds spiralling towards the left (in the direction, that is, which seems proper for a storm and not otherwise sinister) has shocked the forms of the earth into bending and following. There is another life out there, which animates not only the moving sky but the unmoving earth, and which is most startlingly active in *Big Midi Landscape*, of 1961. Here it is the sun which moves, which irradiates the air with a commotion of light, and which sends

71. *The Valley,* 1973

its vigour over a flooded earth. How can one sculpt the sun? Mason's answer is to shape it like a swirling and erupting volcanic crater which flows out over great circles of sky. This really is the sun of the Midi, omnipotent and god-like, whose influence also carries all over the lower sky through ranks of serried incisions. They remind one, irresistibly, of the brushwork of Van Gogh, which is, after all, perfectly appropriate, given Mason's admiration for him, and given Van Gogh's own expressive landscapes, many of them painted when he was himself in Provence. Indeed, Mason's sun resembles Van Gogh's — for instance, in the chalk-and-ink drawings *Wheat Field with Sun and Cloud* and *Wheat Field with Rising Sun,* and see also the exploding stars of *The Starry Night* and *Cypress against a Starry Sky,* all done nearby at Saint-Rémy — and suggests a similar devotion to the energy of light.

The sun is also an eye, with a drilled pupil, which faces the eye of the artist. It resembles the eyes of his human figures, since its gaze is not calm or abstracted but active and intense. And it resembles his own gaze in that, while lighting simply on what is there, it also charges the visible world and composes it into a single rhythm. It seems natural for an artist to see the sun, the source of light, in his own image, and before Mason's power of looking — as before Van Gogh's, where the power combines similarly with reverence — one could almost agree with the old belief that the eyes see not by receiving light rays but by emitting them.

The importance of the landscapes is that they enable Mason to confront the energy of the natural world, and also to develop an intuition of two levels of being, not far from any of his works, but which is only clear in these, and in *The Grape-Pickers* where it culminates.

138

72. *The Luberon with its Valley,* 1973

The axes of the previous works are still present, but already in *The Luberon*, and in the smaller *Luberon* of 1962, the strong horizontal spreading out of the work and the pulling in of the viewer down a road which winds back and continues, for the eye, in the central pleats of the mountain, are subordinate to the sighting of a lower and a higher part. The plain is nature known, through cultivation and through the making of crisscrossing roads, while the mountain, with its irregular and shifting folds, is its own master, a wildness above. It leads away into a far distance which is entirely 'other'. Mason writes of the mountain that it 'stands solemn and enigmatic above the smiling plain',[2] and one remembers that the 'man-made mountain' of the slag-heap in *A Tragedy in the North* is also 'enigmatic', it too being a sign, though with a quite different emotional charge, of the unknown above one.

Similarly in *The Approaching Storm*, while the land is where we are, and while a path leads the viewer inwards towards a glade or even a grove (to an intensification, that is, of place, and of our sense of place), it is again the upper world of the swirling sky — the world, in a sense, beyond landscape — which is the region of energy. This is explicitly so in *Big Midi Landscape*, whose sun is the spiralling source of life and of the whole work.

In all these bronze landscapes, Mason renders what he chances to see around him but also explores the world we inhabit, in terms of nature and the beyond of nature. Away from the city he confronts, if not the sublime, certainly the elemental: the earth, the fire of the sun, the air of the storm cloud, the figurative water of the mountain waves. He makes it difficult to accept that landscape is an inferior art since, although human behaviour is not being investigated and human presence

139

73. *The Luberon,* 1960

is only suggested, in cultivation and distant dwellings, he calls out and celebrates fundamental feelings, of pleasure and of awe, which humans experience on the earth and under the sky. According to the text on Anne Harvey which I quoted earlier, the aim of the artist is 'the meeting of the real with thought', 'the union of things with the mind', and one might even think that the realisation of that aim is particularly formidable in landscape, or can be, since the real to be dealt with, the things which appear, belong to an inhuman otherness.

More importantly, those encounters will certainly influence *The Crowd*. Mason agreed to my suggestion, when we were looking at this work, that the slow mounting of its front figures followed by the rapid mounting of the rear figures resembles the disposition of plain and mountain in *The Luberon*, and recalled the fact that he had been at the Royal College of Art when it was evacuated to the mountains and lakes of Ambleside, where he spent his one term doing a single drawing of the mountain opposite. The Luberon seems to have reactivated memories of the Lake District, and to have suggested the rising of the farther part of the crowd towards an otherness beyond humanism. If he modelled *The Crowd*, moreover, in such a way as to open it to elemental presences — ocean waves, a procession of clouds, a dance of flames — was it not because he had recently

been considering precisely these things, in their alien yet familiar power? While this is certainly an urban crowd: pedestrians in the street, it is also humanity seen or imagined in its deepest environment, the sky and the earth.

And there is more, since the shaping of *The Crowd* into distinct or combining rows of figures, which derives from Mason's observing of the descending crowd on the boulevard St Michel, can be likened also to the folds of the Luberon. The heaving of the mountain is not unlike the heaving sea of *The Crowd*, and even the breaking of its 'wave' at the rear returns, no doubt unconsciously, and occurs at a similar point. One even realises that *The Luberon* is the origin in Mason's work of that central motif of the falling wave, whose first return will be in *The Falling Man* of 1963.

It is strange to discover the importance that landscapes have had for Mason's art, though it is true that they function mainly as a rich resource for other kinds of work in which the human figure predominates. *The Luberon* prepares *The Crowd*; they all prepare *The Grape-Pickers*. They have also been instrumental in the vital changes to epoxy resin, the first use of which was to make landscapes, and to colour, which was first applied to *The Approaching Storm* and to a smaller version of *Le Roucas*. Nor did Mason's exploration of landscape finish there. In the period when *The Departure* and also

140

St Mark's Place were consecrating his move to polychrome sculpture, he made two new reliefs, *Le Roucas* and *A Procession of Clouds*, while 1974 saw his most intense work ever on the Provençal landscape and his most concentrated effort to approach the meaning of natural place. He painted the new reliefs, he reworked, enlarged into resin and painted three of the original reliefs (the fourth, *Big Midi Landscape*, followed in 1975), and as well as a number of ink drawings, he did a series of important gouaches. The works were shown, along with *St Mark's Place*, in the 1974 exhibition at the Pierre Matisse Gallery, and were seen for the first time in Paris in 1977, at an exhibition organised by Jean Clair, *Papiers sur nature*, at the Fondation nationale des arts graphiques et plastiques. 1974 was also the year in which he painted the enlarged *Month of May in Paris* and, most significantly, because of the two worlds involved, the year at whose end he made, while in Provence, the quite different and indeed antithetical small relief which is at the origin of *A Tragedy in the North*.

His concern in the new and in the remodelled works is, as ever, to express as vividly as possible what, according to his own energy of looking, he sees to be there. Hence the greater singularity in the modelling of vines and trees in *The Approaching Storm*, whose evidently vegetable life may owe something to *The Departure*, and the enhanced drama of its wind-filled and trumpeting clouds, which announce the fiery smoke of *Monument for Guadeloupe*. Hence, throughout the reliefs and the gouaches, the violet distances, as the expected blues warm in the southern light, a phenomenon Mason observed in the Luberon and also in Cézanne. Hence, indeed, the necessity of colour: to permit a 'more precise reading' of the Midi landscapes, of the white rocks and

paths amid cultures and vegetation;[3] to allow Mason to celebrate the spectacular skies of the south (which cause him to doubt the supposed superiority of northern skies, and to adduce a similar celebration in the landscapes of Italian Classicism and Mannerism);[4] to add further animation to the scene through the contrast of red and green, most dramatically in *The Approaching Storm* and *A Procession of Clouds*, where a deepening sun sends reds into the clouds themselves but also into the trees responding below them. And hence above all the presence, for the first time in his large sculptures, of painted shadows. I have quoted Mason's comment that a cast shadow 'makes one believe in the existence of the thing painted', and it is interesting that the short text from which this is taken: 'Sur la lumière' ('On Light'), begins once again in a consideration of landscape.[5] For Mason shadow is 'fugitive'; it marks the passing of time, minute by minute. Its presence 'underlines' (the writing is graphic) 'a palpable immediacy, whereas its absence denotes an 'unreal eternity', and may have the effect of detaching 'landscape' from 'nature'. In the gouaches Mason often places shadows in the foreground, so that the eye takes in the shadowed reality of trees or vines before descending into a sunstruck valley. Midday at Ménerbes in particular could easily have become, in Mason's use of the term, a 'cosa mentale', with its valley below, its white-walled town and its distances which merge with the sky. Shadows give it the weight of localised reality, while rows of vines also, rolling away like waves of the sea, speak of successive moments and of the reign of time in the here and now. Although the compositional lines of the work are clear, moreover, they are not stressed, their purpose being not to draw attention to the organising eye of the artist but to allow the genius of the place to reveal itself.

74. *The Luberon Mountain,* 1962

75. *The Vineyards in Winter,* 1973

One comes in these few phrases on something essential in Mason's view of things: his equation of the immediate, the palpable, the real, with existence through time, with compliance to continuous change and flight. A landscape is present in so far as it both greets and therefore reverberates the sun under which it is slowly passing, and stands in its own shadows. A person is present, one might think, in his body as made visible by light and also in the visible shadow which is not the body but is inseparable from it, like the other side of being. Yet if shadows give the sense of reality, it is the sun which displays the earth, and which causes tracts of colourful nature stretched out beneath it to be 'bathed in light' (to return to 'La Foule') and to wear 'a mantle of light'. In the scenes under a full sun in particular, the earth in the light is simply there, it is *evident*, in the beautiful etymological sense that it makes itself to be seen completely. The polychrome reliefs take one to the limit of that evidence. The passage from ink drawings

to bronze reliefs and then to coloured reliefs is almost the full history of Mason's art (the final move is to very high relief, represented in the landscapes by *The Grape-Pickers*), and is the means by which a natural world becomes progressively more present, as it swells against the sculptor's hands and then appears to his eyes in its true colours. In these unpeopled landscapes — and one should note not only how unusual a form is landscape sculpture but that the meaning of these works depends in part on a deliberate exclusion of the human figure — a world not so much of plenty as of plenitude is *there*, offered to the human gaze, its appearance having something of the force of an epiphany. For there is a religious dimension to these works, which one must be careful nevertheless not to misunderstand. In the lecture on Rodin, Mason will say of Van Gogh that as 'one of the greatest draughtsmen of all world art' he was 'truly humble, a true worshipper', and of Cézanne that the 'essential nature' of his work was 'contemplative

76. *Midday at Ménerbes,* 1974

prayer' and that he 'painted nature all his life almost on his knees as an act of worship'. Cézanne is seen on this occasion as being on the right side of the divide between nineteenth-century art and modernism (he is on the wrong side in the different terms of the earlier essay on 'Manet et Cézanne'), and as being among the 'holy men', as Mason had called them in a note on Miklos Bokor, who, working 'under the wind and the rain and the excessive sun', had produced 'the last great sacred painting.' In the same note he also describes 'the essential moment in the life of a painter' as when he 'falls to his knees before Light', and calls painting, quite simply, 'an act of worship.'

I have mentioned Mason's frequent quoting of Goethe's dictum, that the genius of the world is greater than one's own, as a sign of the orientation of his art — away from self, and even away from art, to a reality far more consequential than either. To talk of worship, however, is to enter another region, as Mas-

on says quite explicitly in the interview he gave Michael Brenson: 'one can go further than [Goethe]. I mean, the ultimate desire would be religious, you know, I mean higher than oneself, or . . . something higher'.[6] In the landscapes there is an intuition of this something higher and unnamed, as the movement and energy of a natural world hint at a further and more powerful level of otherness, in the bursting sun, the spirited clouds and even the merely terrestrial mountain, moving with a kind of telluric presence. It seems to be by aiming for that further hint that he is able to close so powerfully with the simple realities of the here and now. Or as he writes himself, again in the note on Miklos Bokor and in perhaps the most far-reaching of all his many suggestive statements, the being of the genuine artist 'goes so resolutely Elsewhere that he becomes inhabited by the Outside.' How does one make contact with a reality outside the self? By aiming beyond it. How can one be sure that such a reality is met with at least in part on its own

143

terms and is not entirely accommodated to the intentions of the self? By seeing it as opening, as it were, on its farther side to a more distant Reality. One goes from here to there by way of elsewhere. The lesson is particularly timely, one realises, in a period when the very notions of 'reality', 'world' and even 'outside' are questioned, not without reason, and often dismissed.

The note on Bokor, for an exhibition of his work at the Galerie Janine Hao, was written in 1964 — very soon after the making of the early landscapes. Even 'La Foule', where Mason claims that 'Outside, above all we are present in the celestial', dates from only the following year. Both texts belong to the period of *The Crowd*, and the first also may have in mind an urban light and an outside of people and of streets. Like the comments on Van Gogh and on Cézanne, they are clearly of the first importance for our reading of all of Mason's works, and the memory of the Luberon cannot be far away, since it is there that a kind of worship was evidently enacted.

Only a kind of worship, however, since Mason believes in no gods, and while his art contains intimations of the sacred, its wonder is directed finally to this world as bathed in Light, seen, that is, in its own celestial possibility. The great sun of *Big Midi Landscape* is not Helios or Phoebus Apollo, or the visible sign of an invisible light beyond. For Mason writes in 'Sur la lumière': 'The sun is the sign of reality', which is a formula both unexpected and exact. Instead of being a sign of something else, the sun signifies what is — itself, and the sky and the earth on which it shines. It is neither a symbolic sign as in numerous religions nor an arbitrary sign as in large areas of modern thought, but the luminous presence of the real. If there is an epiphany in this and in the other landscapes, what appears is the world made manifest.

So what would happen if human figures were placed in the landscape? A few years later, in 1978 (after other activities to which I shall return in the next chapter), Mason and his wife spent a whole autumn in the house near Ménerbes, 'and glorious day followed glorious day. I watched the vines turn red, gold and brown and our farmer friends Marcel and Raymonde Trouyet carrying on picking their Alphonse Lavallée and muscat table grapes in the fields alongside the house'.[7] I quote Mason's own commentary for the pleasure — and, indeed, the 'glory' — which was at the origin of the sculpture that would follow, and for the *naming* of the actual people and things which will enter the work and which will contribute by their local particularity to its wide and general meaning. After making some watercolours, Mason conceived the idea of a large polychrome sculpture on the theme of *The Grape-Pickers* and, once the formal features of the work had been slowly discovered (and after a further delay for important matters to which we can again return), he made a small model in 1981 which now exists as a bronze, and in 1981–1982 executed the sculpture itself, beginning with a full-scale drawing on the wall of his studio. It was shown for the first time in London, at the Arts Council retrospective of 1982–1983.

He peoples the landscape after carefully preparing the terrain, from which he takes only a few rows of vines. For what he needs is the earth and its fertility, so that his human figures can become part of the terrestrial exuberance, while all he requires from what is above them is the sun itself. After the brilliant night scene of *The Departure* and the damp day of *A Tragedy in the North*, *The Grape-Pickers* is a view in full sunlight, where the humans are themselves evident, and where the sun is not to be taken for granted but is 'the second subject of the work'.[8] It is present in its effects, in the yellow and often dazzled leaves, and in the wife's squinting and shading of her eyes — human eyes yielding before the greater eye above. The man's left eye is even circled and creased like the sun of *Big Midi Landscape*, and one finds other representations of the raying of the sun's light in the folds of his trousers and in the gathering of the woman's dress at the waist. The woman is even a kind of gold sun in the midst of the work, with the fingers of her interestingly up-turned hand imitating once again its emitting of light. She also carries the sun on her head scarf, as does the man on his straw hat, and as does the young man in the distance on his shock of blond hair — which is the culminating point of the work, in fact, and, like the summits of the vines where he is situated, of its reaching for the sun.

The sun makes its presence felt, and although the man and the young boy next to him are simply picking grapes, they also bow, and bend the knee as in an act of worship. While actually finishing *The Grape-Pickers*, Mason told Michael Peppiatt: 'I seek to express and, if possible, to exalt the world immediately surrounding me and which I know'.[9] To exalt: to raise aloft, to elevate to a high or a higher degree. In *The Departure of Fruit and Vegetables* Mason exalts Les Halles by the quality of his depiction, and the man with the box of oranges then makes an offering of the things represented and of the sculpture itself to the night sky. In *The Grape-Pickers* Mason exalts vines and the people who work them, and the grape harvester then bows for him towards the Light.

He bows in a world of successive vines and successive moments, where the 'sign of reality' is brought to completion by what seems to be its contrary, by 'the

77. *Le Roucas,* 1970

78. *A Procession of Clouds,* 1970

soft shadows of an October afternoon'.[10] They lie gently under the vines, and they also draw the human figures into the reality of place: by encroaching on them, as with the woman, who wears the shadow of the vine on the dress she is wearing, or by altering their colour where they turn away from the sun, as most noticeably with the young man, who is divided between light and shade. It is important, in fact, that the sun is absent, and that the 'second subject' of the work is more precisely 'its warmth and light'. The work is not concerned with sun-worship but with homage to humans, to the natural world which sustains them, and to the warmth of illumination in which they are bathed.

Mason has also found a new way with painted shadows, since the sculpture is all light when seen from the left and all shadow when seen from the right. As he says, this 'mutation in space can only be a sculptural phenomenon', providing a visual and kinetic pleasure unavailable from painting, and rather than being a mere violation of 'the sculptural surface', it enhances 'the sculptural form', since it adds to its possibilities.[11]

It also enhances the role of the spectator. He looks as usual into the work rather than at it, and as usual he is obliged to be active and mobile, but as well as participating in the work he collaborates with it, since it is his own movement from side to side which causes the work to ply between a world made glorious by light and a world made real by shadow.

Two major changes to the original design also involve the viewer more inwardly in the work, and place its human figures more deeply in nature. The vines were at first to move directly away from the front in a perspective cone towards a background of trees. Mason was dissatisfied with the similarity to *A Tragedy in the North*, 'with leaves instead of paving-stones and trees instead of the colliery buildings',[12] and it is a fact that each of his large compositions has its own unique plan. 'Then one day, returning to the house, I lifted my head and saw the field in question from the other direction. It climbed up and curved over.' (Note once again one of the signature tunes, as it were, of Mason's creative impulse: 'I lifted my head and saw'.) The removal of a

146

79. *The Approaching Storm,* 1974

background, the dipping down of the vines over a far slope, mean that the viewer is drawn in endlessly and that the figures in the scene are in a world that goes on seemingly for ever, on an earth which both rises towards the sun and descends happily to the here and now.

The other problem was that the empty alley left by the fact that the grape-pickers work every second row, emptied the composition when seen straight on. The fact that Mason did not consider simply placing his human figures in each of the alleys is an indication of the particular fidelity of his realism. The solution came two years later when, during a sleepless night, he 'saw' the field turned obliquely, the rows appearing in diagonals with their summits 'piled one above the other and the figures nestling in the foliage.' (He may have been remembering Japanese screen paintings or the far slopes in Uccello's *Battle of San Romano* in the National Gallery, though he had no need to since, if he was thinking of anything, it could have been the angle of the folds along the mountain in *Le Roucas* or in the gouache of *The Luberon with its Valley*). The effect is to create the

most comprehensive of all rising movements to the right, which pulls the viewer into the joy of the work, and more especially to provide a continuity of vegetation for the human figures, a vine-world in whose foliage they 'nestle'.

For this is the work in which humans are at home on the earth. There are few of them — this is Mason's only large composition without a crowd — and three are nearby, which leaves much of the vegetation unpeopled and present for its own sake. The lines of the man's forehead repeat the furrows of his earth. Surrounded by a dazzling abundance, one eye closed, he seems to feel his way, bent over the vine so as to be in a kind of communion with it. A vein appears on his arm like a vine shoot. The young boy next to him also bows, and is so low as to be almost part of the vine, his hair itself hanging like grapes. The woman standing is clothed in the shadow of the vine, and holds grapes in both her hand and her mouth — a detail from life just right for suggesting her participation in the exuberance which she surveys.

80. *Big Midi Landscape*, 1975

81. *The Luberon II,* 1974

82. *The Luberon I,* 1974

83. Following pages: *The Grape-Pickers,* 1982

This is another vision of the world's plenty where, in a multicoloured field of soft colours (and a colour scheme which is, as always, unique), the human figures stand among spiralling vines and handle further spirals in the form of bunches of grapes, and where one might again wonder in what dimension they perform their task, and in what way the woman rises from the vines and from their shadows. The young man in the distance also holds grapes, but his cooler remoteness and mere standing to the work represent a more reflective mood, and maybe set off the lyricism with a necessary prosaic touch.

The difference between the first three large polychrome sculptures and *The Crowd*, in fact, is not so much that they include a setting, of market, colliery or vineyard, as that they set human figures in a densely rendered world to which they belong, in a variety of ways, and which serves to extend them. And the sculptor also belongs, in this case partly through the very design of the work. Although Mason only discovered it later, the five rows of vines resemble the five fingers of a hand, and the resemblance is accentuated by the presence of several actual hands and also by the multiplicity of vine leaves, whose five-fold structure is made clear in the green veins and red leaflets of a single leaf conspicuous under the man's chest. The hand-like shape of the work reminds one of the sculptor's hand, become part, in a sense, of the world which he is representing.

And what is that world? One sees that his principal characters are a Man and a Woman. The man, naked to the waist and so exposed to the sun and to the natural world, is also another study of the male torso. As in *The Falling Man*, it is again the armature of the body which interests Mason, and which leads to a kind of modelling perhaps recalling Michelangelo's yet very much Mason's own, with its clarification of the gnarled structure of the rib-cage, the spine, the shoulders. If the man is bone, moreover, the woman is flesh, and an emblem of the fertility and largeness of the natural world. They complement each other perfectly, and become the man and the woman of a rediscovered Garden. They are by no means Adam and Eve — we know their names — and they have neither the youth nor the particular beauty of origin, yet they preside over one of the rare large works of Mason's which is wholly glad, and which is also the culmination of a long series of works where there is no darkness. This is not Eden, but it is the real world, of working and of ageing, at its height, in the attainment of its possibility. It is the raising to a higher power of the actual grape harvest as described in one of Mason's notes, a time 'of fulfilment and great charm'.[13] The work is indeed full-filled, and is held in a 'charm' akin to the 'enchantment' of *The Departure*.

Mason is a city-dweller and the maker of mainly urban works, yet his human figures are often in contact with a natural world. Not only are the market workers of *The Departure* immersed in fruit and vegetables, but the crowds of *The Month of May in Paris* and of *The Latin Quarter* are protected by a great tree stretching over them, the holiday-makers of *The Costa Brava* are out in the sun (with a parasol at the rear which links the sun to the colours of the artist's palette), while the combatants of the *Monument for Guadeloupe* shed their blood on to the rich grass of the island. Mason also moves, as an artist, between the North and the South, and travelled literally in a recent past between Paris and Ménerbes, between a northern city and a southern countryside. In *The Grape-Pickers* he has chosen to concentrate in a single large sculpture all his feelings for the south, and for the earth, and also to produce the necessary counterpart to *A Tragedy in the North*. Without the existence of *A Tragedy*, *The Grape-Pickers* might have seemed illusory, in its disregarding of catastrophe and grief, of winter, rain and tears. Without *The Grape-Pickers*, *A Tragedy* would have been incomplete, one part of the whole. After the elegies and the tragedies, *The Grape-Pickers* is a kind of georgic, which rises from the detailed study of work on the land to become a song to the earth and to the sunlight, a near-idyll about human being in an exuberant nature.

The exuberance is in the repetition, of vine leaves and of vine rows, and also of patterns on the earth. And while repetition declares, more evidently here than anywhere, the joy of multiplicity, of a world that goes on for ever and that can take one in imagination away from where one is, it also augments the presence of the present, it goes *in* for ever and makes where one is progressively more real. As with the bricks of the houses in *Wheeleys Lane* and the cobble-stones of *A Tragedy in the North*, where each repeated object reinforces and deepens the emotion concerning home, each of the hundreds of leaves of *The Grape-Pickers*, while bristling with the knowledge of an unending vegetation covering the earth, is also further evidence of Mason's feeling for the field alongside the house and, for the viewer, a further attraction into the scene.

84. *The Grape-Pickers* (model)

Repetition, which is a fact of the universe, becomes strange as soon as one focusses on it. It is full of possibility; world-views can be derived from it. Its unthreatening forms usually suggest the inexhaustible profusion of a world much larger than ourselves, and so correspond perfectly to Mason's sense of the world's superior genius. They can also draw one, however, into the unmeasurable copiousness of a local instance, as into the leaves of a single tree, and such is also the case with *The Grape-Pickers*. It is this concentration which places the work beyond narrative. It hints at narrative in that it tells the story of grape-pickers harvesting table grapes in the south of France, but the event is far from unique, and there is no date beyond 'an October afternoon.' The small number of characters (as in Racine, where the effect is nonetheless quite different) means a landscape peopled but not crowded, where the 'crowd' is a crowd of vine leaves.

The woman, moreover, does not participate in the action. She is part of the work, and is even drawn back into it through the bending of her arm, but, alone in her half of the work and turning in a direction different from that of the other figures, she observes the viewer from out of its depth. Covered in orange and violet, she is beyond the red and the green, and wears the colours of the sun and of its shadows. As if belonging both to the earth and to the sky, she holds grapes in one hand and the sun in the other. To meet her gaze as one scans the work is to encounter a kind of goddess of plenty, suddenly and silently there, who, in so far as she speaks, speaks grapes, and who, if she carries an intimation of the numinous, is also decidedly real, her heavy form pressing against the vine. Like the 'maraîcher en majesté' of *The Departure*, she dominates a work of which she is the eventual meaning. Like Solitude in the *Monument for Guadeloupe*, she is the fecund woman who simply *is*, while her husband, like Delgrès, is the man who *does*. The fact of the work's being beyond narrative shows also in the slow and absorbed nature of that doing.

The work is even, in its way, contemplative. It does not, of course, invite the viewer to consider it from a distance; on the contrary, the woman stands to greet him, and the fact of her looking at him and thereby coming out of the work into his world is emphasised by the screening of her eyes. Nor does it present the viewer with a shadowless eternity, but it does draw him in to a moment of real time which lasts and deepens under his gaze, and to a kind of beatitude. It is not an immobile pattern, and its vines stir with the life of their reaching forms and their altering colours, yet their waves are comparatively placid, and while the work certainly moves and changes as the viewer moves, the rapid new relationships in the other works are deliberately reduced and slowed by the small number of forms rising into the air and articulating the space. Its energy — which includes the working of the humans and the working of the vines themselves under the heat — is more inward than in the landscape sculptures, and is close, from the beginning, to what I take to be the final inner quietness of *The Departure*. It manages, moreover, to be both pensive and full. Even in the least crowded and the least variegated of his large sculptures, Mason includes 'everything' and works by proliferation, by the teeming of difference over the sameness of the vine leaves. He shows a way of achieving an art of gradual illumination quite different from what seemed more modern in the early 1980s, the still influential simplifying and paring down of Barnett Newman and Mark Rothko. He recovers, in fact, an older art and an older thought, where the gravest bliss is compatible with, and indeed passes through, a this-worldly experiencing of the abundance of the real, the quiddity of its forms, the life of its persons and things.

Notes on Chapter VIII

[1] Birmingham 1989, p. 91.

[2] *Ibid.*

[3] Arts Council 1982, p. 42.

[4] *Ibid.*, p. 43.

[5] Centre Georges Pompidou 1985, p. 78.

[6] Interview in Claude Bernard 1977.

[7] 'The Grape-Pickers', in Birmingham 1989, pp. 105–6.

[8] Arts Council 1982, p. 50.

[9] 'Responses', in Arts Council 1982, p. 12.

[10] Arts Council 1982, p. 50.

[11] *Ibid.*

[12] 'The Grape-Pickers', in Birmingham 1989.

[13] Arts Council 1982, p. 50.

85. *A Monument for Montreal. An Illuminated Crowd,* 1986. Photo: Pierre-Louis Mongeau

IX

A TOTAL WORK

The *Grape-Pickers* was finished in 1982, in a period when Mason was being accorded major recognition — he was sixty years old — and yet still facing, from some quarters, rejection of his works and dismissive criticism. As well as his shows with Claude Bernard in 1977 and Pierre Matisse in 1980, he was given one-man exhibitions at Villeneuve-les-Avignon in 1977 and at Auxerre in 1980, and was shown in a number of important group exhibitions: in 1979, *La nouvelle subjectivité* at the Palais des Beaux-Arts, Brussels (landscape sculptures and gouaches); in 1981, *Paris–Paris 1937–1957* at the Centre Georges Pompidou (*Barcelona Tram*); and in 1982, *Aftermath: France 1945–1954*, the inaugural exhibition of the Barbican Art Gallery (*Barcelona Tram* again), and *Paris 1960–1980* at the Museum des 20. Jahrhunderts in Vienna (*The Departure, The Month of May in Paris* and several drawings. *The Departure* was the exhibition poster. The works neighbouring Mason's in the main hall were by Balthus and Giacometti). *The Crowd* was installed for the summer in Lyon in 1980, for the *Deuxième symposium de sculpture* where it met with considerable acclaim, and was shown the following year at the exhibition *Anthropos* in Vienna. In 1983, noticed by Barbara Lloyd, he was invited to join the Marlborough Gallery and in 1984 in Paris was given an individual exhibition on the Gallery's stand at the F.I.A.C. in the Grand Palais, where he showed, along with some small bronzes, *The Grape-Pickers*, landscape sculptures and watercolours, and the subject of this chapter, *An Illuminated Crowd*.

The culminating moments of the period are the showing of *A Tragedy in the North* and of a number of landscape sculptures in the International Pavilion of the Venice Biennale of 1982, and above all the retrospective exhibition, *Raymond Mason: coloured sculptures, bronzes and drawings 1952–1982*, organised by the Arts Council of Great Britain and shown at the Serpentine Gallery, London, from 27 November 1982 to 9 January 1983, and subsequently at the Museum of Modern Art, Oxford, from 6 February to 27 March. The

opportunity to display the range of Mason's works, from *Man in a Street* to the recently completed *Grape-Pickers*, was magnificently seized, the only really notable absences being *Wheeleys Lane* and *Birmingham. In Memoriam*. The catalogue included an introductory essay by Michael Peppiatt and the crucial 'Responses' to Peppiatt's questions by Mason himself, from which I have quoted frequently. The BBC programmed an *Omnibus* film they had made on Mason's work for 28 November 1982, so as to coincide with the show.

Despite a winter closing time of 4 pm, the Serpentine Gallery attracted a record attendance of 30,000 visitors, and although this is no proof of the quality of the work, it is a fact to be taken into account when considering that work, especially in the light of Mason's explicit ambition to make contact with as large a public as possible. The critics, on the other hand, were uniformly aghast at what they thought they saw, and found telling phrases to say so. That failure of the glance of the well informed can usually be ignored, but here it is another fact, and relates to what is almost the secret virtue of Mason's work, its property of not seeming original, of not looking, immediately, like great art. And another frustration followed. As a result of the exhibition there was a possibility of the Tate Gallery acquiring *A Tragedy in the North*. Although many visitors stopped to peruse the work, however — because of its size it was placed for twenty-four hours in the main hall rather than in the usual room for deliberations — the Trustees eventually refused it.

The entry to the Marlborough Gallery will lead us to something of specific importance in the exhibitions of the period. The Marlborough was a new experience for Mason, where he was aware of the presence of younger artists like Avigdor Arikha and Red Grooms (who is now his son-in-law) and in particular of their draughtsmanship, of that 'probity of art' on which his own work has always proved itself. His belief in the inceptive role of drawing is part of a human and artistic allegiance to a visual world, and it is eminently satisfying that in 1984 he appeared in the exhibition organised by

Marlborough Fine Art, Tokyo, under the title *International Masters of Figuration*. He was in the company, among others, of Arikha and Grooms, of Auerbach and Bacon who had been fellow artists at Helen Lessore's Beaux Arts Gallery, of Botero, Bravo and López García from the Galerie Claude Bernard, and of Kitaj and Larry Rivers, representatives of an Anglo-American grouping of artists whose thinking about art has sometimes meshed, as Mason has realised, with his own.[1] The importance of the exhibition is that it brought together figurative artists of different generations and quite dissimilar tendencies, and that it happened to recall the work of certain other galleries as well as the Marlborough in encouraging a kind of art which could once have seemed inessential to the age but which was now demonstrating its continuity and its weight.

For in the same year the perceptive Richard Morphet organised at the Tate Gallery *The Hard-Won Image*, in which Mason was also represented, by *The Grape-Pickers* and *St Mark's Place*, and could point in the catalogue to other and similar enterprises: to the *Eight Figurative Painters* exhibition held at the Yale Center for British Art in 1981–1982 and to the Arts Council exhibition *The Proper Study: Contemporary Figurative Paintings from Britain*, which was about to open in New Delhi. Already in 1977, moreover, Jean Clair in an essay on realism had been able to make a similar grouping of current exhibitions, which included Mason's showing of *A Tragedy in the North* and other works at the Galerie Claude Bernard, *Papiers sur nature* at the Fondation nationale des arts graphiques et plastiques, Paris, in which Mason was represented (by Luberon works), *Surrealismus und Sachlichkeit* (Surrealism and Objectivity) in Berlin and, most appropriately, the large Gustave Courbet exhibition at the Grand Palais in Paris and the Royal Academy in London.[2] In 1976 there had also been the aptly titled *The Human Clay*, an exhibition which Kitaj had organised for the Arts Council.

Jean Clair had argued that abstraction, by becoming, as it were, the authorised history of modern art, had marginalised everything else, making it difficult for a viewer properly to respond to Hopper, say, to Dix or Grosz, to Chirico or Carrà, to neoclassical Picasso, Derain after his Fauve period, Morandi, Balthus and to many others who together had created a different history, and who had continued, in fact, a more ancient and unbroken history, that of figurative art. Richard Morphet returns to the argument in the catalogue of *The Hard-Won Image*, and further opposes the claim — which is so easy to make and which bedevils the recognition of poetry or music as much as painting and sculpture — that 'the only art of a period which counts is that of its avant-garde'.[3]

In his Rodin lecture Mason noted similarly of *The Hard-Won Image* that many painters in England, though few sculptors, were evidently working outside the 'international conformity'. The exhibition included among its forty-six artists Blake, Coldstream, Hamilton, Hockney, Kitaj, Moore, and also Bacon, Auerbach, Freud, Kossoff, Michael Andrews and others who had been with Mason at the Beaux Arts Gallery, along with John Lessore and Helen Lessore herself, whom Morphet acknowledged as a key figure underlying the concept of the exhibition. (Her two paintings on show, *Symposium I* and *Symposium II*, contain portraits of Mason drawing.) The values and continuities which Mason had always upheld, while certainly in no way triumphing, were at least finding recognition. Figurative art was both enjoying a revival and demonstrating that it had never died. (His reward was to have his own works described by the critics of the exhibition as 'despicable', 'appalling' and 'of unparalleled horror'.)

86. *An Illuminated Crowd*, 1980

Although Mason's art is very much itself, there are occasionally interesting links to be made with those other realisms of the century, which are not necessarily a matter of influence but simply of a shared reality and of certain partial similarities of seeing. To think of Edward Hopper, for example, is to realise that his urban forms, though not their atmosphere, are relevant to *St Mark's Place* — an 'American' work — and in particular the long horizontals punctuated by careful verticals, the lettering, and the rhythm of repeating and not exactly repeating forms in *Early Sunday Morning*. That work also calls to mind Peter Blake, and one remembers that Mason has been a friend of Eduardo Paolozzi since student days and admires the work of Grooms and the early Oldenburg. One learns from the Brenson interview that he welcomed Pop Art, the only modern movement for which he felt enthusiasm, because of its 'generosity' and the fact that its practitioners were 'going out of themselves' and 'enjoyed what surrounded them'. While the

principles of Pop Art are quite foreign to his own, and while anything treated in his sculpture has a totally different presence and meaning, his delight in the vivid depiction of everyday scenes and objects is, at the moment of his return to exuberant colour, both a necessity of his work and a fact of the period.

It is even more useful, before turning to Mason's most ambitious work, to take the opportunity of these exhibitions and arguments to pause again on the idea of figuration. Mason's reflections, as well as his practice, take one from the simplest and yet maybe surprising implications of a commitment to figurative art into some of the heights of what it means to be a realist. Frank Auerbach is clearly right to see 'a real barrier between the sort of painter who is arranging things on a surface for their own sake and the sort of painter who has a permanent sense of the tangible world'[4] (though most painters of the first sort would no doubt wish to qualify the words 'for their own sake').

87. Above and left: initial studies for *Monument*

For an artist to sense the permanent presence not of *a* but of *the* tangible world involves a quite fundamental orientation of moral as well as perceptual activity. Yet one way of defending an art which seeks to render that world is simply to say that it is more interesting. Part of Mason's objection to what he called at the time of the Arts Council retrospective 'the non-sense and non-communication of abstract art' comes from a conviction that repeated patterns, for instance, are only 'exciting' when they are attached, as in that final tableau of Hogarth's *The Rake's Progress*, to something like a living hand, a fan, a door — to a human form and to other forms of the visible.[5]

Hence his resurrection of 'likeness' and of the gift for 'catching' it. Is it some sickness in our way of considering art, or a deeper mistrust of the world of appearance, or a shallower disdain of the unsophisticated, which can make us scorn the gift? Mason writes that when showing his 'prosaic efforts' at catching a likeness in his drawings as a schoolboy he witnessed 'the wondrous awe with which normal folk regard' such ability, and accuses the art establishment of having partially dried up 'this marvellous source which has flowed since the beginning of time'.[6] To say that something in a painting is 'like' something outside it has become a philosophically bold assertion, and it is true that likeness is not sameness and that the difference between the model and its representation is also of consequence. But to go along with the simple notion that making recognisable images has always been the particular and the basic talent of the visual artist is to cut through all the theories about the inevitable self-enclosure of the work and the blindness of the sign. To say that a cherry tree painted by Balthus is like an actual cherry tree is only the beginning of a discussion, but it is at least a beginning.

Not that seeing is itself simple. Bacon refers to 'the mystery of appearance',[7] and in the unexpected formula (one might have supposed that mystery was hidden behind appearance) one realises both why it is that we need visual artists, among others, and why, as Bacon also writes, realism has to be 'continuously reinvented'.[8] Appearance is difficult and inexhaustible; likeness changes with the changing of the thing seen in our way of seeing it. What Mason shows the viewer differs less from what the viewer has already seen than is the case with many artists, and yet exceeds what the viewer has seen more than with any artists but the most powerful. His realism is not like any other — no successful realism ever is — and to assume that one has met it before in very inferior work (at Madame Tussaud's, for example, or a funfair) is a sure recipe for being unable to see Mason at all. One also knows from the words

inscribed on the small relief of the mining disaster that 'REALITY' for Mason, as for others, is not simply given but needs to be discovered (through the authority, perhaps, of memory), and that it is also liable at any moment to appear, with sudden power. It is worth reminding oneself that the question for the figurative artist is not, or not first, how to render what is there but how to find, in the furthest reaches of the immediate, what truly is there; and that realism is not a technique, but a quest.

Likeness is also charged, of course, with the artist's intentions towards the world and towards his representation of it. There is always in art, as Lucian Freud says of his own painting, an 'intensification of reality'[9] (as if reality were not quite sufficient, or one's ordinary perception of it were, for some reason, inadequate), and in Mason's case we have seen a desire to 'exalt' reality, on the part of someone willing to describe himself as a 'worshipper of the visual world'.[10] Yet he also writes: 'I think of reality not as order, but rather disorder. The outer world has to be dealt with by the inner mind, and that's where the art and the artist has to come in'.[11] The association of outer and inner is the familiar combination of the figurative and the abstract, but the reference to reality as 'disorder' suggests a further, demiurgic role for Mason's energy. It implies that, if painting or sculpture is an 'act of worship' before 'a great marvellous world encompassing a vast field of liberty and possibility',[12] it is indeed an act, in which the artist is privileged to collaborate with what he reveres.

The coincidence of world and thought also leads into the most vexed and the most revealing question of all, that of beauty. Here, too, Mason speaks plainly of what he believes, and can free one yet again from shyness to admit what is both unthinkable in this late, disappointed and undeceivable age, and obvious once seen. What did he encounter when he entered the Birmingham School of Arts and Crafts? 'The great subject itself. Beauty'.[13] There was the beauty of great art, of music, and of the outer world, and there was the beauty of Birmingham itself. All Mason is present in the footnote in which this culminates: 'I've already repeated [the word "beauty"] several times and I do so without a blush. That, in case our contemporary art world has forgotten, is what art is all about.'

He does not define beauty but points to its effect and to how and where it occurs. Already in 1951, before *Man in a Street*, he writes in French, for an exhibition of works by Xavier Coll: 'To arrest one's movement in the real, to cast one's being . . . for an instant into matter, is the authentic miracle among men. This terrestrial miracle is what we call beauty, the state of grace between a man and his project'. Beauty is the perfect union of the inner and the outer, of the artist's intention and the work which finally springs to meet it. The work is a real and material thing in which not only the complex processes of the artist's mind, but the unceasing movement of his person through time and even a moment in the history of his being, are gathered once and for all. This realising of the artist, this deployment and discovery of riches, has so much the effect of a miracle, of the receiving of grace, that the vocabulary which seems appropriate to it is that of religious transcendence.

Although the thinking centres here on the artist himself (and the word 'project' takes one back to the contemporary Existentialism of Sartre), it does so because it is the artist's perception of beauty in the world which fires the work, and because he is inevitably the first person to have the task of judging whether beauty has been achieved. Mason's intention, moreover, given the orientation of his art towards the public, is something he expects to make clear. For of course he also thinks of beauty as involving the viewer: 'I won't satisfy anybody if the sculpture is not *beautiful*. The subject of the work situates it in the world and in history. Beauty transcends that reality and brings happiness'.[14] Just as reaching forms and intensely moulded eyes fix a sculpture physically in space, so its subject locates it mentally in place and time — and co-operates thereby in giving it permanence by securing it as densely as possible in reality — while beauty, which is the transcendental end of the work, brings not composure or aesthetic delight or pleasing melancholy but, according to another simple and refreshing word, happiness. That the creator of *Birmingham. In Memoriam*, of *The Departure*, of *A Tragedy in the North*, should make no allusion to the sadness of beauty is a sign that there is little or no sense in his work of exile or longing, and that beauty, along with the emotion it brings, rises beyond the work and constitutes, where necessary, for the artist as for the viewer, a countervailing hope.

He also rewrites his basic proposition in less personal terms in a passage, again in French, which was not included in the final version of his text on *The Departure*: 'Then I allow myself to imagine that when Idea finds its substance there is a light, as it were, which salutes the miracle. The name for this state of grace would be Beauty.' The capitalised Idea suggests that what enters and animates the inert substance of the work is more than the artist's thought, intercepted in its flight, and that the work becomes exemplary of the realising of human thought itself. On one occasion he goes even further, though with some reluctance. In the interview at the time of *A Tragedy in the North* and *The Aggression*, he says of energy that it is 'my way of infusing . . . the divine spark into my work, so that people can

believe it', and adds: 'I think that beauty . . . is literally the state of grace when . . . the [divine] spark has been captured in the material . . . it's a miraculous moment . . . [B]eauty isn't linked to any particular form. It's just a state . . . of capture'.[15] This sounds, and may well be, Promethean; but at the same time Mason seems to sense, in and beyond the artist's project, in and beyond Idea, the presence of something else, as if to encounter beauty were to be in contact with a superior force which had better remain nameless but for which an ancient metaphor such as 'the divine spark' will serve. It is a question once again of the nature of reality.

One finds all this at work supremely in *An Illuminated Crowd*. Here, the most profound disorder is persuaded into the order of thought and of sculpture. The search for human reality and its beyond is the most universal, and also the most overtly symbolic, in a piece which is figurative in both the artistic and the poetic senses of the word. Beauty is tried to a limit; the happiness it brings is in tension with the most far-reaching unhappiness; the miracle it constitutes and the 'light' which greets it may even be a theme of the work.

The sculpture takes one back to 1978. In the autumn of that year Mason planned *The Grape-Pickers*, the most ambitious of his Luberon works and the one which finally peopled the landscape. He also planned, in that same season, *An Illuminated Crowd*, the most ambitious of all his works, which he describes as 'a landscape of faces',[16] because of the distance from which it would be seen and the rise and fall of the surface. One moves from the seeing and understanding of landscape to a landscape-like articulation of a human theme and shaping of a human crowd; in the light, perhaps, of his judgment in the text on 'La Foule' where, having compared the 'vision of continual metamorphosis' created by the motions of a crowd to the movements of nature, of clouds and waves and fire, he nevertheless declared the entire superiority of the vision in the street: 'by its human significance it far surpasses [natural movements] and attains to drama.'

He made a group of drawings which had as their origin a crowd watching a bonfire in front of the Hôtel de Ville in Paris, with a view to sculpting as large a work as his studio could hold, about eight and a half metres long. Having made a maquette in 1979–1980, however, he was persuaded by Yves Bonnefoy that too many years would go to the making of the full-scale work — even for Mason, who is surely unique among modern sculptors in the years he is prepared to devote to each of his large works — and so 'I decided to satisfy myself with the original model'.[17] In fact a transformation occurred.

This small version was painted to suggest an effect

of illumination and placed in a perspex box which reduces the scale to co-operate perfectly with a contrary impression of vastness. It thus became a sculpture in its own right, and was shown in the 1980 exhibition at the Pierre Matisse Gallery in New York and for the first time in Paris in 1984, on the Marlborough stand at the F.I.A.C. In 1980, while he was still working on it, he was invited by the Louis-Dreyfus Property Group of New York to make a sculpture for a future plaza in central Montreal, and saw this as the opportunity of realising his original intention. The plan did not work out immediately, and the years 1981–1982 were taken up with *The Grape-Pickers*. In the latter year Mason expected to be providing not a sculpture for the esplanade but a relief sculpture for the lobby of the building behind it, but having succeeded in getting his first project accepted he worked from 1983 (the year of his entry to the Marlborough Gallery) to the summer of 1985 on the monumental sculpture, from a new and remodelled maquette but with the original title. It was the first work to follow his Arts Council retrospective and was also, appropriately enough, a further amplification of his vision. He had fortunately realised by then that it would be possible to have the maquette enlarged to an intermediate size in plaster, which he would rework, and then enlarged again to the dimensions he had originally envisaged. The enlargements were undertaken at Brie-Comte-Robert near Paris, under Mason's constant supervision, by the studios of Olivier Haligon, who from that moment became a friend and the principal collaborator for all Mason's important works. The final version, in polyester fibreglass reinforced with steel and painted in polyurethane, was erected in June 1986 on the plaza at 1981 McGill College Avenue, Montreal, in front of the startlingly beautiful BNP building designed by the architect René Menkès.

An Illuminated Crowd is a deepening of *The Crowd*. In the interview with Michael Brenson in 1976, Mason

88. *An Illuminated Crowd* (detail)

had stated: 'I said at the time [of finishing the earlier work] that I hoped to . . . do *The Crowd* again with people thinking about things, but I'm not there yet'.[18] One sees how ambitious Mason had been in *The Crowd*, and one also sees the nature of that ambition. *The Departure*, which was completed, and *A Tragedy in the North*, on which he had been working, were not attempts to realise the hope, because of their defined occasions and subject matter, any more than *The Grape-Pickers* would be. Without in any way being lesser works, they did not have as their theme what for Mason is the largest theme: the human crowd itself. *An Illuminated Crowd*, on the other hand, which again signals the human universality of its concern in its title, moves away from the occasion of a civic bonfire and of people assembled to watch it, and returns to the undefined and indeed unlimited scope of the first large composition. It rethinks the bronze with expressions and emotions, and with something else which had been introduced into subsequent works and which finds here its fundamental role. A move from one racial type to another repeats, along with the passage from emotion to emotion, the 'journey in space'[19] of *St Mark's Place*, and enlarges the sculpture similarly in the mind. In the monument, the races imply a compacting into the work of all human geography as well as all human nature.

The hints of drama in *The Crowd* are also multiplied and made visually explicit in *An Illuminated Crowd*, which progressively ceases to represent an actual and ordinary throng of people that one might encounter in front of the Hôtel de Ville or along the boulevard St Michel, and becomes instead a composing of separate scenes of violence, of death, of rising naked from darkness, and so necessitates a different form. *The Crowd* dispenses with decor, in its reaching for unconfined and 'oceanic' generality, while retaining nonetheless the perspective which draws in the viewer. *The Departure* returns to a setting which participates in the meaning of its human characters, and even (almost) encloses the vision of plenty and the moment of its leaving within a box-like structure recalling the street reliefs. The frame is then abandoned. *A Tragedy in the North* is enacted in a setting like that of a tragic play. *The Grape-Pickers* has a simple back-drop, and in so far as it also has a setting of vine rows, it includes these in the midst of its human figures, who work on a continuing earth rising and falling under the sun. *An Illuminated Crowd* finally introduces for the first time, and partly by reason of its formidable ambition, figures greater than life-size, and places them, also for the first time, in a work which is free-standing. It remains, in fact, the only free-standing of the large works, and contrives, in this way, as in others, to be, like each of them, unique.

89. Projected study for *An Illuminated Crowd*

Already in the small version, the sufficient reason for the absence of perspective (which will lead Mason to devise ways of drawing in the viewer from every side) is that the front and the back of the sculpture do not correspond to a foreground and a background. To be able to follow the changes from the illumination at the front to the obscurity at the rear one needs to see from the side, while the very idea of a long progression from light to darkness requires a stretching-out of the sculpture which is quite unlike *The Crowd* (though very like the equally free-standing *Aggression*). Yet despite the fact that one can look at the work from any angle, it still has a suggestion of right and left. Mason thought at one stage of indicating the 'degrees of emotion' on the base of the work: 'illumination, hope, interest, hilarity, irritation, fear, sickness, hunger, violence, murder and death', as a further and interesting means of 'punctuating and accentuating the stretch of space'.[20] He eventually decided to limit himself to the words 'Obscurantism' and 'Enlightenment' joined by a double-headed arrow, and wrote them on the base of the small version, on the side which places enlightenment on the right and obscurantism on the left. He could have written on the other side, and of course the viewer need only cross to that side for the bearings to be reversed. The photograph of the small version shows it, nonetheless, illuminated from the right, and the monument also is usually presented from the same side or from the front or the rear. The stretching-out of space is in itself basic to Mason's sculptural vision, with its suggestion of space being occupied to the full, as in the distance created at the front of *The Departure* from the man leaning slightly backward on the left to the man straining and bent forward on the right, or of an elsewhere being entered, as in the departing vehicles of *Barcelona Tram* and *Carrefour de l'Odéon*. At the same time space, or rather direction in space, also engages for Mason, traditionally and yet tenaciously, with idea. The stretching of space, as of a person's extended arms, goes from the 'sinister' or 'worthless' left to the 'dextrous' or 'true' right.

There is also a movement, for the first time, to either

end of the work. Mason writes of the 'degradation of the subject and its descent into hell — or its resurgence'.[21] In the smaller version, the eye travels to actual darkness or to actual light; in the case of the monument, where the nature of the ground enables Mason to compensate for the absence of painted meaning, the work literally descends and rises over four different levels, while viewers and passers-by also submit to the metaphorical suggestions of going down or going up as they advance over steps. (It was in 1982, while visiting René Menkès's building with a view to providing a relief sculpture, that Mason thought of drawing directly into his sketch-book the *Illuminated Crowd* as it could be modified so as to stand on the levels of the esplanade. The new arrangement was so right that it continued unchanged into the final work.) One sees again the power of simplicity — of simplicity, that is, at its most difficult. *An Illuminated Crowd* is not, in either version, a work at the cutting edge of the exploration of the human condition. It returns to fundamentals, which it finds original and contemporary ways of probing. It reminds one of the possibilities — of falling or of rising — in the richly central and symbolic, and also realistic and quotidian, *Falling Man*.

The play of light and dark returns us to two of the most traditional and therefore most familiar and recognisable metaphors for describing, to the eye of the mind, a human nature and a human destiny which are 'between'. The physical stretching of space between right and left promotes a metaphysical stretching of the human crowd between right and wrong, in all the many stored-up senses of the words. And while light has already been 'celestial', and while actual shadows have been present, with the suggestion that they represent 'the power of the unknown in everyday reality' ('La Foule'), this is the first appearance of painted shadows, following the painted reflections of *A Tragedy in the North*, and almost the first appearance of darkness in the fullness of its meaning — in the first work where Mason also portrays 'our failing nature'.[22] As nature fails, so the light 'loses itself in the crowd' (a telling phrase no doubt suggested by French), and this leads to other original ways with paint. In *The Grape-Pickers* an apparently unsculptural use of colour will send afternoon sunlight into the work from one side and will render the other side as in shadow. Here, on the smaller version (the monument is quite different in this respect and will need to be considered later) a strong and low source of light, as in the original instance of a bonfire, illumines the front of the work and sends highlights way back over the heads, on which Mason paints splashes of light rather as in *A Tragedy in the North* he painted splashes of reflections. The light slowly gives way, not only to darkening shadows but, at the rear of the work, to a shimmering of purples and blues which delivers a kind of Miltonic 'darkness visible'. The light itself shines in darkness, and Mason picks out indentations on bodies and clothes, and also the contours of patches of light, with red lines, which suggest, according to the position of the figure, the presence of life or the threat to life.

The new meaning of the crowd requires a new form; the new form requires new means of composition. The mass of sixty-five figures becomes visible — becomes, that is, understandable to the eye — first through a number of conspicuous reachings of the sculpture out into the surrounding space: from the horizontal pointing arm at the front, through a man hoisted on someone's shoulders and an even more dramatic, because unexpected, vertical arm which is the summit of the model, to a tall head and a pointed hood, to the prominent knee and elbow of a man falling backwards, and finally to a foot overlapping the base at the rear. That rising and descending curve is a shape which means, and which is accompanied by another curve falling from left to right when the sculpture is viewed from behind, from the splayed fingers of the upraised arm to a man lying prone. And so one might go on, for a work which faces in all directions needs to be made intelligible whatever the angle of the viewer. It also needs to be alive and to 'move', and as well as precisely calculated displacements for the eye from one expression or gesture to another, and two actual portrayals of rushing bodies — in a work where, in contrast to *The Crowd*, most of the figures are still — Mason contrives, especially towards the rear, an agitated rhythm which passes to and fro among differing yet repeating heads, fists, angles, moods. The sheer activity of what became the third level is perfectly caught in the photograph of Mason at work on the monument taken by his friend Henri Cartier-Bresson, one of several photographs by him which perceive Mason sharply in relation to his work or his environment.

There is also a tide-like movement passing through the work — Mason writes of its 'undulation' and of the 'flowing' of the monument over the 'cascade' of levels[23] — which ends at the rear in a falling wave. There is also some suggestion of a landscape over the top of the work, with its large expanse and its irregular and changing surface, though of a landscape quickly replaced for the viewer by his focusing on heads and on their expressive and entirely human faces. It is by giving attention, however, to certain key moments of the composition

90. *An Illuminated Crowd*. Photo: Iris Hao

that one sees its power, and that one understands again why Mason said to Michael Peppiatt: 'For me the elaboration of the inner structure is all-absorbing and is probably my best contribution to present-day art'.[24] The truth, one might say, of all his works is in their inner structure, to attain which the viewer must become all-absorbed in seeking it, and this is most of all the case, as I have tried to show, in the large compositions, where the structural elaboration is almost infinitely complex. Mason's last phrase is also to be heeded, as is the reference not to art in general but to the art of the present.

The man pointing is the entrance — by the sociability of his gesture, of his body turned inward towards others and of his appearance of inviting the whole crowd to look — to the simple human closeness at the van of the work. A woman clasps her son in front of her; an elderly man has his arm round his wife; a father has settled his daughter on his shoulders. The 'pleasing variety' of sculptural positions is also a variety of human holding, which contrasts with the rear of the work, where the figures either hold themselves, through sickness, hunger, despair, or lay hands on others, to assault or to murder. Several mouths are open near the front, as if hungry for the light — in one case a tongue is lolling out so as to suggest the symbolic nature of the work, while in another a cigarette is sticking to a lip so as to fix the symbolic vision in the contemporary world — again in contrast to the rear, where the hunger which is experienced is grimly physical.

The main function of the pointing man, however, is of course to lead out of the work. Like the drunk of *St Mark's Place* and the Pole of *A Tragedy in the North*, he is the most evident link with the viewer, and in the catalogue note for the 1991 Marlborough exhibition in London, Mason sees his oncoming arm as protruding on to the pavement so as 'to arrest the passing gaze' — a banal expression until one realises that arresting the viewer's gaze: slowing a passer-by into a source of attention and turning an aptitude for looking into an ability to see — is both a universal end of Mason's art and a theme of this particular work. The eyes of the man who points and those of the man he is alerting are deep-set, quite unlike most of the other eyes, and suggest a power of seeing, like that of the contrasting, protuberant eyes of the young mother, and also an intense depth of gaze. At the rear of the work, just as arms cannot point because they are bent or wrenched or inert, so one man's head is hooded and the eyes of the final figure are closed.

The man pointing is a development of a similar figure in the Washington monument, who was present from the earliest project, executed in 1976. He is also the familiar figure who asks a question, through the reaches of his look and through the sheer length, as it were, of his pointing. His arm, which Mason describes in the Rodin lecture as an 'advancing spiral' and whose spiral form is emphasised by the folds of his sleeve (especially in the monument and by the strokes of the pencil in one of the drawings envisaging the installation of the work on its future site), is a sign of life, but what it points to is unknown. From as early as *Barcelona Tram*, where people are being 'carried away to their destiny', Mason has made a number of works, which would include *The Departure*, possibly *The Falling Man* and even the slice-of-life *Carrefour de l'Odéon*, which move to the right and towards something vital and yet absent. This opening of what is represented in the work towards what is not representable culminates here, and we shall need to return to it.

At the rear of the work, three or perhaps four men fall in sequence, rather like a dying wave or like a series of stills of the same figure, his head gradually turning as he slumps to the ground. A head is bandaged, stomachs are hugged from hunger, a fist is raised in pain or protest. All the positions are interesting, the most telling being that of the prostrate figure, one of whose legs is awkwardly bent under the other in a final defeat of the body. The last two figures are also naked to the waist, and the modelling of their torsos returns, as does that of the man in *The Grape-Pickers*, to *The Falling Man*. This is important for Mason's study of the torso, where one sees the same handling of the architecture of the upper body, the same exposition of rib cage and spine. In the man falling one also notices again the open angle between the diagonal spine and the horizontal ridge along the ribs, which in *The Grape-Pickers* will lead the viewer's eye from the man to the woman. As the clothes come off, moreover, the bodies which are revealed are once again classical.

The reference in the final figures, who are quite naked and who form a double personage, is also classical, the effect of which is to take the classical origin of Western sculpture into the work's representation of human origin, and into what is both literally and metaphorically the work's turning-point. The figures are of evident sculptural interest, in the strangeness and broad suggestiveness of their relation to one another, in their presentation to the viewer, as he arrives at the rear, of an upside-down head, in the arm apparently supporting the head as it falls backwards, and in the hanging arm which contrasts with the raised and pointing arms elsewhere. The supine figure, who is dead, is also bound to remind one of the man falling backwards from the lintel of the left-hand panel of Rodin's Dantean *The Gates of Hell*, and thereby confirm one's sense that the rear of the work is a descent, not into the Christian Hell but, as Mason's small 'h' makes clear, into an unspecified hell of death and darkness. Dante may himself come to mind, since an arm of the man lying prone seems to have sunk into mud. The most remarkable fact about the lolling head, however, is that, while its mouth is open, its eyes are closed. This is the figure whom the viewer would expect, when the rear of the work faces him, to be looking in his direction, like so many others since *Man in a Street*. An elderly man does look this way, but with eyes that are uncomprehending or resigned. The eyes of which the viewer is most aware are finally closed to the light and to the illumination far away behind him.

A nearby Indian's eyes are gazing downwards and inwards, rather like those of Rodin's thinker as he broods on Hell. And one sees that the rear of the work, which became the fourth level of the monument, tells its own narrative, which includes final prostration, a falling backwards into horror, and a religious figure who represents, no doubt, the obscurantism at the other end from enlightenment. Once one has seen this device of narrating by juxtaposition, as in *The Departure of Fruit and Vegetables*, one realises how rich the work is in narratives. From the rear, for example, one sees the head of the little girl on her father's shoulders next to the hood of a man threatening a woman with a knife. Since every figure has a specific meaning and since the theme of the work is unbounded, the narrative possibilities are practically endless.

The choice of an Indian, moreover, brooding maybe on illusion and the wheel of rebirth, is appropriate, for as one of the final figures, a white man, tumbles backwards into death, the man who bears his weight, and who is black, rises towards life. This is the perfect turn, in fact, of the sculpture, a masterly sculptural and human idea where, as in the turmoil of races at the ends and beginnings of history, the descent into hell meets, in a single complex figure, a resurgence, a rising on to the knees from the furthest darkness of the work, a raising of the eyes to the distant illumination, a movement towards the front and to the right by a solitary and naked figure who counters the mass of an overwhelming fall. The falling and the rising man are also of solid, Blake-like proportions, as befits a work which begins with a crowd watching a bonfire in Paris and has now become vision and imagination.

That falling and rising figure is the depth of the work, the meeting of its opposing movements in a moment of infinite possibility. On the other side there is another kind of meeting, almost a collision, between a man rushing forwards into the crowd with his coat-tails flying and with his arm upraised, and an equally determined figure facing rearwards who confronts him literally nose

91. In front of the building by René Menkès

to nose. It is via the man with the arm that the viewer is drawn into the work on that side, and impelled towards the illumination, only to see, at this midpoint which became in the monument the junction of the two central levels, the contrary will. The meeting here does not occur way down and far back in dream and myth but in the everyday world of personality and polemic. It takes one to the plane of experience on which degradation and descent, or resurgence, are a matter of choice.

The arm and the hand fascinate. Unless the line of sight is too low, they are always the most startling part of the sculpture, and to see that their vertical punctuates the horizontal ebb and flow of the work, stretches the work upwards and gives further emphasis to other turreting forms, and is also needed, because the sculpture is free-standing and very large, to counter-balance, deep in the work, the horizontal arm in the front and reinforce and take over its action of responding to the movements of the viewer, does not dissipate surprise. The gesture is also dramatic, and accentuates the drama of the whole. Yet in mimetic terms the gesture is unexplained, as if part of its function is to draw attention to a hand. Once again, this is in no sense the sculptor's hand, and the last thing Mason wants is to bring himself to the viewer's notice. For the viewer, however, a hand in the middle of the work and rising above it as if to drive it in the direction of the light, which the other most conspicuous hand is engaged in indicating, can be a moving sign of the work's desire.

Also rising above the sculpture is the head of a tall man, looking squarely at the viewer as he passes down the main side of the work. Surrounded by faces expressing strong emotion, including the invisible face of the highly expressive and inhuman hooded man, and next to the smoke billowing from the darkness at the rear, his look is almost impassive. His power is in his ordinariness, in his being half in light, half in shadow, and in his gazing not to the front or to the rear but across the work. He is the figure who, as in so many other works, addresses the viewer interrogatively from the midst.

An Illuminated Crowd travels from anecdote to symbol, from a bonfire to the fires of hell. Many of Mason's works make a similar journey towards largeness of meaning, beginning with *Barcelona Tram*, but no other, except the quite different *Monument for Guadeloupe* and the *Twin Sculptures* in Washington, actually departs from the portrayal of a visible scene or event. It is as if Mason stops the crowd of *The Crowd* to look harder at what is there. The light which bathes the earlier work gradually loses itself, 'the mood degenerates' and the 'rowdiness at the back of any crowd' gives on to the 'failing nature' which it 'exemplifies'[25] and the darkness which is the end of failing. The viewer, too, sees a crowd and then sees into it, and one realises that this second crowd placed, in the monumental version, in the middle of an actual crowd, is also, like *The Crowd* itself but more troublingly so, a heightened summary of all who view it.

It tells, in a way, the story of Man, between the light and the dark, and as it goes once again beyond narrative it enters vision. Yet while one sees the acts of darkness, whatever shines, at the other extremity of the work, beyond social and familiar good, is only indicated. 'Sickness, hunger, violence, murder and death' are present, whereas 'hope' and 'interest' look to something else. There is certainly 'illumination', but the source of illumination is not made clear. In Mason's speech at the unveiling of the monument, it is 'anything you can think of, a spectacle, a fire but principally, I would like to

think, . . . an ideal', and in the sculpture itself it is whatever the characters see and the viewer does not see. In this secular Last — or rather, present and continuing — Judgment, with its tall figure who, though not central, nevertheless divides the ways, an artist who worships light and who aspires entirely to exalt life and the world around him, takes the cruelty and the killing which had previously appeared only recently and only in *The Monument for Guadeloupe* and *The Aggression*, involves them in a more profound and mythic darkness which had never occurred before and which he gathers in this work once and for all, and sets against them a powerful, pointing arm.

In so far as the light is beauty, the whole work is illuminated by its 'miracle', and the darkness itself is answered by the strength of art. But it is important that the light remain undefined. For if a question is posed more evidently in this work than in any other, it is also now the supreme question, to which Mason has in fact often referred. Given the apparent passing of the Christian religion in the eighteenth century, what 'faith' can replace it large enough to encompass the whole destiny of man? And with the eclipse of the Christian story, what subject is sufficiently true and universal to engage the highest efforts of art? The answer clearly begins in humanism, and perhaps specifically in eighteenth-century Enlightenment. The removal of anything from the work (except a billow of smoke) other than human figures is also an answer in itself, as is the horizontal orientation of the work behind the stretching arm and the triangular, prow-like forefront. There is no movement upwards, since the vertical arm does not point, and one remembers Delgrès in *The Monument for Guadeloupe*, rising with the explosion yet looking horizontally in front of him to a future of liberty on earth. But one might also remember 'a thought avid for humanism and for more', and while other works have questioned beyond humanism (beginning once again with *Barcelona Tram*, the origin of so much in Mason's oeuvre), this is the first time that figures in a sculpture have themselves been avid — pointing beyond, panting, and standing open-mouthed. The work is open to what may be. It traces a way, and waits expectantly.

I have been discussing the model and the monument together, but one needs to consider the monument specifically so as to take, as it were, the full measure of the work. The model in its glass box is not exactly a lesser achievement, and its painting is a most powerful and, in sculptural terms, original representation of a light which loses itself in darkness. The monument, however, one of the largest figurative sculptures in the Western world, has the advantage, first, of being able

92. Mason at work on *Monument* in the Haligon Studios, 1985. Photo: Henri Cartier-Bresson

to react to its surroundings. It espouses and gives meaning to the rising or descending levels on which it stands. The advancing, horizontal arm is a 'counter-part', as Mason has written, to 'the ambient verticality' of North American architecture.[26] The portrayal of humans is the necessary complement to the geometrical modern building behind. This last is of great importance to Mason, in fact, who has referred on more than one occasion to the need to place in front of modern architecture not 'a cube on its point' or any other abstract sculpture but human figures. The square-paned façades are ideally suited in their turn to capture and emphasise the undulation of this new crowd.

The monument also reacts to the light. Because of its siting in the open air, it was not possible to paint shadows, which would have been contradicted by the sun, and despite the addition of a literal descent, something is inevitably lost. What is gained is a further sympathy with place, and also a different effect of beauty. The monument was pistol-painted by the Haligon studios in a colour which Mason had chosen (and which he had checked against the colour of the building behind by travelling to Montreal with a piece of painted resin from the 1985 Marlborough exhibition in New York), and in his own words 'the sculpture is light ochre in colour, singing before the blue glass of the building'.[27] 'Singing' suggests the final agreement between the sculpture and its surroundings, a chord of colour from a sculpture which represents universal humanity and an architecture which implies and indeed receives human presence and which goes, through the shape of the square panes of its façade, to another and very different origin of art. The flooding of the whole work with a glowing colour also means that the figures at the rear are equally bathed in its light. Rather than a darkness which matches and reveals their condition, what may at first seem an inappropriate colour answers their condition in the manner most appropriate to art, by the power, that is, of beauty itself.

The sheer size of the monument also affects the modelling of the figures and one's response to them. There is a boldness and simplicity of line and form, most noticeably in the head of the man falling backwards and in figures at the front, in the heads and clothes in particular of the man pointing, of the man next to him, of the interestingly grouped 'mother and child'. In the 1976 interview with Michael Brenson, Mason had said of the great pediment of Olympia, which he had seen only in 1971, on an itinerary planned for him by James Lord: 'There is something in a certain period of Greek Art [the suspended moment between archaic and classical] which is essential for me [and] which I have not yet attained, that is, this great drama within a simple rendering of human form and clothing'.[28] His own figures in no way vie with the art of Olympia, but in their simple strength and by means of an observing eye and a modelling hand which are thoroughly contemporary, they do attain to an essential, heroic drama in a dimension larger than ours. Since the torsos at the rear, while they too may remind one of the art of the Greeks, are also decidedly Mason's, *An Illuminated Crowd* both recovers a great tradition of sculpture and achieves originality — where else is there a work like this? — without being avant-garde.

Mason had also told Brenson of his ambition to produce 'a total work . . . utilising form and colour very strongly, and very purely in as much that the subject will not necessarily be all important, [and] there'd be absolutely no decor.' In the event, the monument which *An Illuminated Crowd* finally became disallowed the use of polychromy, but it is still the closest that Mason has come to that total work. It 'represents the world', no less, of human races, ages, emotions, gestures and actions,[29] and it composes the whole into a serial movement back and forth between the depth of darkness and the beyond of light. It enables one to read anew, moreover, what Mason writes of composition: 'What . . . is composition but bringing everything together, including the emotions from grin to grimace'.[30] There is the bringing-together of everything in the work, which is the requirement for any sculpture or painting, but there is also the bringing together, in a work, of Everything. Just as realism is not, at root, the making of realistic art but a discovering of the real, so composition is — or can be — not only the composing of a work of art but a composing of reality.

Notes on Chapter IX

1 See 'Responses', in Arts Council 1982, p. 15.

2 Jean Clair, 'Si réalisme il y a . . . ', *Nouvelle Revue Française*, no. 300, Paris, 1 January 1978, p. 101.

3 Richard Morphet, *The Hard-Won Image: Traditional Method and Subject in Recent British Art*, The Tate Gallery, London, 1984, p. 9.

4 'A conversation with *Frank Auerbach*' (Catherine Lampert), in Frank Auerbach, Arts Council, London, 1978, p. 19.

5 'Responses', in Arts Council 1982, p. 15.

6 'My Early Artistic Life in Birmingham', in Birmingham 1989, p. 12 and p. 13, note 3.

7 In David Sylvester, *Interviews with Francis Bacon,* London, 1975, p. 105.

8 Interviewed by David Sylvester, *Repères, cahiers d'art contemporain*, no. 10, Galerie Maeght Lelong, Paris, January 1984.

9 'Some thoughts on painting', *Encounter*, vol. 3, no. 1 , London, July 1954, p. 23.

10 'Responses', in Arts Council 1982, p. 13.

11 'The Torrent of Life', in Birmingham 1989, p. 33.

12 *Ibid*.

13 'My Early Artistic Life in Birmingham', in Birmingham 1989, p. 13. The footnote I refer to is number 6 on page 14.

14 'Responses', in Arts Council 1982, p. 13.

15 Interview in Claude Bernard 1977.

16 'Illuminated Crowd', in Birmingham 1989, p. 103.

17 *Ibid*.

18 Interview in Claude Bernard 1977.

19 'St Mark's Place . . . ' and 'Illuminated Crowd', in Birmingham 1989, pp. 96 and 104.

20 'Illuminated Crowd', in Birmingham 1989, p. 104.

21 *Ibid*.

22 Arts Council 1982, p. 49.

23 'Illuminated Crowd', in Birmingham 1989, p. 104.

24 Arts Council 1982, p. 13.

25 *Ibid.,* p. 49.

26 'Monument for Montreal', in Marlborough 1991.

27 'Illuminated Crowd', in Birmingham 1989, p. 104.

28 Partially translated in Claude Bernard 1977.

29 From Mason's speech at the unveiling of the *Illuminated Crowd*, Montreal, 25 June 1986.

30 'My Early Artistic Life in Birmingham', in Birmingham 1989, p. 13, note 5.

93. *New York City,* 1987

CITY PANORAMAS

The Grape-Pickers, where Mason looks literally to the here and now, to a grape harvest in autumn by neighbours in a vineyard near his house, concentrates a kind of contentment of belonging, beneath the sun and in the presence of the earth's plenty. It records extravagantly, yet raises appearances and accidents into a whole and permanent image, and resembles, rather, a *Departure* without the departure. *An Illuminated Crowd*, devised almost at the same time but moving rapidly from a remembered occurrence to a general reflection and from observing to inventing, differs from the other work both in going to the darkness of the human condition and in watching for a light elsewhere. Placed between *A Tragedy in the North*, the *Monument for Guadeloupe* and *The Aggression* on the one hand and *The Grape-Pickers* on the other, it unites the two directions and in thought goes further than either. Just as *The Grape-Pickers* is a necessary complement to *A Tragedy in the North*, moreover, so *An Illuminated Crowd* replies to *The Crowd*.

Mason's sculptures work with and away from each other to form a single developing whole, rather like the plays of a great dramatist. He does not make repeating series, but is one of the very few artists to change his subject entirely with each work, to explore and fill, with each new theme, a large and distinct domain of ideas and emotions, and to contrive for every occasion a singular and never-repeated sculptural form.

An Illuminated Crowd was installed in Montreal in 1986, and was an instant success. It has become one of the sights of the city, and although its use as a background for fashion parades, Ford car displays and as the logo of a TV station, along with its being an obligatory stopping-place for tourist buses, have nothing to do with its worth, they must be a source of legitimate pleasure for Mason, and they speak yet again of his ability to reach the public and to interest people. In the same year he lectured on Rodin at the Hayward Gallery and was invited by the Tate Gallery to talk on the Ecole de Paris, of which he had established himself as a late but prominent member, and, more importantly,

The Crowd was installed in the Tuileries Gardens, at the personal instigation of the Minister of Culture, Jack Lang. Two big, outdoor sculptures were now visible in major international cities, and both had been shown the previous year in Mason's second retrospective, which remains the most notable and the most complete of all his exhibitions. It was held at the Musée national d'art moderne in the Centre Georges Pompidou, Paris, from 11 September to 11 November 1985, and subsequently at the Musée Cantini, Marseilles, from 14 December 1985 to 17 February 1986. The catalogue includes twelve short and essential texts by Mason, many of them hitherto unpublished, along with new essays by Yves Bonnefoy and Jean Clair, and French translations of essays by James Lord and Michael Brenson and of Mason's 'Responses' to Michael Peppiatt. The exhibition was accompanied by an audio-visual presentation of the work, *Les sculptures de Raymond Mason*, made by Bernard Clerc-Renaud.

The retrospective came about through the efforts of a curator of the Musée and a long-time supporter of Mason's, Gérard Régnier, who had written warmly of his work under his pen-name of Jean Clair and had already placed him in key exhibitions: *Papiers sur nature* in Paris in 1977, *La nouvelle subjectivité* in Brussels in 1979, and above all the Venice Biennale of 1982. Régnier wanted, not a display of the five big works in the five rooms of the Galeries Contemporaines (as at one stage seemed likely), but nothing less than a total survey of Mason's work, which he eventually obtained. Mason had delayed the installation of *The Crowd* in the Tuileries so that it could be included. *An Illuminated Crowd*, silhouetted against a giant wall painted in the same deep blue as the building in front of which it was to stand in Montreal, was visible from the street and attracted considerable attention. The whole exhibition drew a good audience from the start and, after a ten-day closing of the Museum occasioned by a strike, maximum attendance and long queues. No national newspaper reported it, however, despite the almost official status of a retrospective in such a venue, and the

94. *Panorama of Paris,* 1959

Museum itself failed to follow its normal practice of purchasing one of the works. Only Jean-Baptiste Para, in a chronicle published in the review *Europe*, not only recognised the merit of the work but ventured the kind of judgment on which one stands or falls, by suggesting that the exhibition would finally prove that Mason 'is to be reckoned among the greatest artists of our time'.[1]

A year after the erection of *An Illuminated Crowd*, Mason produced a nearly five-foot-tall relief of *New York City* in unpainted polyester resin, which would be followed in 1989 and 1991 by similar views of, respectively, *Rome* and *Paris*. These are a new form of big city relief which owe their origin partly to the larger resins of the Luberon, whose lightness first enabled Mason to produce works for the wall on this scale. They also continue a type of work where Mason excels, the urban panorama. His panoramas range widely in time and in the medium used. They begin in small bronzes of the

1950s and, while the masterpiece in the genre is no doubt the oil painting *Birmingham. In Memoriam*, the most sustained deployment of the particular gifts required to make them is found in a series of incomparable ink drawings. Many works of the Luberon, moreover, sculptures, watercolours and again drawings, are related to the type through being landscape panoramas, and need to be borne in mind for our purpose here, which is to pause before moving on to the three other large compositions so as to consider a gamut of works where further resources and further meanings of Mason's art are to be discovered.

The panoramas of Paris begin with a small plaster relief of 1953, later cast into bronze, which represents the view looking south from the Sacré-Coeur. So as to salute, not the streets but the whole of a city which he had known for seven years, Mason climbed to the best point from which to survey it. The artist is no longer 'man in a street' but almost man in the air, and although the scene is spread essentially across one's view, with

a decidedly horizontal row of façades all along the foreground (this is the year of the spreading-out, at eye level, of *Barcelona Tram*), the rapidly receding gullies of the roads draw the eye way in over a prospect shaped for allure. After the fine and relatively homogeneous buildings over most of the foreground, there appear in the middle distance great works of architecture rising above the roof lines, on the left and on the right, the two clusters seemingly joined, appropriately, by the long lines and emerging summits of the almost hidden Louvre. This is the place of art, one might say, itself extending across the view so as to colour one's reading of the whole. Beyond it are the further distances of the less distinguishable and then barely visible Left Bank, which merge into what look like surrounding hills, as if Mason also wishes to present the city in relation with the earth and its folds. The sky, too, participates in the scene, through the unceasing activity of its clouds. The bronze even glints with reflected light, and seems to lay its 'mantle' on the human city.

This is a somewhat lyrical elucidation of the work, whereas David Sylvester was probably right, in his review of the 1954 Beaux Arts Gallery exhibition where it was first shown, to compare it in style to 'the type of decoration sometimes found on cigarette boxes sold as souvenirs'. He was also right, however, to add that the work's effect is nevertheless 'altogether serious and rather compelling'.[2] Through the perfect organisation of its masses, and despite the shallowness of its relief (it is only an inch deep), or maybe because of the disparity between all its measurements and the immeasurable and literally unbounded scene which it represents, it does compel recognition of a certain view or vision of Paris, a generous and animated place seen, from above, to throng all around one and to meet, in a whole, the equally active presences of earth and sky.

The white epoxy resin *Paris* of 1991 returns to the same view, where the most conspicuous change after several decades is the Tour Maine-Montparnasse, noted without affection almost in the middle of the horizon and serving as intermediary for the eye between the rising dome of the Panthéon and the Eiffel Tower. The much larger scale of the work and the slightly higher angle push the middle distance further back and allow the illusionistic rendering to reach over the whole of the large foreground and so draw the eye more successfully into the fascinating crevices of the streets. Above all, the work is less severely composed. The astonishing control of visual complexity by which Mason clarifies the scene, the sureness of touch with which he plots street after street, building after building, disclose a structure, a shapeliness, in the city which is unforced and which includes both strong axes and insistent curves, and create a sculpture whose unity of composition comes likewise from a 'drawing' which elicits order without imposing it.

Panoramas present Mason with works where he has no need to 'multiply the complexity' because complexity of a sort is already in place. The principal achievements among the Paris works are the two big ink drawings of 1959, each of which has the title *Panorama of Paris from the Top of Sacré-Coeur*. They are virtuoso performances, revealing to the full that intellectual and manual power of Mason's draughtsmanship which underlies all his work. The larger of the two draws on an even wider view for a panorama, where a mastery of perspective and a particular concern for the structure of buildings gather selectively a mass of information into a single whole, which goes from lucid volumes of architecture and stretches of thoroughfare to merely suggestive but always readable strokes of the pen wherever distance becomes hazy. It is a view against the light, which contrasts a strong and, in the distance, glittering illumination with almost a second world of attractively mysterious shadow and shadowed spaces. The broad movements of the pen and brush as they impart differing degrees of shade with washes of ink bring an unexpected softness to the view, with a suggestion in places of Japanese calligraphy. A delicacy of shaping causes the scene to spread fan-like from a centre that descends to the base of the paper, where one is most aware of elegantly rendered trees, each one different in form and in treatment, to sides extending progressively as the edges of the view encroach on the whiteness of the paper. The paper itself is delicate, and its creases are visible.

In conveying a kind of large quietness, the play of light and dark also brings to the fore the black and white of the drawing, the absence of any colour but the sepia ink in wash of the foreground. This is part of the lessness of drawing, whose poverty in comparison with the visual world is even more marked than that of painting or sculpture, yet whose accompanying and paradoxical enrichment of that world is all the more remarkable. It is in (figurative) drawing that most subtly, one might think, the visual world reappears, or appears anew. Here, the reappearing is actually shown. The artist relinquishes control of the extent of the scene, which one sees as continuing beyond the right- and left-hand margins of the paper, but he causes the foreground to come into view, to issue from the whiteness of the paper, by beginning the representation of certain almost floating or ghostly buildings from higher than the ground, and by the sinuous passage across the foreground and up to the right which decides, for the sake of the drawing and without reference to the scene, where the drawing shall begin, and which seems to develop the rising view of Paris upwards from the properties of the paper. We pass from illusion, from looking at the drawing as if we were looking at Paris, to figuration, to the recognition that this drawing of Paris draws Paris indeed into a graphic fiction, into a fallacy whose aim is a possible truth. For what appears is not 'appearance'. This is not the sight of Paris which any tourist may have but an exaltation of the visual, a gradual causing to emerge, through the activity of mind and of the moving hand, of a city of light and shade, of a city raised, by being changed, from appearance to presence under the sun.

The other 1959 panoramic drawing of the same view is very different, partly because one is looking not into the sun but with it. It was drawn from even higher up, from the lantern rather than the dome of the basilica, and curtails the view, causing it to run to all the edges of the paper, or of the space for drawing, including the upper edge, where there is no horizon of invisibility or sky. A pure line drawing, it is more constructional, a shaping of the view which, in Mason's words, is 'almost abstract'. The decisive and, one guesses, rapid marks of the pen are less frequent in what shows as a more illuminated foreground and become more serried as one travels into the less distinct forms of the distance. Across the seemingly inextricable skein of the drawing two roads wind back into the scene, dividing it satisfyingly into three unequal sections and giving animation to the whole.

Once again Mason causes a city to appear, not with a few strokes of the pen but with a million, for here too he is, as it were, a 'maximalist'. A panorama is even particularly appropriate for his art, with its etymological claim to be a seeing of 'everything'. And this drawing, though not finer than the other, is more characteristic. He told Michael Brenson in 1976 that he considered drawing to be 'a graphic form of thought',[3] a statement which relates it primarily not to the thing seen but to the seeing mind, and even declared that 'a black line on a white paper' was for him 'an essential

95. *Panorama of Paris,* 1959

description of human thought'. One hears the draughtsman speaking, for whom drawing is not an activity among others but, because he is made like that, the vital exercise of mind and the way of understanding. But he also said, more specifically, that the black line needs the paper, 'the purity of the white', so as to have the quality of 'lightning'. Thought is not seen as contemplation but as action — as a series, indeed, of incisive, fulgurant acts — and it is not surprising that these comments arise from a consideration of the fundamental notion of energy and from a location of energy expressly in graphic work: 'what is the essential of energy in the plastic arts, it's drawing, of course.'

The panorama emerges from, and as, the energy of thought, yet of a thought which, as everywhere in Mason, is not turning on itself but is thinking of *something*, in this case a particular view of Paris. It also realises perfectly some further remarks of Mason's, also dating from 1976, made in a short note beginning 'Ce que j'aime dans le dessin', 'What I like in drawing'. What

he likes is 'rigour', a 'physical, articulated, three-dimensional attack on the paper', as found in Giacometti, where the pencil 'enters from all sides', rather than in Picasso or Matisse, whose lines undulating over the surface of the paper make for a drawing which is literally superficial.[4] The attack in the panorama is quick and dynamic, and one sees that the word 'three-dimensional' goes beyond Mason's apparently effortless command of perspective, which places all buildings as plausible volumes over a perfectly receding plane, and refers to the way his pen-strokes seem to cut into the paper as if raising and lowering it, so that the move is natural from drawing to relief sculpture.

There is a similar energy of thought in one of the many landscape drawings of the Luberon, *Montagne du Luberon* of 1962. As in the reliefs, the drawing brings into evidence the moving masses of the mountain, in part through its lines following the contours of the earth as if modelling them. The density of the drawing, its concentration on the narrow band of the mountain

96. *Rome,* 1989

97. *Paris,* 1991

stretching across an otherwise bare paper, the sheer insistence of the black lines as they judge the effects of
greater or less illumination but seem also, especially in
areas of intense black, to probe for a depth of energy
of presence, make of it one of the most telling of Mason's drawings, and one of the most alive. One of the
most mysterious also, since although the energy of the
drawing is Mason's, the energy which it reaches for and
seeks to capture is not human.

One more Parisian panoramic drawing is of special
interest, *Paris* of 1976, a view in the other direction,
towards the Sacré-Coeur, from a roof along the rue de
Rivoli to which Mason had climbed from the flat of
Henri Cartier-Bresson. (There is a classic Cartier-
Bresson photograph of Mason at work on the drawing,
witty as well as spatially inventive.) The Vendôme
Column, the Opera House and the Sacré-Coeur itself
punctuate a neat rising and then falling horizon, but
what dominates is the receding array of roofs. Their
slopes, strongly articulated at different angles by the

strips of zinc which cover them, both define the view
as seen typically from this height in Paris and send long
horizontal strokes over the work in many different and
aesthetically interesting directions. One sees a stylish
principle of selection in operation, and one sees also,
once again, Mason's mastery of architecture, an art he
would have been pleased to practise.

Although all of the Paris works choose and lay emphasis variously, they have a family likeness and need
to be examined together. The panoramas of London
are quite different. In 1956 Stephen Spender commissioned from Mason a number of drawings to illustrate
articles on Paris and London which would appear in
the issues of *Encounter* magazine for, respectively, April
and May 1957. A visit to the *Encounter* offices in the
Haymarket led to one of the London illustrations, to
another and more finished drawing and to the small
bronze *London* of 1956, all of which are variations on
the view from a window in a side street, looking in a
more or less southerly direction towards Big Ben. The

179

view is shaped, and one is drawn into it, by distinct and retreating lines, but what predominates here is the forms of the horizon. In the drawing in particular the nearby roofs are barely, though clearly, indicated, like the nearby façades, since in London it is not roofs one notices but a profusion of structures rising above them. The scene is made active through a flock of starlings and supremely through a flock, an exuberance, of spires, towers, columns, pediments, domes, chimneys and windy flags. Mason is again responding to the beauty of the copious, and emotion seems to be stirred here by the quite implausible, yet true, wealth of fantastic forms all jostling together as if in a world of their own, to be discovered by rising above the everyday city down below, perhaps on a magic carpet. The variegated forms even resemble members of a crowd, and suggest, though motionless, a similar vision of continual metamorphosis. This unforeseen sighting of a new world suddenly present in the old works well in the bronze, which sustains the vision in a relief more shallow than that of the bronze *Paris*, and even better in the drawing, where the festive character of the work is perfectly caught by the word 'COMEDY' written in the foreground, and accompanied underneath by elegant capitals and decorative oeils-de-boeuf. The word is simply the name of the theatre which happens to be there, yet it announces already that delight in casual and apposite words which is rife in the comedy of *St Mark's Place*.

The panoramas of Rome differ again. The white polyester resin *Rome* of 1989 is a view towards St Peter's and corresponds to the 1976 drawing *Rome, seen from the Villa Medici*. It concentrates on the strong forms of certain major edifices, rising to Michelangelo's great dome, and aims, over this scale (like the polyester *Paris*, it is nearly five feet wide) and over a scene which is large but not immense, for a strict accuracy of line and plane and volume. A powerful three-dimensional solidity is created by the interaction of protruding and depressed forms, by the gradual flattening of the relief towards the back and its ending in a clear sky, and by the standing-out of the buildings against the more indistinct farther bank of the Tiber, with a ridge in the distance of the pines of Rome. A tree in the foreground enhances the solidity of the whole by its bold presence.

The drawing is one of Mason's best, and is of great formal interest. It was done when he was staying in the Villa Medici at the invitation of Balthus, who was its Director, and is the view through a window of the main Medici bedroom. The window itself is present in the scene, and although this is unusual for Mason (who does not include the window of the *Encounter* offices), it is frequent in work by Balthus, and may be in part a homage to a host and a friend. With Mason, however,

the window serves first to draw in the spectator, and since the sill and the interior shutters are rendered in soft pencil lines which contrast with the sharp black lines of the buildings in the further foreground, they act rather in the same way as the deliberately blurred figures at the front of *The Crowd*. The joining of the double windows in the middle and their horizontal partitions also divide the scene into two separate frames, each with its prominent dome, while also emphasising the difference between the room and its view. Most importantly, the window itself is in perspective: the viewer is slightly to the left of centre so that the window's lines close towards the right. A deftly turned perspective is more expressive than perfect symmetry, and gives, as it were, an angle on to the scene. More than that, the frame is not at all a Baudelairean device for deepening the immensity of the view but a means of involving in the drawing the here and now, the place from which one looks. Because of the inclusion of the shutters, moreover, as the perspective goes away to the city — to the almost shadowless city of light and of art — it also comes in, and opens, towards the viewer. The effect resembles that of the buildings flanking the square in *Place de l'Opéra*, except that here there are two places, so that a drawing which presents a panoramic view also presents the place one occupies so as to see it, with even a suggestion of the two eyes through which one looks. It is rather like a drawing of the world and the self, where the self is itself a perspective.

The New York panoramas, finally — the white polyester relief sculpture of 1987 and its three previous drawings, which were done from the office window of William Louis-Dreyfus on the fifty-seventh floor of the Chrysler Building — use the 'portrait' format so as to emphasise, not surprisingly, the sheer verticals of Manhattan. Partly because of a clear and narrowing perspective down two canyons of the city, Lexington Avenue and Broadway, the viewer seems both to plunge and to remount, in a view where everything thrusts up into space and where the horizon consists of the great organ-pipes of the southernmost part of the island. The twin towers of the World Trade Center inevitably predominate, but having noticed the rise of the background from the beginning of Brooklyn Bridge on the left to the top of the towers on the right, which is a fact of the scene, one should then consider the rising of the Eiffel Tower at a similar point of the Paris panoramas, the carefully arranged rise to the Sacré-Coeur in the Paris drawing of 1976, the rise to St Peter's in the panoramas of Rome, and even the flying to the right of the birds in those of London. A depth of meaning of the panoramas is in that rise of the spirit before the spectacle of the human city and its architecture.

Mason's large and very large compositions, which are inevitably few in number, are all indices of the ambition of his art, of his aiming for the masterpiece born of months or years of effort, of his desire to make and to leave truly consequential 'statements'. The panoramas of great cities, of Paris, London, Rome, New York, are also ambitious in their own way. They celebrate the city for which Mason feels such spontaneous warmth not at ground level but from a height where the abundance of the visual world is both a delight and a genuine challenge to art.

Notes on Chapter X

[1] Jean-Baptiste Para, 'Raymond Mason, le relief du vivant', in *Europe*, nos. 679–680, November-December 1985, p. 179.

[2] David Sylvester, 'A New Sculptor', *The Times*, 15 February 1954.

[3] In Claude Bernard 1977.

[4] In Centre Georges Pompidou 1985, p. 77.

98. *London,* 1994

99. Georgetown Plaza, Washington D.C. (northern wall), 1988. Photo: Maxwell Mackenzie

XI

HISTORY

The *Twin Sculptures for Georgetown, Washington DC* are another response to a great city, where height and the angle of view, in this large and indeed double composition, make for a quite new sounding of historical time. The next two works will be linked by the fact that *Latin Quarter* concerns 'the world immediately surrounding'[1] Mason in his present home, and *Forward* the world of his childhood and youth, but it is worth noting now that *Twin Sculptures* and *Forward* are also linked as works exploring history and inquiring into the means and the meanings of that exploration. In both works, moreover, history appears, in the full range of the word's senses, as monumental.

Though completed in 1988, the *Twin Sculptures* take one back to 1976, a year when Mason was working on *A Tragedy in the North* and also on another monument, for Guadeloupe, and when he was commissioned to provide a sculpture for a new plaza in the small township of Georgetown, which stands on the edge of Washington of which it was the cradle. The commission came from the Louis-Dreyfus Property Group, for whom the architectural firm of Skidmore, Owings and Merrill was erecting a pair of buildings, one commercial, the other a luxury hotel in the Canadian chain The Four Seasons. This is an appropriate moment to note the great importance of William Louis-Dreyfus in Mason's career. He has been the major collector of Mason's works, many of which he has placed inside his numerous buildings in France and North America, while two of the most important are on permanent public show: his cast of *The Crowd* standing outside 527 Madison Avenue in New York, and one of his casts of *The Departure* on loan to the church of St Eustache in Paris. He has also commissioned two of the three successfully completed monuments, the *Twin Sculptures* and *An Illuminated Crowd*. Mason's career would certainly have been different but for Louis-Dreyfus's judgment in realising early the value of his work, and generous activity on his behalf over many years.

The successful outcome of the Georgetown venture,

as it happens, was for a long time in doubt, and remained so as late as 1985, when Mason exhibited in his Paris retrospective a series of preparatory works dating from the period 1976 to 1981, along with a large-scale maquette of 1985 showing his twin reliefs in the context of the whole Georgetown Plaza project. Once the commission finally became a reality, Mason sculpted the two elements in plaster and, re-applying the procedure of *An Illuminated Crowd*, reworked them in the intermediate size to which the Haligon Studios enlarged them and then worked them further, and painted them, when cast full-size into resin. They were installed, twelve years after the original commission, in June 1988, and in 1989 were very nearly removed, by one of those reverses which Mason has often suffered, which frequently dog the careers of major artists and so contribute to the heroic portrait. The reason was partly that the United States Commission for Fine Arts should have been consulted about a work visible from a public highway in the historic district of Georgetown, partly that the colours were found 'aggressive' and the whole 'inappropriate' to the site. Although such comments can amuse by the precision of their inaccuracy, it may have been only through the testimonies of a number of prominent public figures, including keepers from major museums and galleries, that the work was saved.

Mason's first thought on receiving the commission was to search for a subject, an event, in accordance with his enduring conviction about what makes for genuine art and what speaks to a public, and to do so by studying the history of Georgetown. He discovered the story of the French architect and engineer Pierre Charles L'Enfant, who had enrolled in the American revolutionary army in 1776, at the age of twenty-two, and had risen to the rank of major. He became the friend of Washington, who later chose him to draft the plans of the federal capital! The two men resided for a month in Suter's Tavern, Georgetown, to review the marshes where the city was to be built. The sculpture would be in two parts, on identical walls facing each other across the plaza, one high up and representing the vivid turmoil of the battles against the British leading to the revolutionary heroes Franklin and Jefferson and finally to L'Enfant and Washington themselves looking across the site of the future city; the other at ground level and showing a modern crowd, some of whom would look up at the visionary scene descried in the clouds.

For all three of the monumental commissions for which he did not already have a subject — Guadeloupe, Georgetown and Birmingham — Mason chose historical sculpture, and immersed himself in an event or a series of events. He said in the lecture on Rodin: 'A major work is a totality. A great theme fires the artist's first thoughts. More often than not literary and historical because in this way he has precise knowledge with which he can deal'. Mason values precise knowledge for its power to focus, to found meaning and to home in on a particular time, to 'the moment lived by man'. *Monument for Guadeloupe* may be a visionary work, yet it is based on numerous, documented specifics, all of which are grounded for the viewer in lines of poetry inscribed around the base of the maquette (from a sonnet to Delgrès by the Guadeloupean poet Gilbert de Chambertrand), which conclude with a whole line devoted to the date: 'C'était le vingt-huit mai de l'an mil huit cent deux', 'It was the twenty-eighth of May in the year eighteen hundred and two'. The exact date figures, indeed, on a great many of Mason's works. For the present work it matters to him, to judge from what he writes of it, that, with a view to studying the plans of the new city, Washington and L'Enfant settled into Suter's Tavern in Georgetown, and that they remained there from 28 March to 30 April 1791. He clearly assumes that meanings of the human situation are to be discovered, investigated and made available for use in human actions originating in the actualities of living, in the ineluctable conditions of time and place, and that the imagination itself — Sidney's 'high flying liberty of conceit' — is the more powerful when it agrees to 'deal with' reality and its insistent but nourishing facts.

The assumption is unfashionable, and certainly alien to post-modern suspicion, to the reduction of 'facts' and 'reality', as of 'world' and of 'truth', to the status of linguistic figments. Equally unfashionable, and disdainful in this case of Romantic notions of the artist, is Mason's attitude to commissions. In the course of an important article published in 1992, he quotes a fellow practitioner as saying: 'the work must come from the artist. One mustn't provide works for public commissions, because that is to fall into a kind of academicism'.[2] I dare say nearly all of us respond warmly to a statement such as that, since most artists, of any art, and most critics and members of 'the public' expect the major artist in particular to be pursuing his own vision,

and wish him not to be distracted from his personal task by requests for work which is apparently to come from somewhere other than deep within. Yet Mason dismisses such talk as 'intellectual stupidity', arguing boldly that a public sculpture should be 'half sculpture, half public', and although his standing against the tide and shocking rejection of what we may be in the habit of taking for granted require a quite discomfiting change of mind, he is surely right. The lapsing of patronage by the Church and the Court has accustomed us to the idea of the career artist and of the private genius, and it is true that the societies in which artists work have radically changed. Yet it also remains true that very many of the works of the past universally acknowledged as especially fine were the results of commissions, and this is signally the case with all the works which Mason himself considers — and he is hardly alone in this — as the supreme masterpieces. Rather than noting the fact as belonging to a particular phase of art history (a phase which turns out to be curiously long), one might think, first, that in his actual commissions, which account for three out of his eight most complex works, Mason renews the tradition and shows how it might function even now.

The addressing of a public through a large and recognisable theme is the constant of his artistic activity, and one sees why, already in the 1960s, he should admire the quite different work of the poster artist A. M. Cassandre. In the text for an exhibition of Cassandre's work which Mason and his wife organised in their gallery in 1966, he suggests (in French) that, through the very fact of being a poster artist, Cassandre brings together 'the essential elements of artistic creation: the subject and the audience', while also submitting to the most obvious demand of the genre, that he renounce 'self-expression'. From this finding of an unexpected and interesting lesson in a minor art, of which others might have said, on the contrary, that it is minor precisely because it disbars the artist from expressing himself, Mason reflects on the large consequences for modern art in general: 'Cassandre has resumed the dialogue with the crowd. This is the essential step. The lost dimension of art can be recovered.' Mason's whole oeuvre is an attempt to recover that lost dimension. And for there to be a dialogue, the artist must have, of course, to use another expression of Mason's which the sophisticated have learnt not to use, 'something to say'. If he is living and thinking and feeling always as well as he is able, and continually sounding the possibilities of his art by learning the laws and virtualities of the medium and perhaps the sense which have made him the kind of artist — sculptor, musician, poet even — that he is, a commission can energise what is there, and may even be the occasion for its appearing. Without seeking self-expression or the furtherance of a solitary quest (which for some artists is the way, undeniably), he can still be working as a whole person and with entire belief and commitment.

One also learns from Mason to extend the sense of a commission. Most or perhaps all of his works have been commissioned in the sense that the invitation and often the imperative to make them has come from outside, from a reality — such as the mining disaster at Liévin or the nature of Les Halles and of its loss — which has itself demanded expression. While seeing the world in the way that only he can see it, because of what he is through his various inheritances, Mason has explored less his view of things than the things themselves, as presences of a world already there and more genial than us.

Here is another simple and apparently unacceptable idea which Mason enables one to think. Not that the question divides neatly into either/or. To acknowledge the wisdom and efficacy of Mason's approach is not to disparage other approaches as foolish and futile. Nor does the approach make true judgment easier in any particular case. Is Cézanne, for instance, a thoroughly

100. Georgetown Plaza, Washington D.C. (southern wall), 1988

modern painter following his lonely way and producing 'Cézannes', or was he too commissioned, as it were, by the Montagne Sainte-Victoire?

Because the monument for Guadeloupe remains as a maquette and the *Illuminated Crowd* is painted in a uniform light ochre, the Georgetown sculpture is Mason's first monumental work in polychromy. Among his works it is also, as always, unique. It is the only large-scale composition in low rather than high relief and, with a considerable panache of originality, it is also a single work in two parts. The two-fold nature of the piece, though not quite so startling as the idea of representing an explosion, is essential to all its effects and meanings. It serves, first, to transfigure the architectural space. The rhythms of the lower part, which faces south, move across to the right and to a pointing arm which extends beyond the corner of the wall and stretches out towards the upper part. As Mason writes, it 'should link the two halves of the complex and give dynamic movement across the plaza'.[3] The upper part, which faces north so as to be visible from Main Street and which is brilliantly painted and lit up at night, as well as raising the eyes to the top of an otherwise bare wall, directs attention yet further, through a second outstretched arm which is in line with Pennsylvania Avenue and points towards the Capitol. The two parts taken together literally give the place its bearings, energising the space from one building to another, lifting the eyes from crowd level and from the actual to a higher level of heroic individuals and of vision, and orienting the old city of Georgetown with respect to the capital city. Meanings cover the walls and reveal the site, and they are the meanings not of the artist (only) but of the passers-by and of the place itself.

All of Mason's monuments, in fact, join forces with the locations which they enter and elucidate. Even for Montreal an already developed work is modified so as to comply with a cascade of steps, which then receive for themselves the meanings of the sculpture. *Forward* will correspond thoroughly with Centenary Square and even with the whole of Birmingham. The *Twin Sculptures* also set out to 'decorate' the plaza (the modest word is Mason's own),[4] and on this level too they operate perfectly. A free-standing sculpture in the middle of the plaza would only have had flat walls to react with, whereas the complex is now made one and the higher sculpture in particular brings 'undulation to the severe bricking of the façade'.[5] It is also interesting that L'Enfant should be indicating in thought 'what is considered to be one of the finest city plans ever conceived',[6] given Mason's continuing concern for architecture and for the human city, and his own talent for drawing a panorama.

The work is the culmination of Mason's desire that a sculpture occupy space by reaching out into it, through turreting heads, upraised or outstretched arms, or even open mouths and vivid eyes, since it not only controls the whole of a plaza but doubles the pointing arm so as to reach, high in the air, for the whole of Washington. Remarkably, all of Mason's large compositions take at least one dimension of his work as far as one could imagine it. This dual composition is also the culmination of looking. The viewer, for once, is not looked at — though several looks in the lower sculpture are coming in his direction so as unemphatically to make him what he already is: a passer-by, an onlooker, and himself part of a crowd — since his attention is needed for the looking which occurs within the work, where he is invited to notice that the looks over the left-hand side and over the front are mostly unremarkable, with certain eyes reduced to slits by the sunlight, whereas towards the right, beginning with the wide-open eyes and raised eyebrows of a young woman seen next to a man's conspicuous spectacles, many of the figures have open and pupilled eyes as they gaze, despite the sun, upwards to vision. The lower part of the sculpture looks at the upper, and the upper part looks elsewhere. This is clearly the imaginative centre, the *idea*, of the work, whose creative moments have been the decision to 'relieve' the two walls, the choice of the particular story of Pierre L'Enfant, and the thought of having the story observed by a crowd.

There are many things to see, however, on the way to that centre. The crowd of the lower part is the first genuine crowd — people who happen to be together in the street, are not assembled for any purpose — since *The Crowd* itself; is indeed, with the passers-by of *St Mark's Place*, the only other accidental crowd since the moment when Mason's art, in *The Departure of Fruit and Vegetables*, began not only to depict individuals but to find ways of bringing them together for some kind of communion of spirit: to save, in fact, the modern crowd, which otherwise is random and anonymous. The crowd in Georgetown multiplied considerably from the first small bronzes of 1976 and 1980 to the picture-size study in painted epoxy resin of 1986, and includes some thirty-four figures. The composition again gives the impression of energy, of continual change, of metamorphosis, with passages from stillness to lunging movement, from cursory to dramatic gestures, from figures simply facing each other to a real confrontation, and from near to far, yet the purpose of the relatively low relief is not to draw in the viewer but to engage his attention for the meanings of the crowd and for the crowd's own attention to something else.

One sees, too, the shading, 'drawing' and pared

Major Pierre Charles l'Enfant
1754 – 1825

modelling of this lower sculpture, which ask to be understood. It is appropriate that, looking towards the visionary, the figures on the right should also be looking into the sun, and the fact that the work is not free-standing in the manner of *An Illuminated Crowd* allows Mason to suggest this by painting shadows on bodies turned away from the light or cast into shadow by other bodies. The shadows are purplish-red, in part no doubt because black shadows would have been visually uninteresting (even on Mason's fully polychrome work, shadows are never black), in part because red for Mason is something like the colour of life. All the colour on this lower work is red, in fact, so that one finds shadow 'hollowing eyes', as he writes of it doing in 'La Foule', with red blobs which are the equivalent of the black blobs of his ink drawings. Red is a minimal but striking colour for that part of the work whose role is to intimate human incompletion and to direct the viewer's gaze to another part where all is plenitude and colour.

As colour is strategically reduced to red, so the 'drawing' on the sculpture appears in the form of simple lines, picked out in red, which convey numerous folds in clothes and the clefts of various facial features, notably wrinkles on foreheads. The multiplicity of such lines, and their use to trace contours between, most noticeably, hair and face, suggest drawing quite forcibly and, in a work where the modelling is shallow, they also bring to an otherwise smooth surface the necessary incision and variety. This drawing has always been a feature of Mason's sculptural imagination, but lines etched in red against a single other light colour only occur in the small version of *An Illuminated Crowd*, where the colour scheme becomes more complex as one moves back, and in areas of the last two completed monuments: the lower

part of the *Twin Sculptures* and the advance section of *Forward*.

The modelling is also simplified, bold, and frankly stylised. It resembles that of the monuments in Montreal and Birmingham, to the point where one realises that there is a kind of modelling which Mason has developed specifically for monumental work. The cleanness here of line and form again heightens the drama of what is in fact quite an intense and stirring crowd — consider, for example, the man advancing towards the viewer as if wading through light and shadow — and again combines a suggestion of the heroic dimension of pre-classical Greek sculpture with a sense of the contemporary: the work is clearly produced in the period of, say, Pop Art. The figures are also larger than life-size, and are placed slightly above eye level. Whereas the simplifying of colour and drawing suggests the deficiency of this ordinary crowd, in comparison at least with what some of them see, the simple modelling also serves to enhance them, and to give them their own human grandeur in the here and now.

The viewer also sees that he is to look to the right. He enters through the back and rightward-turning head of a man who was present in the crowd from the earliest bronze of 1976 and who recalls the similar figures of *Barcelona Tram* and *Place de l'Opéra*. The sculpture also turns the corner of the wall, and if one comes to it from the other side one is still drawn to the pointing arm, by its surprising and exciting position, and by the rise towards it of the few figures of this short continuation. When the whole is in view, the sculpture seems to arrow towards the arm, or to narrow like a prow towards a woman posed, by a happy touch of the imagination, as a figurehead, her head raised, her arms and hands held stiffly backwards, her body leaning forward, the whole made plausible, as one realises on approach, by the fact that her husband's arms are around her waist. The arm itself, for which one is also prepared by a cluster of conspicuous arm gestures about the centre of the larger part of the work, is a long spiral leading elsewhere.

It leads upwards to further spiral forms of clouds, smoke, feathers, mane, lace, wigs and hair. For everything above is more dramatic and literally more colourful, the polyurethane rather than matt acrylic paint (necessary so as to resist extremes of weather) conveying the angry heightened red of the English uniforms against the blue of the American, the dying, whitening faces, the swirl of gun-smoke and the confusion of forms in battle, which recall and finally use what Mason had conceived in the maquette for Guadeloupe. This upper part exploits the fact that it turns the corner of the wall, by stretching itself between the extended arm and open hand of a cavalry officer on the right and the pointing arm and hand of Pierre L'Enfant on the left, and by causing the faces of two opposing soldiers to confront each other at the very angle of the building. The two arms also serve to gather into one the long and varied narrative.

In *Twin Sculptures*, too, there is a will to overcome. Violence and death — which occur already, as in *An Illuminated Crowd*, at one end of the work while a pointing arm leads away from them at the other end — are assumed into a larger narrative aiming beyond them. From the battle there emerge the radial plan of the city and the radical project of a new republic. The American flag is formed from the colours of conflict. And perhaps this is even a scene of reconciliation. The dying man is British, but the redcoats contribute to the colours of the enemy flag, and those colours belong equally to the Union Jack.

That the upper part is an expressly fictive work is in fact central to the whole, since what is at issue here is history, and the exploration of history as memory and as imagination. The two parts of the sculpture enact and visualise history as memory by describing two moments in time, one of which is remembered by the other. Separated by centuries, they are linked by the awareness of some of the lower figures, which travels within the viewer's awareness across the space between. For whatever we conceive history to be, like everything else it is nothing for us until it enters experience, and we can only experience it, like everything else, here and now. Hence the contemporaneity and basically commonplace nature of the crowd at our level, and a higher level which is the exteriorisation of their thought, of what they raise to recollection. Had the sculpture consisted solely of the upper part, not only would the work have been more limited but the upper part itself, even if identical to what

101. Study for southern wall, 1987

it is now, would have been different. Everything really does depend on that 'dynamic movement across the plaza', whereby the scene on high becomes not simply an historical sculpture but an image of memory.

Since the scene at which someone is pointing, moreover, is itself pointing, as we gaze into the past we also gaze into a future. As with *An Illuminated Crowd*, it is both sculpturally more interesting and humanly more alluring if what we glimpse is not entirely defined and remains absent. Had the narrative above been complete, the sculpture would have come to an end in a completed moment. The further allure here, however, is that as the viewer travels in that strange new tense, he 'sees' both the future-in-the-past of the perfect city and the present reality of Washington D.C.; both the birth of a nation and the fruit of promise. The revelation in the clouds is at once of destiny and of origin, but the viewer can see what origin has become by observing destiny around him. Some sadness is involved, and the inevitably troubled present may even be visible in the past, since behind L'Enfant there is already a crowd, of what may be ordinary soldiers or future citizens of the Republic. One has raised his arm, perhaps for victory, or to greet the President, but perhaps also to protest.

By the arc of its movement through both of its elements, the sculpture directs attention at what the future in the past always implies — at the conditional — and by arresting movement at the moment of vision, of aspiration and, very pointedly, of new beginning, the *monument* appropriates several meanings from the origin of the word in the Latin *monere:* to remind, to advise, to warn. By disclosing a remembered future it makes continuously present, to the gaze of those who are prepared to see, the suspended moment of the achievable.

It is this admonitory as well as celebratory nature of the work which accounts for the presence of violence in the upper part, but also for the relative ease of its overcoming, compared in particular to the lethal heroism of *Monument for Guadeloupe* and the grieving recognition of *A Tragedy in the North*. What matters most is the level of undertaking and the future that follows success. It also explains the presence of an individual tale where success is combined with failure: that of L'Enfant himself, who was eventually dismissed from the work and died poor and forgotten through having neglected to establish a copyright on his designs, and yet whose city was built. The 'Odyssey' of this young Frenchman, Mason writes, 'should be remembered'.[7] It also makes clear, finally, that the crowd below are just as much the subject of the work as the historical personages above, and one understands more sharply now a statement of Mason's which it is easy to pass over.

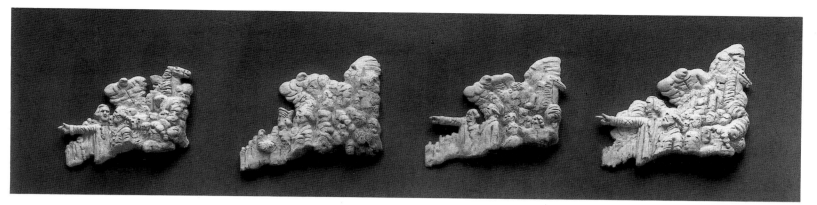

102. Polychrome studies for northern wall, 1987

In 'Sur le contenu' ('On content'), which dates from 1977 and so from the year following the Washington commission, he writes, as elsewhere, of the 'impoverishment of the subject' consequent upon the common disintegration of 'tradition and beliefs'. He continues, however: 'But there are others! If we have abandoned the old beliefs this is no doubt because we believe that we possess new ones. Day by day people are a little more free. Why is it surprising, then, if I consider them the most significant subject for sculpture'?[8] One might have expected a move from the discarding of religious beliefs to the adoption of humanism, but it is the crowd itself, profiting daily from Delgrès's cry of 'Vive la liberté!' commemorated the previous year, which becomes the focus of attention and the subject of sculpture. The loss of belief leads to the depicting of the crowd, which sometimes looks and waits.

We are also in the presence of history as imagination. Members of the crowd read their destiny in the sky, and their searching of the clouds, of those insubstantial forms which have always been noted for their hermeneutic gifts, brings to the fore and even mimes the role of imagination in the discovery and appropriation of history. They see in white vapours a riot of colour, the clashing of armies, the emergence of a nation — with the face of a black man behind Jefferson — and the future transformation of marshlands. The whole, from the suffering of disorder to the surveying of the possible, is composed by distance into serenity, and Mason seems to invite the viewer himself to use his imagination, and to discern in the highest billow of cloud as it turns the corner of the building the feathered headdress and the noble and melancholy face of an Indian chief.

And there is a further level of imagination, since Mason also writes that, in the clouds above, the crowd not only sees decisive events but 'reads the epic poem' of its beginning.[9] Again, this is not loose talk by a sculptor. Not only are the celebrated names of the literally elevated story accompanied by a suggested host of lesser figures, but reference seems to be made quite specifically to the *Aeneid*, where a final victory leads most famously to the founding of a nation by the originating 'father'. The very conspicuous dying enemy soldier may even recall Turnus, killed by Aeneas in the last lines of Virgil's poem, his body 'becoming limp'. Many of Mason's works gain stature from the momentousness of their subject, and it is interesting that, in a period when the two major kinds of poem according to classical and renaissance literary thought have been a problem for writers, he has referred explicitly to two of his sculptures as a 'tragedy' and an 'epic'. I earlier characterised *Birmingham. In Memoriam* and *The Departure of Fruit and Vegetables* as elegies, *A Tragedy in the North*, the *Monument for Guadeloupe* and *The Aggression* as tragedies, and *The Grape-Pickers* as a georgic, with a partly alien terminology offered simply as an aid to reflection. *Latin Quarter*, as we shall see, would be an urban pastoral, where the country itself is present in a huge tree, and where problems are real but are resolved in communal gaiety and in a kind of dance. It is even political pastoral, in the manner of *The Month of May in Paris*, whose very title is a reminder of the genre and a further reference to literature. The other three final large compositions are all, in different ways, epic. *An Illuminated Crowd* is epic by its totalising ambition and by the multiplicity of its characters, while its final figure rising from darkness is the hero as origin. *Twin Sculptures* and *Forward* are additionally, as it were, 'history plays', like the *Monument for Guadeloupe*, and we shall need to consider the reasons for the particular orientation of that latest phase.

If the imagination is capable of epic, of a world, that is, whether in history or in poetry, where names are made, Mason describes the crowd below as 'anonymous'.[10] It is quite literally shallow, a spread-out with little distance, and is divided, moralistically, between those who see and those who do not. In the shadows

189

and strong sunlight where they walk, a first glance suggests that those who protect themselves from the light have a perfectly straightforward reason for doing so, but a second glance reveals the wide-open eyes of the cloud-gazers. A man round the corner looks downwards while holding a newspaper. Why should he look up since he already possesses a form of history, the chronicle of yesterday, the indiscriminate news which has already grown old? One man is aghast at what he perceives, and covers his mouth with a dramatic gesture reminiscent of *Les Epouvantées*, as if appalled by something that the others do not perceive, or by the distance from himself of epic possibility. Two men in conflict at the rear recall the face-to-face of the American and British soldiers above, but without the motive of war, and seem to demonstrate in this work, too, the 'rowdiness at the back of any crowd'.

The crowd below looks towards the light of history, as reviewed by the imagination, by turning from shadow — like the man by whose back we enter and who is divided between shadow and light — while remaining nevertheless where shadow persists, and continues to mark the passing of time in the actual and the everyday. For there, after all, is where we do live, and although the doubling of the work enables Mason to draw on one of the most enduring of all metaphors, which places the real world below and the better world above, in the only one of his sculptures to look upwards, what the characters see is the clouds of our own skies.

Even the second of the two out-stretched arms is pointing, like that of *An Illuminated Crowd* and like the gaze of Delgrès and the stare of Solitude in the *Monument for Guadeloupe*, not upwards but horizontally in front, to life in time. The work of memory and of imagination is to effect an enlargement of the possible in the here and now.

In this above all intelligent sculpture, which may, indeed, be more rewarding intellectually than visually (through its offer, not of a convenient peg for the thoughts of the viewer but of the opportunity to explore a thought which it has already emplaced), Mason contrives, while satisfying a commission, to interpret the crowd once more, and to interpret history. He also interprets his own art, and art in general. The upper piece draws attention to itself as a work of art. In turning the corner of the building it recalls a narrative capital high up on a column, and it confirms the hint by the face-to-face of the soldiers. Its height can equally suggest a pediment — one, futhermore, which has retained its colour — and also a fresco situated, like some of those which Mason most admires, way above eye-level in a tall chapel. And if the upper piece re-enacts, in a modern sculpture, a small history of essential art forms, the lower piece, quite literally, draws attention to it. The extended arm, which has been a signature of Mason's sculpture since *St Mark's Place*, points away from the work but also points for the first and only time, at another part of the work, so that as one negotiates the plaza one is invited by a sculpture to look at a sculpture. This is, in fact, Mason's most obviously modern and, indeed, modernist work. Unashamedly self-referential, the sculpture is a trope of sculpture, whereby a comparatively realist representation of an urban crowd points away from itself to the manifestation of what even realist art must always be: a fiction, an eliciting of significance, a reading in the clouds of the imagination, a transformation of 'precise knowledge' into accurate vision.

But then there is the second arm. For if the work refers to itself, it also, supremely, refers away from itself. Both references are necessary, and the double reference is a complete poetics of representation. Mason has always insisted that he is not concerned to advance 'sculpture' as such — since sculpture, as such, does not exist[11] — but he has always pointed, at one and the same time, to the all-important inner structure of a work, to its essential abstraction, to the primacy of the aesthetic, and to the all-important need to go outwards to a public and to the world which artist and public share. In its concern for itself and even greater concern for the life on which it impinges, *Twin Sculptures* is an allegory of Mason's art, and one might also take it as an allegory of the well-being of modernism, of a heightened self-awareness serving and heightening an awareness of the real.

It is also an allegory of the spectator. Certain figures of the lower sculpture are themselves spectators, not for the first time in Mason's work, and in so far as they represent the spectator as Mason desires him to be, they reveal him as someone who looks hard and long, not as a solitary individual but as a member of a crowd, and above all not as an aesthete agog for a new art object, but as a whole person hungry for light, for gravitas, for largeness of meaning.

It is fitting, finally, that history, art and the crowd with its thoughts, should come together in a single sculpture. History and art meet to the extent that they are both activities of the imagination, and they meet again in the idea of creative memory. As mother of the Muses, Memory nurtures both Clio and Calliope, both history and epic poetry, and as certain figures of the crowd 'remember', they assemble the originating events of their nation in such a way as to create understanding of the beginning and of our relation to all the possibles of time, and they cause the clouds in the sky to tell a story as large as life.

Notes on Chapter XI

[1] 'Responses', in Arts Council 1982, p. 12.

[2] *Revue des deux mondes*, November 1992, p. 91. To the general heading for a series of articles by various contributors: 'L'art contemporain, pour qui?' Mason added, as his own title: ' . . . et pour quand?'

[3] Birmingham 1989, p. 103, and 'Twin Sculptures for Georgetown, Washington D.C.', in Marlborough 1991.

[4] Birmingham 1989, p. 102, and 'Twin Sculptures . . . '

[5] Birmingham 1989, p. 103.

[6] *Ibid.*

[7] 'Twin Sculptures . . . '

[8] In Centre Georges Pompidou 1985, p. 78.

[9] *Ibid.* 'Distant epic' in Birmingham 1989, p. 103.

[10] Birmingham 1989, p. 103, and 'Twin Sculptures . . . '

[11] In Claude Bernard 1977.

103. *The Crowd,* southern wall, 1988

104. *Boulevard Saint-Michel,* 1986

THE LATIN QUARTER

One's first impression of *Latin Quarter*, on the other hand, is of being looked at, and of being drawn into a scene magically curved by perspective. As students march past, their successive rows fan inwards and backwards to a vanishing point behind the building opposite, but not far behind, in a visual world suddenly compacted just in front of the viewer and intense with colourful life. Even the rue Soufflot, which moves away at a right angle from the boulevard St Michel on whose pavement one is supposed to be standing, has been enchanted into the perspective cone. Parallels have always narrowed rapidly in Mason, but never so coercively as here. In the large composition which most resembles his early street reliefs, one is attracted as if by a magnet into a crowd which passes across the picture plane in the world of the here and now, and then summoned, by following its direction, into the distance of a disappearing road. Because of the scale of the work and the depth of its relief, by walking to the right oneself one can experience the sculptural and kinetic pleasure of discovering the length of that road, and of sensing that, through its being raked back into the work, the distance into which it recedes is a further possibility of the familiar world.

The hyperbole of the perspective brings a similar excess to the movements of the human figures. The young man on the extreme left has his body and one leg facing front while his head and the other leg turn right. His bent leg makes an angle of ninety degrees. The effect of this posture, which may at first seem merely stilted, is to swing the whole work round and forward and to suggest, by the increased expressivity of awkward gestures, a greater than usual animation in the marching lines. Figures on the right, poised with their knees raised unrealistically high, complete the turning arc and, despite their apparent stiffness, gather the animation and carry it forward. One might again think of Bruegel (whom Mason greatly admires),[1] and in particular of his *Peasant Dance*, which had already suggested the kissing lovers of *The Departure of Fruit and Vegeta-*

bles and which may have contributed here — in the only one of Mason's large sculptures where there is a good deal of walking by entirely visible bodies — to the setting in motion of the motionless. These thoroughly contemporary figures have nevertheless found ways of moving which are Mason's and not Bruegel's, and he has also managed to avoid the exemplary 'walking men' of Rodin and Giacometti.

The compressed perspective becomes necessary because of the new angle on the crowd. In *The Crowd* itself the lines of passers-by approach the viewer head-on and withdraw from him as on a pavement, whereas here people walk past in profile in successive lines along a road. (Both sculptures represent a crowd on the boulevard St Michel, in fact, one coming down, one going up.) For the first time Mason represents the other inspiriting view of 'men in a street', his forty years' experience of the 'march and counter-march of students', where the spatial facts are quite different: 'As wave after wave went by I experienced the proximity of the nearest student to my gaze then, tunnelled between each row, a distant glimpse of the opposite pavement. This tunnelling always seemed to be a sculptural possibility'.[2] One knows the tunnelling from many other works and its central importance in Mason's spatial imagination (a 'tunnel' draws one into a work, opens and explores the dimensions of a visual world and promises distance, rather like a real street drawing one into itself), and one might also note the persistent metaphor of the waves. Seen from the side of the work, the marchers are once again a sea of heads; seen from the front, they pass by like breakers. Because of that ever-changing proximity, the 'composition must beat out the rhythm of inclined angles to suggest the march onward', and the movement is also assisted by the raised feet that one sees on looking down the otherwise empty tunnels, by such studied details as the fact that the longest stride occurs to the right of the contrasting stillness of a tree and that the person striding is impelled by a hand pushing in the direction of the work as in *An Illuminated Crowd,* and finally by the stretching of the sculpture

105. *Latin Quarter,* 1987

between figures on the left leaning back and figures on the right leaning forwards, and between the colours of the flag on one side and the same colours repeated on the clothes of the young man on the other.

The viewer participates in the animation of the figures, who move across to the right in orderly fashion. Is there a reference here to the more solemn procession of *The Departure*? That conspicuous hand with the spread fingers also occurs at the front of the work, like the hand of the man with the gouged eyes, while the youth on the far right carries a rucksack strapped to his shoulders which can remind one of the man with the overalls and a laden cart. For if Mason's emotion goes out in the earlier sculpture to the market workers, to the place of plenty which they serve, and to the loss of that 'paradise', it goes out here to another paradise, that of the students, of their Quarter, and of a youth which is not lost but marches past and round in continual renewal.

As another kind of procession, the students are also, and even more clearly, a spectacle, while all across the rear of the work are spectators. A demonstration is a form of street theatre, in which a crowd organises itself so as to be seen, and *Latin Quarter* culminates Mason's delight in bringing to the fore, and into the action, the looking which is the main affair of the visual arts. Yet he emphasises even more plainly the fact of being looked at. In a work situated a few paces from his home,

he causes a young man at the front to welcome the viewer more frankly and smilingly than ever before, returning thereby to the perhaps rather strangely smiling man of *The Crowd* and also renewing acquaintance with the beginning: *Man in a Street*, a first relief where the observed already looks back at the observer. The real surprise, however, is not that the young man's gaze is immediately doubled in that of the person behind him, but that almost wherever one looks one meets someone else's gaze. Even spectators, who are ostensibly interested in the students, seem to lean so as to get a sight of the viewer, in the same way that certain of the students crane their necks. The tunnel in front of the viewer, which might have emptied the sculpture as did the alley in the original design for *The Grape-Pickers*, takes one past gazing students to spectators on the far pavement who seem equally concerned to discover one's presence. An additional perspective cone is created, in fact, on this side of the work, by all those gazes focusing on a second vanishing point, one's own eye. Here is another entirely original sculptural form — which Mason, as always, will not repeat — an unprecedented means of renewing and increasing the power of a work both to lure the spectator in and to go out in his direction.

The advancing cone reminds one again of the 'all-important frontal dimension between sculpture and onlooker', which had led most remarkably to the blurred foreground figures of *The Crowd* and to the Pole of

194

A Tragedy in the North, with his seeming attempt to restrain a woman fleeing out of the sculpture altogether into the viewer's world, and which leads here to yet further prodigious inventiveness. It also reminds one that Mason's work, as it offers itself to the viewer, has a design on him and expects to control his response. It is fitting that Mason should describe the effect of gazes which converge on the viewer by an ancient term from rhetoric: they suggest 'the persuasion of exuberant youth'. The young man at the front, like the miner of *A Tragedy in the North* though in a quite different work, comes out of the sculpture bearing its message, and also seeking to sway one into the same youthful exuberance.

Taken together, the two perspective cones pull the work through and beyond realism. Whereas *An Illuminated Crowd* begins in a possible street scene but moves quickly to overt symbolism in a site of the imagination, the realist figures of *Latin Quarter* remain in their world, which is that of student demonstrations in the locality where they occur, but just as the scene has been seized by a powerful charm which bows it inwards so that it becomes a turning and eternally returning place of happiness, so a further charm has caused the students to direct their own happiness outwards, quite implausibly, towards the viewer as spectator.

Yet the two cones also offer an interesting solution to the problems of linear perspective in its endeavour to represent visual reality. When looking to the side as well as to the front one sees objects apparently diminishing in size as they recede, since parallel lines close together in all directions and not only into the distance before one. Although one perceives this along an actual street, however, by turning one's head, over the smaller scale of even quite a large sculpture a diminution towards the edges would merely appear bizarre, and in any case Mason always invites the spectator to move from side to side and to view the changing configurations of the whole. The marching figures on the right and left cannot be smaller than the figures in the centre, and the only vanishing points are behind the work or in front of it. Nevertheless, as well as exaggerating perspective Mason also removes, as it were, the picture frame, and causes the foreground itself to curve back at the edges. The nearest figures of the rows on the left and the right are further away from the front of the work than the nearest figures in the middle, and give the illusion of lateral perspectives. At the same time, the oncoming cone creates a kind of interior perspective which places artist and viewer, more evidently than before, in the same space as what they sculpt or observe.

We are looked at in part so as to be captured for a sculpture whose dimensions are also explicable in terms of the need to involve us. ('My big works', he told an interviewer, 'are conceived in size so the spectator could imagine himself actually in the work, participating in the action').[3] The looks also further the particular emotion of the work. Commenting on *Latin Quarter* in a television film, Mason suggested that 'when you see twenty thousand or more students grouped together to say something, you feel a great emotion',[4] and he notes in his text on the work that, for the students too, 'however grave the nature of the demonstration it is invariably accompanied by the exhilaration of sharing a common cause'. For the purpose of the sculpture he suppresses the knowledge drawn on for *An Illuminated Crowd*, and even the conviction of the 'rowdiness' or 'violence' to be found at the back of 'any crowd',[5] and perhaps recovers, indeed, a more persistent conviction about human goodness. Certainly in this work he intends to communicate, as 'wave after wave' of students goes by, an exhilaration before youth, and also before multiplicity, before the sea of heads, the rank on rank of windows, the leaves of the tree.

The colours of the work derive from the emotion and express it, through the numerous recalls which fascinate the eye and compose the whole, and especially through the new pastel colour scheme which gathers into itself the clothes of the students and the spectators, the trunk and leaves of the tree, and even the awnings and roofs of the buildings. All the Latin Quarter and its people have been coloured by the warm tints of an emotion, for which the usual colour contrasts, whereby objects placed next to each other spring apart, are replaced by easy passages and harmonies. The architectural forms have been correspondingly simplified. All that survives from the close detail of the actual buildings, and also of certain preparatory drawings and watercolours, is a decorative lintel, while an area of the façade opposite has been left bare. In comparison with that of previous works the architecture can seem bland, until one realises that its simplicity allows us to focus on the human figures, and that the relative blandness of the figures themselves serves a necessary end. One may come with some surprise on these students where, despite the discovery of a black man and of an older man with a lined forehead, no 'journey in space' is offered across races or ages or expressions, and where most of the modelling is homogeneous. The clothes, too, are lightly indicated as against, for example, the straw hat of the grape-picker. Heads are moulded, faces are painted, with none of the near concern for individual presence in, say, *A Tragedy in the North*. Mason's task, however, is not to describe individuals but to catch the burst of youth — the work is precisely a demonstration of youth — and to set a kind of flame passing lightly from one participant to another.

106. *Le Boul' Mich'*, 1986

107. Study for *Latin Quarter*, 1986

The flame passes over the whole work, in fact. For *Latin Quarter* is after all the name of a place, not the description of an event, and the only words on the sculpture, 'LE/ST MICHEL', have been invented for the occasion, so that, by apparently designating an hotel or brasserie, they can name the boulevard which is the axis of the Quartier Latin and the thoroughfare of emotion for anyone in love with the place. The architecture constitutes a setting which insists on returning here as part of the substance of the work and as entering, as in *The Departure* and *A Tragedy in the North*, the experience and the being of the human figures. It is even shown to correspond. The alignment of the numerous windows answers the alignment of the students. The 'crenellated roof-tops' echo, through an aesthetic requirement which combines once again with the construction of meaning, 'the zigzag lines of the front row of heads'.[6]

Because of the nature of the emotion which this place and these figures create, there is also little shading on the work and the shadows are subdued. The viewer is looking, to be sure, at the relatively northern light of Paris and not at the southern light of Provence, but the young people also seem to tread lightly on the roadway. Unmarked, hardly characterised and yet undeniably there, they belong without needing to impinge weightily, in a breezy work where, over against the infinitely deepening belonging, ease and richness of the sun- and shadow-filled *Grape-Pickers*, there is for once an almost total absence of contrast. The eye can certainly travel from the blond hair and clean-shaven face of the young man at the front to the dark hair and beard of the person beyond him, and thence to the grey hair of the older man, to a young woman and to the black man, but all this is concentrated in a single area of the whole, rather like the expressive gestures of *The Crowd*.

Yet *Latin Quarter* is also an urban reply to *The Grape-Pickers*. It, too, is a work of unthreatened joy in the open air, of kinship with others and with a place made real by time (the quarter has been 'the home of this ancient university, the Sorbonne, for eight centuries')[7] and made familiar by neighbourhood. As *The Grape-Pickers* is situated in the field next to Mason's house, so the scene of *Latin Quarter* 'confronts me every day I step outside my courtyard'.[8] The difference is in the kind of permanence which is seized and celebrated, the ever-recurring harvest under the unchanging sun or the continual renewal of unformed youth and of the idea of youth. The work is an image not of Place itself but of Here, of the visual world into which the artist had stepped day by day for forty years, from one or other of his successive flats, and which he fills not with ageing but with youth, with the students who are 'its rightful inhabitants'.[9]

It is typical of Mason's work that this acknowledgment of otherness (the scene is not his but theirs) is accompanied by a large emotional investment of his own. The extra degree of happiness in the students comes, one can assume, from his personal happiness with them and with the place. They look outwards on a second perspective cone in part because the joy of the work is returning to the artist. The tricolour, which means the Revolution and therefore accords perfectly with protesting students and with the very notion of the modern crowd, is also France, the adopted home. The theme itself of the Latin Quarter resumes decades of Mason's human and artistic activity, and returns, indeed, to *The House of the Soul* of 1949–1950, which he has described in a letter as already 'a synthesis of all that assails his eyes in the Latin Quarter', including the dome of the Panthéon which is visible here at the end of the rue Soufflot.

Is one justified in also seeing a representation of Mason himself in the work? This could hardly be intentional, given his express desire to go out of the self towards the subject and towards the viewer. A strongly built young man with abundant wavy hair, at the end of a row of students to the right of the tree, has nevertheless turned fully and rather improbably in our direction, with a look which is open but impossible to read. Like characters in several earlier works, he looks out at the viewer and at the artist from the back of the sculpture, and also from the midst of youth. He is not Mason — though he does resemble Mason when young — and to read too much into him would unbalance the concerns of the whole, yet the interest for the spectator of the work is likely to be increased by this discreet presence of the partly-other, possibly of the ageing sculptor's earlier self.

Of course Mason is equally responding to a place which, independently of self and even before being represented and enhanced in a work of sculpture, has a quality which he perceives in all places that have themselves entered the imagination and been transfigured into signs of possibility, homes of transcendence in the here and now. He had referred to the transforming 'magic' of Les Halles and its harbouring of the 'wonders of nature', and now writes of 'the magical inclined plane of the Boul' Mich'.[10] With many other artists or writers the words would be no more than conventional expressions of elation, but with Mason one learns that words are always used with the directness and accuracy of his sculpture. He is aware of the good fortune of living in a site made special by history, by the other art of architecture, and even by the descending or rising level of the ground, a site which much of his art also inhabits and by which it is privileged in return.

108. *The Latin Quarter,* 1988–89

His particular emotional involvement and personal reading of the scene necessarily affect the politics of the work. The marching students are distant echoes of the Revolutionary crowd, and are associated with the student crowds of May '68, the most recent event to have tried to recapture the transformative energies of the Event itself. By chance, Mason was present in the place de la Sorbonne at the very moment when that still considerable episode and would-be apocalypse began, and immediately made a drawing, on the spot, which is of no small historical interest. He was greatly enthused by the whole affair, in fact, and did many drawings and lithographs of the scenes in the Latin Quarter including the last barricade, which was erected in the rue Monsieur-le-Prince just outside his flat. The largest work celebrating the moment, *The Month of May in Paris*, is a pondered and surprisingly angled response to the imaginative uprising, which shows the crowd at the foot of the boulevard de Port-Royal preparing to watch a student march on the Charlety Stadium. These are not the students themselves but onlookers for whom the students will become a spectacle, as if Mason at forty-six, though sympathising keenly with the students, is concerned to depict the rest of a society which needs to benefit from their action. The milling crowd is specifically waiting, and one might think the same of *The Crowd* itself, begun earlier but finished in the same year. *The Month of May in Paris* places the faithless and waiting modern crowd in relation to a revolutionary hope, though at a distance from its as yet absent source. Mason then raises the particular occurrence to the level of an image, by also situating the crowd under the tree of liberty, growing from the head and thought of the central figure, and by choosing a title of wide literary and mythic resonance.

A decade later, in 1978, he returned to the idea — to the quest for sufficient meaning — and with *An Illuminated Crowd* envisaged another assembling of people waiting expectantly for something, which may again be a political, revolutionary ideal, visible to certain of their number but still absent from the work. After almost another decade, the theme insists once again, and the politics rise even more swiftly into image as Mason gathers all student marches into the ever-repeating Student March, which passes under the same Tree. For although the 'exhilaration of sharing a common cause' is apparent, the cause itself is undefined, while the origin of the work is very precise. In the course of a student demonstration against an education reform on 5 December 1986, a young student, Malik Oussekine, died in the rue Monsieur-le-Prince as a result of one of the many clashes with the police. Although the circumstances are quite different, one inevitably thinks of *The*

Aggression. Mason heard the skirmishings but was writing his Rodin lecture late that night and had to leave for London the next day prior to giving the lecture at the Hayward Gallery on the 10th. He had time just before setting out to make quick sketches of the silent march of students mounting the boulevard St Michel to the nearby Cochin Hospital where Malik's body was laid. It is this march which is represented in *Latin Quarter* of 1987, a smaller, unpainted version of the definitive work, which was first shown as a plaster, along with drawings and lithographs, in Mason's *Latin Quarter* exhibition of the same year at the Marlborough Graphics Gallery in London, and then, cast into resin, in the Birmingham retrospective of 1989. It represents a truly defiant march of demonstrators, with few smiling faces and with a young man at the centre who confronts the viewer, his mouth open as if shouting a slogan. Already in the many preparatory drawings and watercolours, however, the mood has lightened, and by the time of the large, polychrome sculpture of 1988–1989, the work smiles at the viewer, the meaning of the march has become universal, and the 'tragic' grounds for it entirely irrelevant. In a note of January 1987, Mason recounts the death of Oussekine in his street, but goes on, after lamenting the fact that since May 1968 the district has been progressively emptied of students, to rejoice that, when the students turn out to demonstrate, 'miraculously' the Latin Quarter 'regains its soul'. In a text for the first showing of the large version in London, at the Marlborough Gallery in 1991 (it had figured in Mason's one man show in Paris in 1989, on the Marlborough stand at the F.I.A.C. in the Grand Palais), Mason ignores altogether the actual inception of the work by writing that it is 'not entirely based on the famous month of May 1968'.

A fist is still raised, and is of great sculptural importance since, like the raised arm of *An Illuminated Crowd*, it is visible from all angles and responds to the viewer's movements. It signifies, however, not protest against a government measure or against the police but the protest of youth, the energy of young life marching through the world. It signifies, in fact, a kind of faith. When referring in his note of January 1987 to the 'exhilaration' of the students, he also writes: 'I breathe more deeply during these moments when commerce and traffic stop and the handsome architecture is graced solely by human forms'. To 'breathe deeply' is to participate in a better life with a larger rhythm. He writes above all, in a passage not retained in the text for the Marlborough Gallery catalogue, of the 'pure élan' of many thousands of united students, and concludes: 'one cannot escape the thought that hardly anything separates them from a great and permanent belief.'

109. *Souvenir of May 1968*, 1986

And the tree, once again, is of great significance. It carries over from *The Month of May in Paris* the symbolic suggestion of the May tree and of the Jacobins' tree of liberty, one of those many images by which the French Revolution, apparently the result of rationalising political theory, already endeavoured to understand itself and to found its meaning in myth. And it implies, of course, that the season has changed, and that for the purpose of the sculpture we are not in an actual December but in a figurative May. As a tree of hope, moreover, it is also a tree of life, which towers above the crowd and, taking advantage of the high relief, sends its branches and foliage back over the humans as if to protect them. (It even has 'wings', though it may be over-ingenious to think of it as a natural substitute for the archangel along whose boulevard the students are advancing and whose name is written on the opposing façade.) The authority of the tree is reinforced when its trunk and foliage are recalled in the flagpole and its waving flag, and when red and green, in their pastel variants and in company with other colours, course over its trunk.

That trunk is interesting, in fact, as painting. In a letter to Frances Morris of 6 July 1990, concerning the lithograph of *The Month of May in Paris* which had been acquired by the Tate Gallery, Mason writes: 'ever since my first hours in Paris over forty years ago, I have been fascinated by the peeling bark of the plane tree, thinking, that if all abstract painting was as good, the world would be a better place.' The last phrase is not a flourish, I believe, but is seriously meant: in 'Les mains éblouies' Mason had called the 'artistic' as opposed to the literary side of Rembrandt his real contribution not only to painting but to 'this world'.[11] This is a celebration of the power of art as well as a sharp comment on abstraction, and indeed on the plane tree and on any visual object, whose design and colouring may well reveal themselves, on inspection, to have the qualities of abstract work, to follow no laws but their own, and in a way to baffle the idea of representation. Why, on the trunk of a plane tree, that particular shape in the bark, or this particular hue? Mason's painted trunk is certainly a vivid figuration of a unique and specific type of tree, yet it also foregrounds (literally) the random harmony of shapes and colours chosen and disposed for reasons which are aesthetic.

This conspicuous and beautiful piece of 'figurative abstraction' also brings into view what Mason has often reiterated, that once he is engaged in a long-term sculpture whose elaboration will demand months or years, most of his concerns have already become abstract, since what he has to make, while addressing a public and carrying a theme to completion, is a work of art. It is important to note, in fact, given Mason's commitment to realism and given his dismissive references to certain kinds of abstract art, that abstraction itself is in no way inimical to him. He told Michael Brenson: 'I feel that every artist working today must . . . have an abstract period, because he is then dealing with the formal essence of pictorial art.' The point for Mason is then to move on, to treat such a period as an apprenticeship, and to use its lessons in the representation of the visual world so as to accomplish 'a more total work'. This is, naturally, a point of view, yet for anyone who believes that art is an exaltation of the world it may well follow that without figuration there is no world to raise and without abstraction no art by which to raise it.

The 'politics' of the sculpture, as anyone can see, are an emotional engagement with an ideal for society rather than the espousal of an ideology or programme, or the demonstration of wrongs to be righted. The students are themselves the life for which previous crowds have waited, and it is interesting to find that among his own notes Mason has a newspaper clipping in which Tolstoy is quoted as saying what I believe Mason himself might have said: 'The aims of art are incommensurable with the aims of socialism. The mission of the artist should not be to resolve a problem irrefutably but to oblige us to love life.' It is also worth noting that, although socialism corresponds to Mason's class origin and to a certain generosity in his response to others, in his usual trenchant way he cuts through the sentimentalism and dread of snobbery which beset many self-approving intellectuals, refusing to produce 'popular art',[12] defending Manet's rendering of a comfortable middle-class world on the grounds that it was the world he knew and believed in,[13] and telling Jane Farrington in the unpublished interview of May 1988: 'I can't support . . . the political creed . . . that wishes the worker to unite and to remain a worker anyway. I mean the worker must have the possibility of escaping that.'

Latin Quarter is not a political statement but an image. It is another large-scale composition dealing with history, but the history has been deliberately generalised. And so, therefore, has story. Here, too, one sees what Mason meant when he told Michael Brenson that, wanting an art that would contain everything, he also wanted it to 'contain' narrative. The sculpture goes once again beyond narrative, moving from the *chronos*, the merely passing time, of any particular student march to the *kairos*, the meaningful time — the apparition, almost the epiphany — of marching Youth, of May, and of Here.

Hence the unusual interest of a photograph by Roger Guillemot of Mason with the completed sculpture in his studio. (It can be seen on the cover of the catalogue for

110. *The Latin Quarter,* at the F.I.A.C., Paris 1989

Mason's exhibition at Marlborough Fine Art, London, in 1991.) Already in the television programme of 1989, *Raymond Mason — A Full Meal,* one sees the ageing sculptor at work on the tree and on the young man in the foreground (and also, at great speed, on related drawings), but in the photograph he poses carefully so as to be perfectly related to the work. He sits in front of it eating the apple of knowledge, which he is cutting or carving with a knife, while all that innocence stretches

behind him. Like so many of his own figures, he looks at the viewer. One sees at one and the same time two of the fundamentals of his art, which are clear to reflection but which the photograph elucidates for the eyes: the full response to a place and to a happening which are close to the point of intimacy and involve him completely, and the authentic act of going out of and away from himself, to something at once autobiographical and objective, familiar and other.

Notes on Chapter XII

[1] 'Responses', in Arts Council 1982, p. 13.

[2] 'Latin Quarter', in Marlborough 1991. I continue to quote from this text.

[3] In Marlborough 1985.

[4] *Raymond Mason – A Full Meal, 1989.*

[5] Arts Council, p. 49, Centre Georges Pompidou 1985, p. 74.

[6] 'Latin Quarter'.

[7] 'Raymond Mason – A Full Meal', 1989.

[8] 'Latin Quarter'.

[9] From an unpublished note of Mason's dated January 1987.

[10] 'The Departure of Fruit and Vegetables . . . ', in Birmingham 1989, p. 90; 'Latin Quarter', in Marlborough 1991.

[11] In Centre Georges Pompidou 1985, p. 75.

[12] In Marlborough 1985.

[13] 'Manet et Cézanne', in Centre Georges Pompidou 1985, p. 81.

Above and right: *The Latin Quarter* (details)

XIII

BIRMINGHAM

In the same year that the *Twin Sculptures* were installed in Washington, 1988, a commission was confirmed for another monumental sculpture, to be erected in Mason's home town of Birmingham. He had been approached the previous year by Birmingham City Council, on the recommendation of Vivian Lovell of the Public Art Commissions Agency, to provide a sculpture to stand in front of the projected International Convention Centre in Civic Square, which would itself be renamed Centenary Square and entirely relaid. He had supplied a small model, the *Study for the Birmingham Monument* (1987) in painted clay, along with a descriptive text, and secured the assignment without a competition being announced. The undertaking of the work was part of Mason's return to Birmingham, for in 1989 his third large retrospective was held at the Birmingham City Museum and Art Gallery, from 27 April to 18 June. As a result of seeing the BBC television film of Mason's work broadcast at the time of the London and Oxford retrospective of 1982-1983, a childhood friend, Hilda Brown, had made contact with him, and persuaded Evelyn Silber, a curator at the museum, of the appropriateness of a retrospective in Mason's native city. The exhibition, *Raymond Mason: Sculptures and Drawings*, was organised by Evelyn Silber and Jane Farrington, and was dedicated by the artist to Hilda Brown, who had died shortly before the opening. The catalogue includes an essay by Mason, 'My Early Artistic Life in Birmingham', a transcript of his conversation with Richard Cork, 'The Torrent of Life', which had been broadcast on Radio 3 in 1985 at the time of the Paris retrospective, a poem by Roy Fuller, 'After a lecture on Rodin (By Raymond Mason)', and two essays on the work: 'Raymond Mason and the English Narrative Tradition' by Jane Farrington, and 'Raymond Mason — an Exalting Life' by Sarah Wilson, who had become an enthusiastic supporter of Mason's in the early 1980s and had secured for him important opportunities to lecture. The exhibition coincided with Birmingham's centenary, and as well as showing among its seventy-two items *Birmingham. In Memoriam,*

Wheeleys Lane and another watercolour from the 1958 set, *View of a Canal and Cemetery*, it included drawings for the future monument in Centenary Square.

Public recognition was gathering. In 1988 *A Tragedy in the North* had been exhibited in Wakefield Cathedral as part of the Wakefield Festival, while 1989 also brought the showing of the Central Television film on Mason's work, *Raymond Mason — A Full Meal*, an interview with Martin Kemp in the Radio 3 series 'Third Ear', promotion in the French Ordre des Arts et des Lettres to the rank of Officier, and a one-man exhibition on the Marlborough Gallery stand at the F.I.A.C. in the Grand Palais in Paris. The Birmingham exhibition, which received support from the Arts Council of Great Britain and the Henry Moore Foundation, also toured with continuing success to the Manchester City Art Gallery (15 July to 3 September) and the City Art Gallery, Edinburgh (23 September to 12 November), and in 1990 a cast of *The Crowd* was installed in Madison Avenue, New York. On 12 June 1991, the Birmingham monument was inaugurated by the Queen, as part of the opening of the new International Convention Centre. The story, nevertheless, has the usual coda. Local political and journalistic interests hostile to the party which had commissioned the sculpture organised a campaign to have it removed, which harried Mason well into the following year, while an exhibition in October and November 1991 at the Marlborough Gallery in London, which had *Latin Quarter* as its centre-piece but which also included the painted plaster of the Birmingham monument along with preparatory works and a number of works derived from his public sculptures, was ignored or assailed by critics.

Work on the monument — to be known as *Forward*, from the City of Birmingham motto — could only begin after the completion of *Latin Quarter*, which Mason produced in 1988 and 1989 and which had itself been delayed, from the moment of its conception in late 1986, by the preparation of the *Twin Sculptures*. Mason proceeded as with *An Illuminated Crowd*, making a one-third-size plaster in his studio (contending anxiously with time and knowing that the effect of plaster on his lungs made the work dangerous and would disbar him from any further large compositions), and then exhaustingly reworking the separate pieces as they were enlarged at Brie-Comte-Robert by the Haligon Studios, before finally painting the whole, in steel-reinforced stratified polyester resin, with polyurethane paint. From its beginning in the small model, the form is once again unique. The first four large designs, *The Crowd, The Departure, A Tragedy in the North* and *The Grape-Pickers*, are all remarkably deepened high reliefs which derive, though dissimilar, from a painter's sensitivity to perspective, to a rapidly diminishing scale that, by being fictive, fascinates and involves the viewer. *An Illuminated Crowd*, which is not, like them, a scene, though it begins in one, is the only free-standing work, which goes out by its forms into the surrounding crowds and reacts with their buildings, and equally offers itself to be circumscribed by the pedestrian and so becomes also an interior, and enters, by its meanings, the inner shape of that slow-moving consciousness. The Washington monument goes to the other sculptural limit, and as the only large work in low relief invites less involvement than thought, concerning our relations to time, while *Latin Quarter* returns to perspective but so as to develop it to an extreme, with a view to the most effective suasion of the spectator and his most irresistible attraction into the otherness of recurring youth. As a perfect final touch, *Forward* combines free-standing with relief sculpture, in a creative freedom which one associates with late works. It can be walked round and yet the figures decrease in size towards the rear, according to perspective when seen from the front. Buildings are present, though not as setting. One can read the work, in fact, as beginning in the simple and 'pictorial' perspective of the raked streets and buildings at the rear seen from the side, and then emerging as free-standing, though with a continuing increase in scale, the transition being made possible by the ambiguity — sculpturally so intelligent and inventive — of two diagonal files of people at the back, who grow larger both as they approach the spectator viewing them from the side along a perspective and as they advance towards the larger front of the work.

The sculpture also appears as a procession, and yet it contains several figures standing or sitting. It is loose of all expectations, in fact (more so, perhaps, than any other of his works), and each of its moves has meaning. In this last of his works to fulfil all that Mason, like Picasso as he sees him, requires of great art, namely composition, history and size, and in his final achievement of what he sees, in the lecture on Rodin, as the successful aim of Rodin himself but as something 'lost'

in our time: 'a work of art capable of standing alone, rich in intentions, totally realised and recognisable to all', he draws on numerous sculptural resources for what is in many ways a recapitulation of his art and of his life, and a questioning, via a public celebration of Birmingham informed by 'precise' and public 'knowledge', of what it means to live through time.

For there are three sections to the work, and as it reaches for origin as represented in the rear section its scale diminishes (according to an ancient metaphor which 'sees' time as if it were space), yet its colour grows. Or rather it 'deepens': as one leaves the 'light ochre with vermilion red accents' of the front for 'browns with touches of violet' and 'the famous red' of Birmingham brick, where the drawing is now 'accented with black',[1] one also approaches the deeps of a past coloured with memory and emotion. Whereas several corridors elsewhere lead through the work, like streets of the city, in this warm and enclosed first world perspective draws one in and makes one at home as within one's own farthest memory. The houses of the childhood scene are even smaller in scale than the people who parade past them, and are treated, persuasively, as a child might treat them. A factory, on the other hand, seems enormous, and even rises from the work's cliff-like rear end to send out a living spiral of smoke from its towering chimney. It stands for the peaceful giant that stood opposite Mason's house and is the occasion for his art to home to his beginning, and to the 'redbrick factory' about which he had been convinced in as early as 1965, according to his letter to Marie-Laure de Noailles, that it was probably what, as a sculptor, he 'had to say'.[2]

A procession of working men and women likewise returns Mason to his working-class beginnings, while a procession of children on the other side, who follow their Quaker school teacher as 'a reminder of Birmingham's pioneering for education of the poor',[3] also resembles the dream-like world of children which no doubt accompanies us all. The whole of the rear of the work is heavy with inwardness, where not realism but reality is the aim, the presence of a remembered world in its true colours and proper dimensions. After *Latin Quarter*, which moves back through time from his present home and the architecture of his immediate horizon to his young manhood in Paris, *Forward* moves further back to the home and the architecture of origin, to his youth and childhood. Though by no means his final works, these two sculptures adjacent in time use, for the purpose of art, of subject, of communication, the virtual chiasmus of most people's lives, anticipation followed by memory, a trajectory out and back, and in this case Birmingham, Paris: Paris, Birmingham.

The sculpture emerges — grows, like a human being

208

112. Study for *Forward*, 1988

113. Following pages: *Forward, Centernary Square. Birmingham,* 1991

— from that origin of smallness and immensity, and reaches, at its centre, certain figures of the father. Part of a car, smooth and stylish, recalls Mason's father as pioneer motorist, gifted mechanic and taxi-driver, while its conspicuous front wheels repeat a large factory wheel and so also link the father's work to the life-work of Birmingham. A car designer leaning on the bonnet holds a pencil in a jaunty gesture pointing it forward, and suggests another use for the working hand. Whatever emotion has been caught at the rear, the car and draughtsman seek to free it. Whereas *Birmingham. In Memoriam,* which looks backwards and downwards elegiacally to a disappearing past, remembers Mason's mother (whose recent death gives to the painting a particular poignancy), *Forward,* a work which appears from the past but which also continues into the future, remembers and indeed memorialises his father, who like his son 'could make anything with his hands.' This is not an offer to psychoanalyse, but a simple observing that Mason's masculine, persuasive art does indeed return

to and emerge from the streets and passers-by of his childhood back there, that as an urban artist he can take pleasure in his derivation from a great and, in English terms, central city, and that the figure who leads the work towards the front, smiling and with concentration, is associated with his father.

The personal dimension of the work is even stronger than usual. The sculpture as it advances, however, is freighted with impersonal, historical thought and so relates to the previous monument, for Georgetown. As history too the movement forward meets with some resistance. What is the time of the work? Concerning his portrayal of the Birmingham politicians, Neville, Austen and Joseph Chamberlain, Mason writes that their generations form 'an interesting sequence where historical time becomes sculptural space'.[4] As a pageant-like vision with the sharp exactnesses and sliding imprecisions of dream, the work may enter and control time for the viewer stepping backwards or forwards along it. Its space imitates real space to the extent that to walk

is often to walk through time — one need only step round to the back of the thoroughly contemporary International Convention Centre at which the work points to find oneself in a nineteenth century of canal and industrial buildings in red brick — while adding from the past what only art and thought can raise, the figures of the dead. And it may be on account of their presence that the sculpture seeks as soon as it emerges from the world of the beginning, to arrest time.

Consider the wheels. In order to 'bridge the giant space', Mason writes, 'the circles of the wheel continue to spin throughout the work', as one of the many ways of bringing multiplicity into unity. The car wheel, though stationary, suggests the movement forward, but the huge wheel of a steam engine turns on itself, so as to still time, or turn it in its tremendous power. Situated near the centre of the work, it resembles the wheel of time, and its circle is repeated on the torso of a nearby 'stalwart' and yet defunct iron-worker.

Consider also the molten metal being poured from yet another circle. Mason is drawn, as a sculptor, to extremes, to movements that only art can stop, whether of smoke, or clouds, or falling, or an explosion, or simply flapping flags. To sculpt a descending liquid is to enter an infinite moment of timelessness — or maybe of time-fullness, since the experience of a timeless moment is equally replete with time, as if an absence of time were also its perfect presence. The stillness of visual art, as enacted and revealed most fathomlessly in Vermeer's *The Milkmaid*, always invites the viewer to a new inness of outward attention by which to penetrate that fictive moment, that unreal stillness whose end is to make visible a real that has been transfigured, and *Forward*, by concentrating on a time which is there, about the middle of the work, slows and holds time so as also to poise the viewer between time past and time present and future. The whole work pours time through itself, combining the two levels of the *Twin Sculptures* and hesitating between the inevitable movement forward and the warmth of then. The timespan of *Twin Sculptures* and *Forward* is similar, modern Birmingham being no older than modern America and 1775 being the date both of the outbreak of the War of Independence and of the opening of their foundry by James Watt and Matthew Boulton, but whereas the distant American work remembers, from the light and shadows of the present, a past vividly coloured and projected as an imaginative fresco, the near-to-home Birmingham work colours with intense tones a past seen to be disappearing, and exercises its most knowing imagination in the creation of figures to halt time and turn it around in the mind. A sculpture of both the movement and the immobility of time, it refuses to allow time merely to advance. So its

composition likewise serves both to move it forward, by the rise of the base, the increasing size of the figures, the diagonal axes which 'enforce everywhere the onward march', and to link the rear to the front, by recalling the tall chimney, for example, 'the precise symbol of the city's prosperity and the age of steam',[5] in the raised arm of the main figure, whose hand as he strides into the future is still 'the industrious hand' of the past.

That this allegiance to the past transcends nostalgia is clear from the Lady of the Arts. A figure from Birmingham's coat of arms, she 'turns around to throw a kiss to the past', as a homage to the 'glorious past when for a moment in history, Birmingham, the first manufacturing town in the world, was unique'. As the lady who presides over the arts, however, is she not also the Muse, or rather, the mother of the Muses, Memory in person? Active in *Twin Sculptures*, she is physically present in *Forward*. She remembers, for Mason, the downstairs window, the street and the factory where his art began, and maybe even his actual art, since the colours of façades and roofs at the rear are those of *Birmingham. In Memoriam*, of 1958, while the human figures within an urban setting recall his fundamental subject matter. Behind her, the double helix represented on a frontal block takes one right back to the spiral of passers-by in *The House of the Soul* of 1949–1950, to which one had already returned, as to its architecture, with *Latin Quarter*. As these references to Mason's art also serve the larger purpose of celebrating Birmingham and, in the case of the spiral, life itself, so two other figures near the Lady refer outwards to Art and the tradition of Art. A jeweller scrutinising a jewelled work through an eye-piece is an emblem of the viewer as rapt attention. The iron-worker stripped to the waist recalls the concern for anatomy, along with narration and perspective, which characterises the pictorial art from the Renaissance to the nineteenth century whose virtues Mason is intent on recovering, and while his head and face are modern, the design of his midriff reaches back, as did male costumes for *Phèdre*, to Greek and Roman torsos. He is the other character from the Birmingham coat of arms, and he too has been gathered into art, so as to recall, as part of a remembering 'monument', an origin, a great source and resource.

The Lady of the Arts, situated just forward of the highly charged central section of the work, turns away from the movement onward not so as to refuse it, and not specifically so as to reject contemporary art or the art of the future — another figure almost next to her is the man with a pencil looking and pointing forward — but so as to return to creative memory, and fold the past and the art of the past into the present. Though

Forward, Centenary Square (detail)

Forward, Centenary Square (detail)

shorter than other figures through being invisible from the knees down, she is conceived on an appropriately larger scale.

Twin Sculptures had enacted the process by which an ordinary crowd appropriates history, one element of the work being present in the consciousness of the other. *Forward* places the various pasts which it shows to the spectator — the pasts of a self, of a city and of art — in the consciousness of an imaginary figure, who is not a citizen of Birmingham like the others but a female genius of the place and transformer of time. She transforms it most clearly for the nearby figures who stride past her and who emphasise, by a contrast typical of Mason, the movement forward. Does one sense in the leading section of the work, too, a certain disinclination? The telling but uniform vermilion red lines on the light ochre move back, after all, not to the deepening blues of the violent shadow-world of the polychrome *Illuminated Crowd* but to the 'famous red' of Birmingham in its heyday. The figures in the rear are at home in their environment, having taken on its hues, whereas the figures at the front emerge from that closely defined place and community into the largeness of the unknown. Mason refers in an unpublished note to the 'essential' colour of the rear, and describes its red as 'the warmth of blood'. He not only remarks, moreover, that *monere* means to remind, but declares: 'I want people to feel an identity with the great red-brick city that was'. 'The great city that was' is the paradigmatic formula of elegy (and of tragedy): the whole work leaves behind a greatness and a vital warmth. Yet the front section, too, is warm in its way: it shines in the light, and glows profusely in the afternoon and evening sun.

It is also strange that, in a work dedicated to moving forward, the bearded man and the boy in the front row are stationary, another man near the front sits with his elbow resting on closed books and contemplates the future rather than entering it, while even the right leg of the central and advancing 'figure of Birmingham' is an immobile column. Behind, are a block and a computer screen on a stand. Yet at the same time the scale here, the modelling of calm heads and expressions and of simple bodies, along with the severe delineating of edges on hair, clothing and of folds in material, aim once again for a classical inheld drama and permanence, under the contemporary and indeed informal attire of shirt, dress, or boy's shorts. The classical reference brings the resource of the furthest past into the art of the present as it envisages the future. In the boldly simple drawing and equally perfect slimness and pose of the left-hand figures, the boy's head resting against the man's hands, the stillness brings attention and readiness to the for-

ward movement, as if the viewer were being shown the quiet and searching consciousness within the advancing bodies.

Perhaps the hesitation is more in the viewer than in the sculptor. One cannot get close to these figures because Mason does not close with them, as he closes most evidently with the characters of *A Tragedy in the North*. In his 1987 text he writes of the group at the front that they 'symbolise' the modern family and community. One recognises them not in their individuality and certainly not in their joy or grief but in their roles, as mother and child, older man and young boy, engineer, businessman, secretary, Asian. The workers and craftsmen behind them also signify not themselves but their calling. Whereas *An Illuminated Crowd* is a 'human comedy' (on the model of Balzac's *Comédie humaine*), with a multitude of characters engaging in a gamut of human acts stretching from the light of our condition to its darkness, *Forward*, while adding historical depth, ignores the range of our emotions and moods and substitutes, for moral and spiritual actions, representative activities. For Mason's purpose is, as always, different. This is not a universal and mostly timeless human crowd but the march of humanity through time as manifested in a specific place.

Hence the further hint of epic. Mason does not use the word itself but he does write: 'After an apparition amid a cloud of steam of men of science like Priestley, Watt and Murdoch, an anonymous crowd of workers, growing ever smaller, finally disappears into the mists of smoke and of time.' His words recall the 'anonymous group' down below in the Washington monument, and if the nameless workers 'disappear' into the mists of smoke, certain named heroes appear — for what is almost a numinous 'apparition' — in a cloud of steam. Their number is repeated, moreover, in the other named characters, the Chamberlains, and in the trio of adult characters across the work's prow, who focus, as does everything else in the work, on the most evidently epic of all the characters, the 'great figure of a man' who leads the march, and who is the first to be mentioned in Mason's texts. Is he also a great figure of Man? *Forward*, the story of Birmingham, is also the epic of humanity, the poetic narrative of humanity growing through time, and it culminates in this figure, in whom, indeed, all of Mason's protagonists come to a head. He is larger than life not because, as in *An Illuminated Crowd*, he and those immediately around him occur in a dimension more ample than our own — the dimension of art, whose magnifying of the real and deepening of attention are a means, a way, to understanding — but because he is a kind of pioneer of the race. It is in *Forward* that the creed of that 1977 note 'Sur le contenu' finds its perfect embodiment. The 'most significant' subject after the break-up of belief and of artistic tradition is 'people', and while the lower crowd of *Twin Sculptures* already sees its destiny in the sky, and its flag in the red tints of the sun on white cloud against the blue, it is stilled and wakeful to possibility, whereas the crowd in *Forward* advances, and is no longer concerned with the conditional and with the necessary disappointment of the actual.

Produced when the Soviet bloc was disintegrating and inaugurated in the aftermath of the Cold War, does *Forward* hanker, then, for an uplifting optimism for which our century in particular has hardly prepared us? In its further organising of the crowd, it certainly gives the largest meaning to the idea of a procession, by showing the procession of humanity itself through time and so transforming the eternal and circling march of youth in *Latin Quarter* into a forward march of all ages into the future. Yet the complexity of the work, its awareness of different times and exploration of different ways with time, distances it from any easy assumption that we are, or could be, en route for better things, while suggesting nevertheless that such a belief, when freighted with worldly knowledge, is one we can desire and need. *Forward* is not a communist sculpture, any more than Mason himself is a communist or even a socialist, but it does strive for a communal ideal, and it also celebrates work. The central figure, as epic hero, is not distinct from the others since he represents the workers in the rear by the hand that he holds aloft, which 'signals that the industrious hand has nowhere been better employed' than in Birmingham. 'Industrious' unites, in a fraternity beyond class, the workers employed by industry and the craftsmen, scientists and professionals who employ their time industriously. The scientists in fact lead the march of workers in one of the pieces derived from the sculpture, whose title, *Workers of Birmingham*, is thereby enlarged. In a letter to the *Birmingham Post* of 17 October 1991, Mason writes: 'When I was a boy Birmingham was a great workshop and its citizens were happy to work and proud of their work. I have attempted to evoke this noble visage of the city.' While much of Mason's early sculpture showed people in the street, *Forward* is the culmination, after an interval, of those subsequent works: *Hand of the Artist*, *The Falling Man*, *The Departure*, *A Tragedy in the North*, *The Grape-Pickers*, which consider work and present it as a value, as an access to oneself, to the human group, or to the earth. It describes work in the city as opening one to long continuities through changing time in a meaningful place. Mason's own work is included, not by design but simply because the viewer is likely to reflect on the hand which has laboured at this sculpture, where

the idea of labour is celebrated. In the different phrasing of the 1987 descriptive text, moreover, Mason writes that the 'hand . . . has been employed to as great a use in Birmingham as in any other famous centre of artistry in the history of the world.' He both raises the artistry of Birmingham, in its crafts and applied skills, to comparison with the usually more prestigious artistry in painting of, say, Florence or Venice, and finds a place for his own activity, for his own 'industrious' or ingenious hand, in a tradition from which he differs and to which he nevertheless belongs.

And the work has a theme beyond humanity, which is life. Spirals throughout the sculpture lead to that representation of a double helix at the front, where the formula of DNA inscribed beneath it, which salutes first the 1962 Nobel Prize of the Birmingham-trained biophysicist and early friend of Mason's, Maurice Wilkins, gives a further sense to the title of the work by revealing the evolutionary mechanism of life itself. It is life, here, which moves 'forward'. The double helix is an elegant résumé or *mise en abîme* of the whole sculpture in its circling advance, and through the associations of the spiral not only with vitality but with the primal waters, it also rehearses, albeit in a sign for the intelligence, the controlling 'myths' of Mason's art.

Yet the sculpture moves, nonetheless, in both directions. Elegy is certainly gathered into epic, the work of the past borne by the great hand into an unseen future. Yet 'sculptural interest' lies in both the 'growing immensity' seen fom the back and the 'diminishing scale' seen from the front, and it is a measure of Mason's imaginative capacity that, in making a second monument moving in contrary directions, he extends it not, as *An Illuminated Crowd*, between enlightenment and obscurity, but between the future and the past. *Forward* displays, not the ends of our condition and the facts of choice, but the relationship to time on which choice is made. As the definitive manifestation of a humanist creed, it relates to the past as resource and to the future as the apprehended possible. It plies between the rolling spiral of smoke and the perfect double helix, between the 'great figure of a man' and the peaceful giant.

In his final large 'crowd' Mason recovers the origin of the word in the Anglo-Saxon *crudan*, to make one's way or push forward, and in the last of his large compositions he goes as far back as possible in his own experience so as to create the work which looks most evidently to the future. One might even describe his whole oeuvre, rather schematically, as containing near the beginning two major elegies to the past: *Birmingham. In Memoriam* and *The Departure of Fruit and Vegetables*, followed by two diverse explorations of a present: *A*

Tragedy in the North and *The Grape-Pickers*, which lead, in the *Illuminated Crowd, Twin Sculptures, Latin Quarter* and *Forward*, to various viewings of the future. All the works, in terms of what Mason calls their 'content', are a developing response to the loss of belief, and all respond, both in their content and in their art, to the loss of artistic tradition. All reach out to the viewer, in accordance with Mason's unwavering conviction as to the proper addressing of a work. Many of them also look out from where they are or even travel away from themselves, as do also, most evidently, *Barcelona Tram, Carrefour de l'Odéon* and *The Aggression*, almost as if to enter the real space of the viewer. Is there another sculptor, in fact, whose works exit so pointedly from their own world into ours?

Forward, which comes alive, as always, through the continuous metamorphoses produced by the viewer's movements, also faces truly in all directions, since almost wherever the viewer is positioned someone is looking his way. While it is difficult to enter, moreover (*An Illuminated Crowd* speaks at all points to what we are and reaches inside our self-knowledge so as to occur partly there, whereas the Birmingham monument is a sequence of historical tableaux), it goes out more thoroughly than ever into the place where it is sited. It rises towards the International Convention Centre, while on the north side, which salutes not, as does the south, the industrial life of the city but its commitment to music, theatre and also education, an instrumentalist marches as if towards Symphony Hall and an actress curtseys diagonally to the Repertory Theatre. As it receives the sun, furthermore, the aim for the sculpture, as Mason told a journalist, is that it should 'light up' the vast Centenary Square.[6]

It does indeed, and it also reaches out to the whole of the city. It emerges from the city centre, and in particular from the School of Art and the Museum and Art Gallery. As the Lady of the Arts blows a kiss to the rear of the sculpture her greeting travels beyond the work to the hub of the city itself. Figures in the piece direct one's thought to other areas, the jeweller, for example, to the Jewellery Quarter, while the buildings and the crowd of objects gather in the whole city and also send one's mind voyaging away over it. The 'subject' of the monument, as Mason writes, is 'the city and the citizens of Birmingham', and even more comprehensively than with the monument for Georgetown, the subject of the work coincides with its location. It invites one to look elsewhere, to discover where one is. And it is not only a matter of topography, for Mason also writes that 'the impression of remote space' which comes from looking down the reducing scale of the figures not only increases the dimension of the sculpture, as perspective always will, but 'stretches the space' of the square itself. The monument seems larger than the square in which it stands, and to gaze through it is to penetrate to a farness of space and also of time. The viewer is at once here, now, and elsewhere, then.

He is, indeed, at a kind of centre. It is again Mason himself who directs attention to the other apparently simple and popular image at the front of the work, where 'the criss-cross of fingers and folds' on the chest of the leading figure 'emphasises the heart and the denomination of Birmingham as "The Heart of England"'. A large man with a working hand whose other hand is on his heart takes one inwards to the personal and heart-felt core of the work (situated three streets away from Wheeleys Lane) and outwards to an awareness of the sculpture at the heart of Birmingham and Birmingham at the heart of England. As the monument 'reminds' by descending through time and 'foretells' by facing the future and 'puts in mind' by radiating in all directions, it too becomes, like the early *Place de l'Opéra,* a work of art in a vast and windy square which draws one gradually into Place. The sense of place and the art of place have always been a fundamental concern of this artist who has lived most of his life abroad. The Birmingham commission, coming when it did, allowed him to bring his work full circle, by returning his thought and heart to what was for him the place of origin and the very origin of place.

Notes on Chapter XIII

[1] From Mason's descriptive text of 1987 for Birmingham City Council, 'A Monument for Civic Square'.

[2] See the end of the interview in Claude Bernard 1977.

[3] 'A monument for Centenary Square, Birmingham', in Marlborough 1991. I continue to quote from this text unless otherwise stated.

[4] 'A Monument for Civic Square'.

[5] *Ibid.*

[6] 'Larger-than-life tribute to Brum's golden age', *Independent*, 5 June 1991.

[7] 'The Departure of Fruit and Vegetables . . . ', in Birmingham 1989, p. 90.

114. *Forward, Centenary Square* (detail)
Photo: Roger Guillemot

XIV

TO CONTINUE IS TO BEGIN AGAIN

There are very many works of Mason's that I have not discussed, and that await discovery. They include innumerable drawings, for which a monograph is needed. They also include, for example, two painted portraits of the writer Roy Fuller (a friend), and an over-life-size portrait bust of Béatrice de Rothschild, begun in clay in 1959 or early 1960 though only finished, in plaster and after an immense labour of doing and undoing, in 1962. They might have included other works, the commissions which Mason has had reluctantly to decline and which one can only regret. The most public of these was for a sculpture to be placed in the new Paris Opera House, the Opéra de la Bastille, which was inaugurated with considerable trump in 1990.

And the oeuvre, happily, continues; the 'unremitting work' announced so early in the article on Augustus John is still fuelled by the same 'unfailing determination to produce'. It is true that Mason regards *Forward* as the last of his works on a grand scale. Such works require to be modelled in plaster, whereas the state of his lungs after decades of breathing in plaster dust has obliged him to return to clay and to confine himself to low relief. One high relief, *Rue du Bac*, has nevertheless tempted him: a view of a crowd waiting at the end of the street of the title. It is the latest of his several waiting crowds, where time is poised before a variously anticipated future.

Each of the low reliefs, interestingly, is, or contains, a generous homage. Among them is a panoramic view of London seen from a tower on Millbank, which Mason felt he must add to the group of unpainted resins already representing Paris, Rome and New York. A view of the Richelieu Wing of the Louvre salutes the remarkable mid-nineteenth-century statues which grace it, while a view of Stockholm, which Mason visited for the first time to see a retrospective of the works of Sven Blomberg, his old friend from Birmingham days, includes a homage to Blomberg himself in the unusual form of a portrait of him, painting in the sky above the unified architectural forms and pastel shades of the city. The most significant of the reliefs in this respect, however, are two views which celebrate Mason's own street, the rue Monsieur-le-Prince. They even recall, despite their colour, his early work, being scenes of the street in the manner of the bronze reliefs of the 1950s. A central male figure low down in the foreground and facing this way, who also recalls the principal figure of *The Crowd* and who may be carrying the many intricate relationships of the scene in his head, goes back after exactly forty years to the beginning, to *Man in a Street* itself. Indeed, one may also remember *The Departure* in the display of fruit and vegetables; a counter-perspective some way down the road can put one in mind of a comparable effect along the terraces descending on the right in *Birmingham. In Memoriam*; a dog appears, in the smaller relief a spaniel with a Seurat tail, and in the larger a black Scottish terrier next to a little boy; in the larger again a woman's chignon, seen from behind, spirals in the midst of the passers-by. Works which are close to home, in that they represent what Mason sees when he looks to the left as he comes out of his courtyard, gather, quietly, much of his past.

One of the lessons to be learnt from Mason is that by having a subject and single-mindedly pursuing its representation, he also finds himself sounding those large and fundamental matters which come into view throughout his work and make it of such importance. In a time which converges nowhere and by simply depicting, essentially in a few, maximal works, a crowd in front of mine buildings or four people harvesting grapes, he enters and makes visible human 'recognition' in tragedy, or the oneness and exuberance of life under the sun. His focal theme, in fact, is the old one: humanity — so little featured in recent sculpture — and, more specifically, human beings located in place. In those street scenes of the 1950s where he considers that his art truly begins, it is place which predominates, and even when persons and individualised expression move to the fore, place continues to found and to enlarge the human figures, whether it be the market and church of Les Halles, or a streetscape in Georgetown, or a road through Limbo in downtown New York. *The Crowd* has no decor, yet Mason always refers to that surge of humanity as occurring on the slope of the boulevard St Michel. Even *An Illuminated Crowd*, the most universal and unsituated of his crowd scenes, is associated nevertheless with the place de l'Hôtel de Ville in central Paris. Hence no doubt the landscape reliefs, watercolours and drawings of the Luberon: they represent a kind of art which he sees as minor and so suggest an insistent concern for our larger station on the inhuman earth as well as in the human forms of the city. And in seeking to disclose an inexhaustible where for human being, his art reaches, it seems, always to a centre, to the place of opera, to the 'heart' of both of his cities, to the door in *Wheeleys Lane*.

Mason's humans are not abstracted from the places to which they belong, in line with an ancient understanding, not so much spatial as platial, of what it is to be human. One recognises it in one of the early texts to address the question: 'And the Lord God planted a garden eastward in Eden; and there he put the man whom he had formed' (Genesis 2:8), and one sees the urgency of rediscovering a meaningful place in the exclusion from the garden which quickly follows. That particular view of the matter may not mean much to Mason, yet he is unusual in a world now thought to be post-modern and soon presumably to be post even that, through the regressive and potentially innovative stubbornness with which he holds to the superiority, the beauty and the existence of a world beyond self.

Among the artists still concerned for the sculpting of human figures, moreover, he is even more unusual in that, his subject being the crowd, he offers the public representations of itself. He reaches out to his viewers in part by placing them in his sculptures, and in part also by the almost ubiquitous presence of the hand. It is important for Mason that he actually makes his works himself, and reworks the surfaces of all casts and enlargements. In the Rodin lecture he dispraises the marbles (including *The Kiss*), which were executed from clay models by stone-cutters, and continues: 'So let's get back to what Rodin really did with his own miraculous hands.' His own hand constructs the offering and is then extended, as it were, to the public, not through Mason being self-advertisingly present in the work but on the contrary through characters: a compassionate Pole, a cloud-gazing citizen, even a drunken bum, who open the world of the far-from-autonomous sculpture to the everyday world of the spectator. And one also sees, in this perspective as in others, the size of Mason's ambition. He is not concerned to attract connoisseurs or even a large public. The difficulty for the artist now, he writes, is 'the choice of a subject of universal nature

capable of interesting and speaking out . . . to the entire world'.[1] An artist who wants his works to include 'everything' addresses them to everybody.

It is also by immersing himself completely in his subject that, without seeking originality, singularity or avant-garde publicity, he becomes most fully himself; and by always looking for ways, not to 'advance sculpture' or to free it from some non-existent prison but to increase the power of expression of each work as he makes it, that he does in fact advance sculpture and change it continually before one's eyes. By pressing the visible towards the invisible, and by raising a non-dogmatic humanism towards a 'celestial' light, he also proves once again that art is always, however realist and provided that it succeeds, an art of the possible. It is the commitment to a subject, finally, as universal and as telling as he can make it, that leads to his unexpected and generous admirations of quite alien kinds of art. Who would have associated him, for instance, with Francis Bacon? Yet he has often made public the scale of his esteem. Wouldn't one have associated him even less with Surrealism, considering his Realism, his hostility to 'objects', his preference for the diurnal Verdi over the nocturnal Wagner? Yet he came to recognise, according to the interview with Jane Farrington, that 'all the really powerful creators of this century emerged from that movement . . . because it was nourishing the essential side of art which is *what to say*'.

He also advances one's understanding in general of sculpture, through a realism which continually explores its own frontiers. Indeed, like Bacon, Giacometti and Balthus, and like many of the artistic movements of an uncentred but peculiarly inventive century, he advances the poetics of representation. There, after all, in the permanent and unpardoning issue of *mimesis*, of how to relate the work to the world so that both are present and both are enhanced, is the real challenge to thought and, I would suppose, to any form of creativity. And he reserves additional surprises. I have quoted him on the 'disorder' of reality and on the artist's 'capturing' of the divine spark — he also speaks of 'stealing' it — and here are some further comments he made to Michael Brenson in 1976: 'It seems to me that if you can master illusion . . . it's a very powerful gift . . . you're like Mephistopheles, if you wish. You can create a world of your own. You can make people believe all sorts of strange things'.

The interest of these unbuttoned remarks, which add, to an already demiurgic and Promethean image of the artist, a Mephistophelean, is that they were made by a realist. For they recognise the paradox of realism, that the more a representation resembles, the more power it has to deceive. To catch a likeness is to create an

116. *The Richelieu wing of the Louvre*, 1993.

117. *Rue Monsieur-le-Prince I,* 1992

illusion. Mason sees the danger of the greatest gift, and acknowledges that when the 'outer world' and the 'inner thought', the 'figurative' and the 'abstract', meet, what emerges is another world which is neither and both, and is necessary to each. In one direction this is the fiction which heightens fact, the unreal which augments reality and equips one to inhabit it. It is the power of candid illusion, more than of an art which reveals its disguises, to open the world before one. In the other direction, he even says this: the artist's 'desire' is 'to live in his world . . . he's incapable of living unless he can transpose everything into a world.' From someone else this could mean that the work is a mere refuge and substitute for living, yet Mason goes on to state once again his basic ethical argument: 'the artist's movement should be outwards, away from himself', and to claim that the work enables him precisely 'not to turn inwards'. In the act of making, the artist himself is made, by his bringing his world into order — by his rendering his world, indeed, as a *world* — such that the work broadens his own way into the world beyond. That is no doubt why, on this particular occasion when he demands that a work of art contain 'everything', he defines this as 'an allusion to every possible thing one can think about'.

He would seem to have achieved a great deal, in a series of works which are unlike any others and in a gradually developing and echoing whole. Yet critics are often condescending. Histories of art, collections of art theory by practitioners, even companions to the art of the century, almost entirely exclude him. European museums, when offered the 1982 and 1985 retrospectives for tour, cagily refused. Only two works, of an artist now in his seventies, are on permanent display in the museums of the world: an early painting in the Swindon Museum and a cast of *The Falling Man* in the sculpture garden of the Hirschhorn Museum in Washington. One can always have doubts in the face of such uniformity of neglect, though hardly if one remembers the quality of Mason's admirers, especially among his fellow artists. And where his works have been placed in another kind of public building or on public sites, the public itself has made much of them. In the church of St Eustache in Paris and in Montreal, they have gathered a warm following and become objects of a kind of cult, while the bronze *Crowd* in the Tuileries Gardens has been so caressed that Mason rather regrets the shine that it has taken instead of a deepening patina. He is legitimately pleased at the years of interest and affection which these works have aroused and at the notoriety which they have attracted, and is clearly right to find the explanation in part in their figurative nature.

In bringing together his conviction about figuration

and his desire for colour he has revived, more decisively than anyone and in large and complex works, the long but also long defunct tradition of polychrome figurative sculpture. If he is as fine an artist as I have been claiming, this is likely to make him a very important artist indeed. He is certainly in the rear of fashion, yet also, with almost equal certainty, in advance of his time. This is a good way of opening the future, and of being deeply, not superficially modern.

Notes on Chapter XIV
[1] In 'Responses', in Arts Council 1982, p. 13.

118. *Rue du Bac*, 1994

RUE MONSIEUR-LE-PRINCE. PARIS 6ᵉ.

119. *Rue Monsieur-le-Prince II*, 1992

BIOGRAPHY
BIBLIOGRAPHY
LIST OF ILLUSTRATIONS
INDEX OF NAMES

BIOGRAPHY

1922
Born in Birmingham, England, to Scottish father (hence his second name Greig) and English mother. Father a pioneering motor mechanic, mother from a Birmingham publican family. Educated at St Thomas's Church of England Junior School and George Dixon's Secondary School, Birmingham.

1937-39
Scholarship place at Birmingham College of Arts and Crafts.

1939
Volunteers for military service in Royal Navy. Invalided out in 1941.

1942
Royal Scholarship for painting at Royal College of Art, London, then evacuated to Ambleside, Lake District.

1943
Leaves the RCA to return to Birmingham where he shares a studio for six months with fellow artist Sven Blomberg. Earns a living painting portraits. They put on a joint exhibition in their studio. Presents himself at the Slade School, then evacuated to the Ruskin School of Drawing and Fine Art, Oxford, of which he becomes a member. Friendship with fellow student Eduardo Paolozzi.

1944
Turns to sculpture under guidance of Ralph Nuttall-Smith. Lives in the Ashmolean Museum and profits from its sculpture galleries.

1945
Moves to London (Sun House, Fane Street, West Kensington) and rejoins the Slade School on its return. Visits Henry Moore in Hampstead.

1946
Exhibits in London with Sven and Mimi Blomberg and leaves with them for Paris. Enters the Ecole nationale supérieure des Beaux-Arts, Paris, with a scholarship from the French State. Decides to settle in Paris where he still lives.

120. With Harry (Sven) Blomberg in the days when they shared a studio

121. Mason sculpting a nude in stone in his house in Fane Street

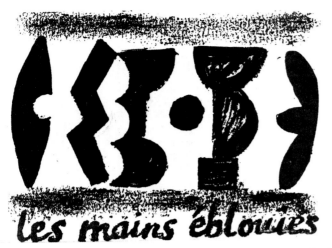

122. Invitation card for the exhibition at the Galerie Maeght

1947
Renounces the Ecole des Beaux-Arts and leads a makeshift existence with young painters Serge Rezvani and Jacques Lanzmann in an empty mansion on the edge of the Seine. Participates with them in the exhibition *Les Mains éblouies* at the Galerie Maeght. Makes the invitation card and exhibits coloured abstract sculptures.

1948
Meets Alberto Giacometti and forms a life-long friendship.

1949
Exhibits at the Salon des Réalités Nouvelles but abstraction already 'bores him to death' and in the trail of Giacometti he returns to figurative work.

1950
Exhibits with his companion the painter Mimi Fogt at the Hôtel Crystal, Saint-Germain-des-Prés. Visits Barcelona.

1951
Travels to Greece and Crete.

123. Mason newly installed in his studio, rue Monsieur-le-Prince 1953. Photo: Douglas Glass

1952

The low relief *Man in a Street* which Mason considers the beginning of his career. Second visit to Barcelona. Acts as interpreter between Giacometti and Henry Moore at the latter's exhibition, Musée national d'art moderne, Paris. Mimi Fogt introduces him to Picasso at Vallauris.

1953

First high relief *Barcelona Tram*. Takes a studio in rue Monsieur-le-Prince in the Latin Quarter where he still works.

1954

A second and more important meeting with Picasso in the South of France. First exhibition at Helen Lessore's Beaux Arts Gallery, London; invited by Henry Moore to visit him at Much Hadom. Meets and begins friendship with Francis Bacon.

1955

Has his second crucial artistic encounter, after that with Giacometti, when he meets Balthus at the house of Carmen Baron, who gathered together artists, writers, musicians such as Balthus, Max Ernst, Man Ray, Cassandre, Francis Poulenc, Jacques Prévert.

1956

Meets Janine Hao, later to become his wife. Sculpts *The Idyll*.

1957

Place de l'Opéra.

1958

Mother dies. Returns to Birmingham to find that the city of his childhood has become irrevocably altered. Paints *Birmingham. In Memoriam*. Buys a house near Ménerbes on a hillside facing the Luberon mountain range.

1958-59

Carrefour de l'Odéon.

1959

Designs stage-set and costumes for *Phèdre* by Racine for the Marie Bell Company at the Théâtre du Gymnase, Paris.

1960

With his wife opens the Galerie Janine Hao adjacent to his studio. The inaugural exhibition is of his own work. The activity of the gallery continues for six years with exhibitions by Anne Harvey, Michel Charpentier, Charles Matton, Miklos Bokor, Gaston-Louis Roux, Mayou Iserantant, Pierre Bégou, Sven Blomberg, Léopold Levy, Cassandre and Balthus.

124. Working on *The Idyll*

BEAUX ARTS GALLERY
7 BRUTON PLACE, W.1

AN
EXHIBITION
OF
DRAWINGS and SCULPTURES
BY
RAYMOND MASON

PRIVATE VIEW: Thursday, February 11th, 3 - 7
Open until March 13th, 10 - 5.30; Saturdays 10 - 1

125. First exhibition with Helen Lessore, 1954

126. The Carrefour de l'Odéon next to the Passage du Commerce — St. André by Balthus

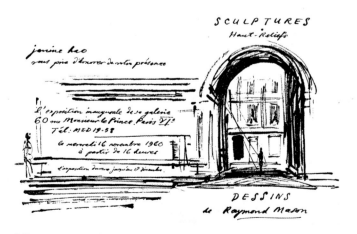

127. Inaugural card for the Galerie Janine Hao

1962

Awarded the William and Noma Copley Foundation Prize, Chicago, on the recommendation of Marcel Duchamp.

1963

Joins the Galerie Claude Bernard, Paris, then uniquely devoted to sculpture. (Would later form a quartet with César, Roël d'Haese and Ipoustéguy.) One-man exhibitions in 1965, 1971, 1973, 1977.

1965

The Crowd first shown at the Galerie Claude Bernard, May 1965.

1966

The final exhibition of the Galerie Janine Hao, *Drawings and Watercolours by Balthus,* brings the visit of his

128. Janine Hao in her gallery during the Raymond Mason exhibition

D'AFFICHES

PEINTRE

A.M. CASSANDRE

GALERIE JANINE HAO

60 RUE MONSIEUR-LE-PRINCE
PARIS
VI

JUIN 1966

129. Original poster by Cassandre

130. The Galerie Janine Hao with original plaster of *Carrefour de l'Odéon*

231

New York dealer Pierre Matisse and the encounter of the latter with Mason's work. Visits Alberto Giacometti on his last evening in Paris.

1967
Joins the Pierre Matisse Gallery, New York. One-man exhibitions in 1968, 1971, 1974 and 1980.

1967-68
Works at the Fonderia Bruni, Rome, on the casting of two examples of *The Crowd* and the entire exhibition for New York. Frequent visits to the Villa Medici where Balthus is director from 1960 to 1976.

1968
Draws the May revolts in the Latin Quarter. Shows the front frieze of *The Crowd* in bronze in *The Obsessive Image,* Institute of Contemporary Art, London.

131. *Rome, seen from the Villa Medici*, 1976

132. Mason and the minister André Malraux in front of *The Crowd* at the inauguration of the Centre National d'Art Contemporain, 1968. Photo: Martine Franck (Magnum)

133. Drawing in Les Halles market. Photo: Michel Boffredo

134. The beginning of the *Departure* . . . 1970

135. . . . and its end

Exhibits the original plaster of *The Crowd* and other works at the inaugural exhibition, *Trois Sculptures,* at the Centre national d'art contemporain (CNAC), Paris. Exhibits *The Crowd,* bronzes and drawings at the Pierre Matisse Gallery, New York.

1969
Principal exhibitor of group exhibition *The Crowd* at The Arts Club, Chicago. Exhibits in the International Exhibition at the Wiener Sezession, Vienna, and begins close friendship with its director, the painter Georg Eisler.

1969-71
Creates his monumental piece *The Departure of Fruit and Vegetables from the Heart of Paris, 28 February 1969.* First shown at the Galerie Claude Bernard (spring 1971) and then at the Pierre Matisse Gallery (also 1971). Exhibits *The Crowd* and other works in *Les Chemins de la Création,* Château d'Ancy-le-Franc, Yonne, France, organized by his friend Louis Deladicq.

1973
Exhibits in *Sculpteurs du XXe siècle,* Musée des Beaux-Arts, Calais. One-man show, *Watercolours,* Galerie Claude Bernard. Exhibits *St Mark's Place. East Village, New York* and coloured landscape sculptures and gouaches, *The Luberon,* at the Pierre Matisse Gallery.

1975
The Crowd installed for the summer in the Jardin des Tuileries, Paris. Gives slide lecture on his polychrome compositions at the Musée national d'art moderne, Paris.

1976
A version of *The Departure* is installed in the Church of St Eustache, Paris (the church which figures in the sculpture). On Christmas Eve before the congregation of midnight mass, the audio-visual service of the Centre Georges Pompidou presents on giant screens a hundred images of the sculpture prepared by Bernard Clerc-Renaud, accompanied by an improvisation on the great organ by Jean Guillou. *The Aggression at 48 rue Monsieur-le-Prince. June 23rd 1975.* Begins studies for Georgetown, Washington D.C., but the project is suspended. Is contacted by the architect, Jean Le Couteur, for the execution of a Monument to Louis Delgrès, Pointe-à-Pitre, Guadeloupe. Admired by Guadeloupean sources, the model is not accepted. Returns to the Villa Medici as sculpture advisor for the Prix de Rome.

1977
Monumental piece *A Tragedy in the North. Winter, Rain and Tears.* Francis Bacon, present on the day of its completion, returns with his friend Michel Leiris. Exhibits in *Papiers sur Nature* at the Fondation Nationale des

136. Painting from his house in the Luberon. Photo: Michel Boffredo

137. Mason drawing the roof-tops of Paris. Photo: Henri Cartier-Bresson

138. *The Roof-tops of Paris*, 1976

Arts Graphiques et Plastiques, Paris. Presents landscape sculptures and drawings, with text by Yves Bonnefoy, at the Chartreuse de Villeneuve-les-Avignon. Exhibits *A Tragedy* and numerous other sculptures and fifty drawings at the Galerie Claude Bernard. Henry Moore is taken by James Lord to see the mining sculpture.

1978
Is honoured with the title of Chevalier de l'Ordre des Arts et des Lettres by the French State. Jean Dubuffet visits his studio.

1979
Exhibits in a group show, *La Nouvelle subjectivité*, organised by Jean Clair, Palais des Beaux-Arts, Brussels. *A Tragedy* shown at the Musée des Beaux-Arts, Mons, Belgium. *An Illuminated Crowd*.

1980
The Crowd installed in Lyons for the *Deuxième Symposium de sculpture* and subsequently for *Anthropos* in Vienna. Exhibits *A Tragedy, The Aggression* and *An*

Illuminated Crowd at the Pierre Matisse Gallery. One-man show at Maison de l'Yonne et du Tourisme, Auxerre, France.

1981
Selected for group exhibition *Paris-Paris* at Musée national d'art moderne, Centre Georges Pompidou.

au merveilleux Mason
avec l'amicale admiration de
J Dubuffet

Paris 28/9/78

237

139. Cover for the poetry magazine of Fouad-el-Etre

140. *Mason's studio* – charcoal drawing by Sam Szafran

1982

Completes *The Grape-Pickers*. Exhibits in *Aftermath. France 1945-54*, inaugural exhibition at the Barbican Art Gallery, London, organised by Sarah Wilson, later to become one of Mason's principal advocates. Exhibits and has the poster in *Paris 1960-80* at Museum des 20. Jahrhunderts, Vienna. *A Tragedy* in the International Section of Venice Biennale. Exhibits in *La Délirante, revue de poésie*, Centre Georges Pompidou. Retrospective exhibition, *Raymond Mason. Coloured sculptures, bronzes and drawings, 1952–1982*, organised by the Arts Council of Great Britain and shown at the Serpentine Gallery, London, and the Museum of Modern Art, Oxford.

1983

Begins work on 65-figure monument for central Montreal, Canada. Joins the Marlborough Gallery, London and New York.

1984

Exhibits in *The Hard-Won Image*, group show organised by Richard Morphet, Tate Gallery, London. One-man exhibition on the Marlborough Gallery stand at F.I.A.C., Grand Palais, Paris. Exhibits in group show International Masters of Figuration, Marlborough Fine Art Ltd, Tokyo. Meets Red Grooms, later to become a member of his family.

1985

One-man exhibition at Marlborough Gallery, New York. Major retrospective exhibition in the Galeries Contemporaines of the Centre Georges Pompidou, Paris, and Musée Cantini, Marseilles, to February 1986.

141. The 1980 exhibition at the Pierre Matisse Gallery, New York with *The Aggression* and *A Tragedy*

1986

Installation of *The Crowd* in the Tuileries Gardens, Paris. Installation of *An Illuminated Crowd*, McGill College Avenue, Montreal. Lectures on 'Rodin. An occasion to discuss sculpture' to coincide with Rodin exhibition, Hayward Gallery, London. Francis Bacon is present, and Roy Fuller, who will write a poem 'After a lecture on Rodin'. Lectures on 'Memories of the Ecole de Paris' at the Tate Gallery.

1987

One-man exhibition *Latin Quarter* at the Marlborough Graphics Gallery, London. Helps in the installation of the Red Grooms retrospective at the Whitney Museum, New York.

1988

Commissioned by the City of Birmingham to execute a monumental sculpture for Centenary Square to face the new International Convention Centre. Model and related drawings for this project shown in Birmingham

Art Gallery. *A Tragedy* installed in Wakefield Cathedral as part of the Wakefield Festival. Installation of twin polychrome monumental high reliefs, Georgetown Plaza, Washington D.C.

1989

Retrospective exhibition *Raymond Mason. Sculptures and Drawings* at Birmingham Museum and Art Gallery, touring to Manchester City Art Gallery and City Art Centre, Edinburgh. Exhibits in *6 Sculptors*, Marlborough Gallery, New York. Is made Officier de l'Ordre des Arts et des Lettres. Accompanies Balthus at the Centenary Homage to Charlie Chaplin, Vevey, Switzerland. One-man exhibition on Marlborough Gallery stand at F.I.A.C., presenting big high-relief *Latin Quarter*.

1990

Permanent installation of second cast of *The Crowd* 527 Madison Avenue, New York.

142. Painting a second copy of *The Grape-Pickers*, 1984. Photo: Hans Namuth

143. Retrospective at the Centre Georges Pompidou, 1985. Photo: Harry Gruyaert (Magnum)

144. Mason's friend Roy Fuller, who wrote two poems about him

145. Jean Clair, curator of the Beaubourg retrospective and many other exhibitions by Mason

146. Unveiling in Montreal with Yvon Lamarre and the collector and patron of Mason's work, William Louis-Dreyfus

1991
Inauguration by HM Queen Elizabeth II of the monumental sculpture *Forward*, Centenary Square, Birmingham, June 12. One-man exhibition Marlborough Fine Art London. Lectures on 'Stepping out of the studio' at Courtauld Institute, London.

147. With Paola Gribaudo and Pierre Levai of Marlborough, New York 1994

1992
Rue Monsieur-le-Prince 1 and 2. Lectures on the architectural content in his sculpture for 'Art and Architecture', London. Fernando Botero flies him to Spain for the inauguration of Marlborough Galería, Madrid.

1993
Exhibits in group show of polychrome sculpture, Marlborough Gallery, New York. Installation of *The Departure* in entry hall of Four Seasons Hotel, Georgetown, Washington D.C. Installation of *A Tragedy* in headquarters of Louis-Dreyfus Company, Connecticut, USA. Low relief *The Richelieu Wing. The Louvre*. Installation of *The Falling Man*, Miami, Florida. One of the speakers on 'Paris Post War', Tate Gallery.

1994
Permanent installation of the original plaster of *The Grape-Pickers* for the Fête de la Vigne, Vézelay, France. Made Honorary Citizen of the town. *Figures de l'art d'aujourd'hui* (eight artists of the Marlborough Gallery), Galerie Marwan Hoss, Paris. One-man exhibition, Marlborough Gallery, New York.

148. *The Crowd* in Manhattan, 1988

149. Unveiling of the *Monument for Birmingham* by Her Majesty Queen Elizabeth II, 1991. Photo: Barbara Lloyd

BIBLIOGRAPHY

1. MAIN EXHIBITION CATALOGUES

Raymond Mason, Galerie Claude Bernard, Paris, 1965. (Abbrev. Claude Bernard 1965.)
Raymond Mason, Pierre Matisse Gallery, New York, 1968. (Abbrev. Pierre Matisse 1968.)
Raymond Mason: Le départ des fruits et légumes du coeur de Paris, Galerie Claude Bernard, Paris, 1971. (Abbrev. Claude Bernard 1971.)
Raymond Mason, Pierre Matisse Gallery, New York, 1971. (Abbrev. Pierre Matisse 1971.)
Raymond Mason: St. Mark's Place, East Village, N Y, The Luberon, Pierre Matisse Gallery, New York, 1974. (Abbrev. Pierre Matisse 1974.)
Raymond Mason: Sculptures et dessins, Galerie Claude Bernard, Paris, 1977. (Abbrev. Claude Bernard 1977.)
Raymond Mason: Polychrome Sculpture, Pierre Matisse Gallery, New York, 1980. (Abbrev. Pierre Matisse 1980.)
Raymond Mason: Coloured Sculptures, Bronzes and Drawings 1952-1982, Serpentine Gallery, London, 1982-83, Museum of Modern Art, Oxford, 1983, Arts Council of Great Britain, 1982. (Abbrev. Arts Council 1982.)
Raymond Mason: Painted Sculptures and Bronzes 1952–1985, Marlborough Gallery, New York, 1985. (Abbrev. Marlborough 1985.)
Raymond Mason, Musée national d'art moderne, Centre Georges Pompidou, Paris, 1985, Musée Cantini, Marseilles, 1985–86, Editions du Centre Pompidou, Paris, 1985. (Abbrev. Centre Georges Pompidou 1985.)
Raymond Mason: Sculptures and Drawings, Birmingham City Museum and Art Gallery, Manchester City Art Gallery, City Art Centre, Edinburgh, 1989, ed. Jane Farrington and Evelyn Silber, Lund Humphries, London, in association with Birmingham City Museum and Art Gallery, 1989. (Abbrev. Birmingham 1989.)
Raymond Mason, Marlborough Fine Art, London, 1991. (Abbrev. Marlborough 1991.)

2. WRITINGS BY RAYMOND MASON

'British Art Schools – Augustus John', New Phineas, University College London, Autumn 1945.
'Les mains éblouies', *Derrière le miroir, no. 9*, Galerie Maeght, Paris, April 1948. Reprinted in Centre Georges Pompidou 1985.
'Xavier Coll', exhibition text, Galerie de Seine, Paris, 1951.
'Anne Harvey', exhibition text, Galerie Janine Hao, Paris, May 1961.
'Miklos Bokor', exhibition text, Galerie Janine Hao, Paris, April 1964.

'La Foule' 1965, in Centre Georges Pompidou 1985.
'Cassandre', in exhibition catalogue *A. M. Cassandre, peintre d'affiches*, Galerie Motte, Geneva, February 1966, Galerie Janine Hao, Paris, June 1966.
'Le marché des fruits et légumes', in Claude Bernard 1971, reprinted as 'Le départ des fruits et légumes du coeur de Paris le 28 février 1969' in Centre Georges Pompidou 1985; English translation by Patricia Southgate, 'The Departure of Fruit and Vegetables from the Heart of Paris, 28 February 1969', in Pierre Matisse 1971, reprinted in Birmingham 1989.
'Le musée' 1973, in Centre Georges Pompidou 1985.
'St Mark's Place, East Village, New York City', in Pierre Matisse 1974, reprinted in *The Tate Gallery 1982–84, Illustrated Catalogue of Acquisitions*, London, 1986, and in Birmingham 1989; revised French version in Centre Georges Pompidou 1985.
'Ce que j'aime dans le dessin' 1976, in Centre Georges Pompidou 1985.
Preface of exhibition catalogue *Pascal*, Villa Medici, Rome, April 1977.
'C'est peu après le jour de Noël 1974...', in Claude Bernard 1977, revised and extended version 'Une tragédie dans le Nord. L'hiver, la pluie, les larmes' 1978, in Centre Georges Pompidou 1985; 'A Tragedy in the North. Winter, Rain and Tears', in Pierre Matisse 1980, reprinted in Birmingham 1989.
'Sur le contenu' 1977, in Centre Georges Pompidou 1985.
'Bien entendu, je pense que le seul sujet signifiant...', *Skira annuel, Art actuel*, no. 4, Geneva, 1978.
'La Dation Picasso', *Cahiers du Musée national d'art moderne*, no. 3, Centre Georges Pompidou, Paris, 1980.
Preface of exhibition catalogue *Szeto*, Galerie L'Oeil de Sévigné, Paris, March 1980.
'Les sculpteurs de l'antiquité...', *Skira annuel, Art actuel*, no. 6, Geneva, 1980.
'Manet et Cézanne' 1981, in Centre Georges Pompidou 1985.
'Je suis assez étonné que l'on n'arrive pas à définir le mot "réalisme"', transcription from a public debate 'La tentation du réalisme dans l'art d'aujourd'hui', Centre Georges Pompidou, 23 February 1981, in *Les cahiers de la peinture*, no. 115, Paris, March 1981.
'The Illuminated Crowd was intended...', in Arts Council 1982, revised and extended version 'Illuminated Crowd', in Birmingham 1989; revised French version, 'Une foule illuminée', in Centre Georges Pompidou 1985. Arts Council 1982 contains numerous short notes on other works.
'Un témoignage des années 50', *Balthus*, Musée national d'art moderne, Centre Georges Pompidou, Paris, 1982.
'Balthus', in Centre Georges Pompidou 1985, from a text for a France-Culture broadcast, December 1983.

'Sur la lumière' (undated), in Centre Georges Pompidou 1985.
Comments on *Barcelona Tram* and *St Mark's Place* in *The Tate Gallery 1982–84, Illustrated Catalogue of Acquisitions*, London, 1986. Extract from comments on *Barcelona Tram* in Birmingham 1989.
'Serge Rezvani', exhibition text, Galerie Callu-Mérite, Paris, April 1989.
'My Early Artistic Life in Birmingham', 'Grand Paysage du Midi', 'Project for Washington', 'The Grape-Pickers', in Birmingham 1989.
Comments on *Ginette Neveu* in *The Swindon Collection of Twentieth-Century British Art*, Thamesdown Borough Council, 1991.
'Jean Leyris', exhibition text, Galerie Jean Peyrole, Paris, 1991.
Preface, 'Latin Quarter', 'A monument for Centenary Square, Birmingham', in Marlborough 1991. This also contains new, short texts on *The Crowd, Monument for Montreal, Twin Sculptures for Georgetown, Washington DC*.
'. . . et pour quand?', *Revue des deux mondes*, 'L'art contemporain, pour qui?', Paris, November 1992.

3. INTERVIEWS

'Conversation avec Raymond Mason', in Claude Bernard 1977; 'Conversación con Raymond Mason', Guadalimar, no. 29, Madrid, February 1978. Translated and shortened versions of an interview given to Michael Brenson in Spring 1976.
'Responses by Raymond Mason to questions by Michael Peppiatt', in Arts Council 1982; French version, as 'Raymond Mason et Michael Peppiatt, Entretien', in Centre Georges Pompidou 1985.
'Introduction and Interview with Raymond Mason', in Marlborough 1985. From an interview given to Cynthia Nadelman, 28 November 1984.
'The Torrent of Life', in Birmingham 1989, transcript of a conversation with Richard Cork, for a BBC Radio 3 broadcast, April 1985.
Unpublished interview given to Jane Farrington, May 1988, frequently quoted in article by Jane Farrington in Birmingham 1989.

4. RADIO AND TELEVISION BROADCASTS

Jean Paget, 'Raymond Mason', France-Culture, 'L'Atelier de création radiophonique', 1972.
'Raymond Mason', directed by Christopher Martin, BBC TV, 'Omnibus', 28 November 1982.
Francesca Isidori, 'A propos de l'exposition Balthus', France-Culture, 'Les nuits magnétiques', produced by Alain Veinstein, 7 December 1983.
Richard Cork, 'Raymond Mason: The Torrent of Life', produced by Judith Bumpus, BBC Radio 3, 'Third Ear', 24 April 1985.

'Raymond Mason, l'homme des foules', directed by Michael Gibson, France-Culture, September 1985.
'Raymond Mason – A Full Meal', directed by Catherine Collis, Central Television, 'Contrast', 14 February 1989.
Martin Kemp, 'Raymond Mason', produced by Judith Bumpus, BBC Radio 3, 'Third Ear', 19 May 1989.
Paule Chavasse, 'Giacometti: témoignages', France-Culture, 29 August 1992.

5. ON RAYMOND MASON

David Sylvester, 'A New Sculptor', *The Times*, London, 15 February 1954.
Robert Melville, 'Exhibitions. Painting', *Architectural Review*, vol. 115, no. 689, London, May 1954.
Eric Newton, 'Art round the Galleries', *Time and Tide*, London, 10 November 1956.
David Sylvester, 'Two Exhibitions of Sculpture', *The Listener*, London, 15 November 1956.
J. Bornibus, 'Raymond Mason', in Claude Bernard 1965.
Gérald Gassiot-Talabot, 'La figuration narrative dans la peinture contemporaine', *Quadrum*, vol. 18, Brussels, 1965.
Patrick Waldberg, 'Raymond Mason ou les espaces ouverts', *Quadrum*, vol. 19, Brussels, 1965.
Jean Bouret, 'Sept jours avec la peinture', *Les Lettres Françaises*, no. 1076, Paris, 15–21 April 1965.
Jean-Jacques Levêque, 'Les couloirs de l'inquiétude', *Arts*, Paris, 28 April–4 May 1965.
John Ashbery, 'Mason, Raysse', *Art News*, vol. 64, no. 6, New York, October 1965.
Marie-Laure de Noailles, 'Journal d'un peintre', *Cahiers des saisons*, Julliard, Paris, 1965.
Patrick Waldberg, 'La ville rêvée et la ville vécue', *XXe siècle*, Paris, May 1966.
Yves Bonnefoy, 'Raymond Mason', in exhibition catalogue *Trois sculptures*, Centre national d'art contemporain, Paris, 1968.
Yves Bonnefoy, 'Proust parlant de Chateaubriand . . .', and English translation by Anthony Rudolf, in Pierre Matisse 1968. Reprinted in Yves Bonnefoy, *Sur un sculpteur et des peintres*, Plon, Paris, 1989.
L. C., 'Reviews and previews, Raymond Mason', *Art News*, vol. 67, no. 8, New York, December 1968.
James Lord, 'Raymond Mason', *L'Oeil*, no. 198, Paris, June 1971.
Tomyoka Taiko, 'Raymond Mason', *Mizue*, no. 2, Tokyo, 1972.
Michael Peppiatt, 'Paris: Summer', *Art International*, vol. 17, no. 7, Lugano, September 1973.
James Lord, 'A Celebration of Sight. The gouaches and painted reliefs of Raymond Mason', in Pierre Matisse 1974. French translation by Annie Pérez, 'Eloge de la vision', in Centre Georges Pompidou 1985.
Phyllis Derfner, 'New York Letter', *Art International*, vol. 19, no. 1, Lugano, January 1975.

Phyllis Derfner, 'Raymond Mason at Pierre Matisse', *Art in America*, no. 3, New York, May–June 1975.

Flora Minervo, 'Un americano a Parigi sono un artista di strada', Bolaffi Arte, Turin, May–June 1975.

Michael Brenson, 'Riding out the abstract tide in Paris', *Paris Metro*, no. 1, 23 June 1976.

Yves Bonnefoy, *Paysages de Raymond Mason*, illustrated by the artist, La Maison du Livre et des Mots de la Chartreuse de Villeneuve-les-Avignon, 1977. Reprinted in Yves Bonnefoy, *op. cit.*

Michael Brenson, 'Lentement et presque en silence . . .', in Claude Bernard 1977.

Gaston Palewski, 'Propos', *Revue des deux mondes*, Paris, January 1978.

René Micha, 'Paris', *Art International*, vol. 22, no. 1, Lugano, January 1978.

Jean Clair, 'Raymond Mason', *Nouvelle Revue Française*, no. 302, Paris, 1 March 1978.

Alice Bellony-Rewald, 'Raymond Mason, le grand art de l'ordinaire', *Coloquio Artes*, no. 36, Lisbon, March 1978.

Michael Brenson, 'Raymond Mason. Urban drama in high relief', *Art in America*, no. 4, New York, July–August 1979.

Michael Brenson, 'At the end of an interview . . . ', in Pierre Matisse 1980.

Nicholas King, 'Raymond Mason tableaux in polychrome sculpture', *Art World*, vol. 4, no. 7, New York, 19 April–17 May 1980.

Lise Bloch-Morhange and David Alper, *Artiste et métèque à Paris*, Buchet-Chastel, Paris, 1980.

Michael Peppiatt, 'Introduction', in Arts Council 1982.

'Exposition de Raymond Mason', *Connaissance des Arts*, no. 370, Paris, 1982.

Heinz-Peter Schwerfel, 'Aus dem Leben gegriffen', *Art*, no. 2, Hamburg, February 1983.

Timothy Hyman, 'Raymond Mason at the Serpentine', *Artscribe*, no. 39, London, February 1983.

Sarah Wilson, 'Raymond Mason', *Artscribe*, no. 39, London, February 1983.

Ben Hinx-Edwards, 'Raymond Mason', *Artline*, London, March 1983.

Richard Morphet, *The Hard-Won Image: Traditional Method and Subject in Recent British Art*, The Tate Gallery, London, 1984.

Michael Brenson, 'Contemporary frescoes rooted in late Gothic art', *New York Times*, 7 April 1985. French translation by Annie Pérez, 'Des fresques contemporaines qui s'enracinent dans l'art gothique tardif', in Centre Georges Pompidou 1985.

Yves Bonnefoy, 'La liberté de l'esprit', in Centre Georges Pompidou 1985.

Jean Clair, 'Un orage de passions', in Centre Georges Pompidou 1985.

Michael Gibson, 'La foule comme modèle', *Connaissance des arts*, no. 403, Paris, September 1985.

Jean-Baptiste Para, 'Raymond Mason, le relief du vivant', *Europe*, nos. 679–680, Paris, November–December 1985.

'Raymond Mason. *Barcelona Tram. St Mark's Place, East Village, New York City*', in *The Tate Gallery 1982–84, Illustrated Catalogue of Acquisitions*, London, 1986.

Helen Lessore, 'Raymond Mason', in *A Partial Testament: Essays on Some Moderns in the Great Tradition*, The Tate Gallery, London, 1986.

James Lord, *Two Sculptures at Georgetown Plaza*, Louis-Dreyfus Property Group, September 1988.

Sarah Wilson, 'Raymond Mason – An Exalting Life', in Birmingham 1989.

Jane Farrington, 'Raymond Mason and the English Narrative Tradition', in Birmingham 1989.

Red Grooms, William Louis-Dreyfus, *The Crowd*, Louis-Dreyfus Property Group, May 1990.

Jean Clair, 'Une moderne nef des fous', *Connaissance des arts*, Paris, October 1991.

LIST OF ILLUSTRATIONS

63. Model for *Monument for Guadeloupe,* 1976, painted plaster (in its box 65×60×45 cm). Coll.: the artist, Paris.

64. Project for Pointe-à-Pitre, Guadeloupe, 1976, pencil in sketch-book (16×20 cm). Coll.: the artist, Paris.

65. Project for Pointe-à-Pitre, Guadeloupe, 1976, pencil in sketch-book (16×20 cm). Coll.: the artist, Paris.

66. Model for *Monument for Guadeloupe,* 1976 (detail).

67. Louis Delgrès, *Monument for Guadeloupe* (detail).

68. Solitude, *Monument for Guadeloupe* (detail).

69. *Monument for Guadeloupe* (details).

70. *The Grape-Pickers* 1982 (detail).

71. *The Valley,* 1973, acrylic gouache on paper (79×104 cm). Coll.: William Louis-Dreyfus, New York.

72. *The Luberon with its Valley,* 1973, acrylic gouache on paper (79×104 cm). Coll.: William Louis-Dreyfus, New York.

73. *La Montagne du Luberon,* 1960, ink on paper (47.5×81 cm). Coll.: Jacques Elbaz, Paris.

74. *La Montagne du Luberon,* 1962, ink on paper (50×81 cm). Coll.: Musée National d'Art Moderne, Centre Georges Pompidou, Paris.

75. *The Vineyards in Winter,* 1973, acrylic gouache on paper (79×104 cm). Coll.: William Louis-Dreyfus, New York.

76. *Midday at Ménerbes,* 1974, acrylic gouache on paper (79×104 cm). Coll.: William Louis-Dreyfus, New York.

77. *Le Roucas,* 1970, epoxy resin and acrylic paint (106.5×178×10 cm). Edition of 6.

78. *A Procession of Clouds,* 1970, epoxy resin and acrylic paint (95×131×15 cm). Edition of 6.

79. *The Approaching Storm,* 1974, epoxy resin and acrylic paint (94×123×10 cm). Edition of 6.

80. *Big Midi Landscape,* 1975, epoxy resin and acrylic paint (106×200×13 cm). Edition of 6.

81. *The Luberon II,* 1974, epoxy resin and acrylic paint (68×106×3 cm). Edition of 6.

82. *The Luberon I,* 1974, epoxy resin and acrylic paint (106.5×178×10 cm). Edition of 6.

83. *The Grape-Pickers,* 1982, polyester resin and acrylic paint (280×325×170 cm). Edition of 4.

84. *The Grape-Pickers* (model).

85. *A Monument for Montreal. An Illuminated Crowd,* 1986, stratified polyester resin, polyurethane paint (314×860×320 cm). Louis-Dreyfus Property Group, New York.

86. *An Illuminated Crowd,* 1980, epoxy resin and acrylic paint (in its box 51×104×37.5 cm). Edition of 6.

87. Initial studies for *Monument,* 1980, pencil in sketch-book (49×39.5 cm). Coll.: the artist, Paris.

88. *An Illuminated Crowd* (detail).

89. Projected study for *An Illuminated Crowd* on the site of the D.M.K. building Mc Gill College Avenue Montreal, 1984, watercolour on paper (49×62 cm). Marlborough Gallery, New York.

90. *An Illuminated Crowd.* Photo: Iris Hao.

91. In front of the building by René Menkès.

92. Mason at work on *Monument* in the Haligon Studios, 1985. Photo: Henri Cartier-Bresson.

93. *New York City,* 1987, polyester resin (143×104×14 cm). Edition of 9.

94. *Panorama of Paris,* 1959, ink on paper (49×86 cm). Coll.: Philippe Roman, Paris.

95. *Panorama of Paris,* 1959, ink and sepia, pen and wash on paper (48×130 cm). Coll.: the artist, Paris.

96. *Rome,* 1989, polyester resin (106×144.5×13 cm). Edition of 9.

97. *Paris,* 1991, polyester resin (102×143×12 cm). Edition of 8.

98. *London,* 1994, polyester resin (105×144×14 cm). Edition of 8.

99. *Twin Sculptures,* Georgetown Plaza, Washington D.C. (northern wall), 1988, stratified polyester resin, polyurethane paint (500×550×80 cm, return on other wall 1.53 cm).

100. *Twin Sculptures,* Georgetown Plaza, Washington D.C. (southern wall), 1988 (286×525×80 cm, return on other wall 2.45 cm).

101. Study for southern wall, 1987, bronze (12×19.7×5 cm). Edition of 8.

102. Polychrome studies for northern wall, 1987, painted plaster on wood (27×120 cm). Marlborough Gallery, New York.

103. *The Crowd,* southern wall, 1988.

104. *Boulevard Saint-Michel,* 1986, ink on paper (50×65 cm). Marlborough Gallery, New York.

105. *Latin Quarter,* 1987, polyester resin (84×117×70.5 cm). Edition of 9.

106. *Le Boul' Mich',* 1986, ink on paper (33×42.5 cm). Marlborough Gallery, New York.

107. Study for *Latin Quarter,* 1986, ink and pencil on paper (35.6×45.7 cm). Marlborough Gallery, New York.

108. *The Latin Quarter,* 1988–89, polyester resin and acrylic (310×350×200 cm). Edition of 3.

109. *Souvenir of May 1968,* 1986, lithograph (44×39 cm). Edition of 30.

110. *The Latin Quarter,* at the F.I.A.C., Paris, 1989.

111. *Forward. A Monument for Birmingham,* 1991, stratified polyester resin, polyurethane paint (505×933×366 cm).

112. Study for *Forward,* 1988, terracotta (12×23.5×10 cm). Coll.: the artist, Paris.

113. *Forward. A Monument for Birmingham,* 1991.

114. *Forward, Centenary Square, Birmingham,* 1991 (detail).

115. *The Richelieu wing of the Louvre,* 1992, watercolour and pencil on paper (65×50 cm). Marlborough Gallery, New York.

116. *The Richelieu wing of the Louvre,* 1993, polyester resin (180×130×20 cm). Edition of 8.

117. *Rue Monsieur-le-Prince I,* 1992, polyester resin, acrylic paint (130×93×14 cm). Edition of 8.

118. *Rue de Bac,* ink, 1994.

119. *Rue Monsieur-le-Prince II,* 1992, polyester resin, acrylic paint (165×118×47 cm). Edition of 8.

120. With Harry (Sven) Blomberg in the days when they shared a studio.

121. Mason sculpting a nude in stone in his house in Fane Street.

122. Invitation card for the exhibition at the Galerie Maeght.

123. Mason newly installed in his studio, rue Monsieur-le-Prince 1953. Photo: Douglas Glass.

124. Working on *The Idyll.*

125. First exhibition with Helen Lessore, 1954.

126. The Carrefour de l'Odéon next to the Passage du Commerce – St. André by Balthus.

127. Inaugural card for the Galerie Janine Hao.

128. Janine Hao in her gallery during the Raymond Mason exhibition.

129. Original poster by Cassandre.

INDEX OF NAMES